OFF THE BEATEN PATH® SERIES

TENTH EDITION

OFF THE BEATEN PATH®
COLORADO →

A GUIDE TO UNIQUE PLACES

ERIC LINDBERG

gpp®
travel

Guilford, Connecticut

All the information in this guidebook is subject to change. We recommend that you call ahead to obtain current information before traveling.

Copyright © 1987, 1991, 1994, 1997, 1999 by Curtis Casewit
Copyright © 2001, 2003, 2005, 2007, 2009 Morris Book Publishing, LLC

Text design: Linda R. Loiewski
Maps: Equator Graphics © Morris Book Publishing, LLC

ISSN 1539-6614
ISBN 978-0-7627-5024-5

Printed in the United States of America
10 9 8 7 6 5 4 3 2 1

Contents

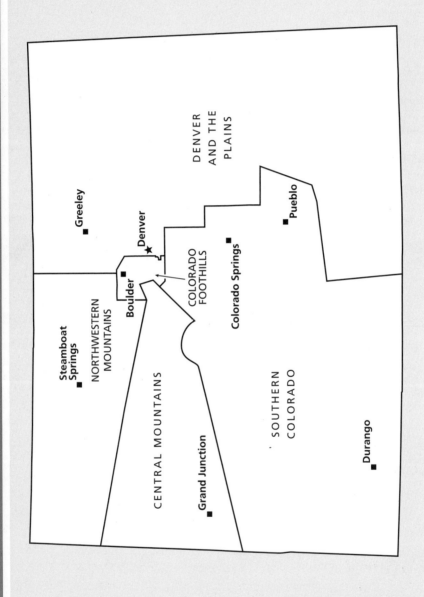

NORTHWESTERN MOUNTAINS

Steamboat Springs ■

Greeley ■

Denver ★

Boulder ■

COLORADO FOOTHILLS

DENVER AND THE PLAINS

CENTRAL MOUNTAINS

Grand Junction ■

Colorado Springs ■

Pueblo ■

SOUTHERN COLORADO

Durango ■

Acknowledgments

This book was written with the help of many people. The author thanks Gaylene Ore, Ore Communications; Rich Grant, Carrina Junge, and Jennifer Elving, Denver Metro Convention and Visitors Bureau; Mike Lane, Steamboat Ski and Resort Corporation; Anne Klein Barney, Durango Area Tourism Office; Jenn deBergezc, Winter Park Resort; Joan Christensen, JC Communications; Beth Buehler, Gunnison-Crested Butte Tourism Association; and his research assistant, Jo McWilliams.

Introduction

It's no wonder that Colorado's cities and small towns frequently appear on those *Best Places to Live in America* lists. The state has so much to offer that many people come and never leave. Even long-time residents constantly find new things to love about the state.

The mountains are perhaps the biggest draw. In spring wildflowers fill the meadows, streams and rivers flow, and life returns to the high country. Summer means long, warm days, afternoon thundershowers, exploring the forests and alpine reaches. In the fall, aspen shimmer golden against electric blue skies and bull elk gather in the meadows to bugle and herd their harems. Winter is the time for thrilling downhill runs through fresh powder, quiet snowshoeing or cross country ski tours deep into the woods, or sitting by a crackling cabin as snow swirls outside.

But there's more to the state than mountains. Colorado is the true west, and just outside any town or city another world begins, where ranches, farms, and scattered rural communities represent the western rural lifestyle. Much of the state's early pioneering history comes from agricultural beginnings on the plains and the valleys.

Colorado's Great Sand Dunes are the tallest in North America. The Pawnee Grasslands Buttes protect a Great Plains geography largely gone from the American landscape. Dinosaur bones can be inspected at Dinosaur National Monument. Rivers run through canyons, awaiting exploration by raft. Historic ghost towns and ancient Native American ruins remain to remind visitors of the first people to call this place home.

Along with the open spaces and natural beauty, Colorado is also a renowned cultural destination. Front Range cities are blessed with world-class performing arts, cuisine to satisfy any palate, a thriving music scene, a high concentration of microbreweries, extensive bike paths and parks, four major league sports teams, and top-notch universities. And perhaps best of all, within easy access of each of these cities awaits the Rocky Mountains.

Colorado Off the Beaten Path® travels to the far corners of the state and covers most points in between. It offers a mixture of unique, less-known destinations and more well-known locales. Both visitors and residents will find new places to explore and keep them busy for years to come.

About the Book's Organization

This book is divided into five regions, with each chapter covering a region of the state.

Author's Note

After attending a Colorado university for two years in the mid 70s, I left the state to see the world. Twenty years and 48 countries later, I returned to decide whether I could call the place home again. It was a quick decision. After 15 years, I constantly discover more reasons to stay. Colorado is not a place where people often boast of having seen and done it all. Exploring the endless miles of mountains, canyons, rivers, and plains alone would take years if not a lifetime. And culture junkies have no shortage of activities; restaurants, plays, sports games, gallery openings, concerts, brewpubs, bookstores, and coffeehouses keep even the most jaded cultural sophisticate busy.

But the reason many choose to call Colorado home is the ease with which one can slip between the worlds of urban and wilderness. Swapping out my car for boots or bike tires or raft, I can climb a mountain, follow a river, or wander through a forest, and be reminded once again of why I choose to live here.

Chapter 1 deals with the Front Range foothills area west of the Denver/Boulder corridor, where much of the state's population lives. Chapter 2 explores the state's northwestern mountains, including Rocky Mountain National Park, Trail Ridge Road, and Steamboat Springs. In Chapter 3 you follow one of Colorado's main arteries—Interstate 70—through historic Georgetown and Glenwood Springs to the Western Slope city of Grand Junction, with side trips along the way. Chapter 4 goes into the state's vast southern region, including the spectacular San Juan mountains, the ruins of Mesa Verde, the unique towns of Telluride, Cortez, and Durango. Finally, Chapter 5 covers cosmopolitan Denver and the sprawling Plains. Throughout the book you will discover unique, hidden places overlooked by the casual traveler.

Happy Trails!

Fast Facts about Colorado

COLORADO TOURISM OFFICE

1625 Broadway, Suite 1700
Denver, CO 80202
(800) 265-6723, (303) 446-2422
www.colorado.com

COLORADO'S MAJOR NEWSPAPERS

The Denver Post (daily), www.denverpost.com
Westword Newspaper (weekly), www.westword.com

TRANSPORTATION: REGIONAL TRANSPORTATION DISTRICT (RTD)

RTD has an extensive bus system in addition to light rail.
1600 Blake St.
Denver, CO 80202
(800) 366-7433
www.rtd-denver.com

CLIMATE OVERVIEW

Semiarid
Short springs
Dry, often hot summers with brief periods of rain with thunder and lightning
Warm, clear fall days with cool nights
Mild winters, except in mountains

Average highs and lows in Denver (temperatures Fahrenheit)

Jan 43/16	Apr 61/34	July 88/58	Oct 66/36
Feb 46/20	May 70/43	Aug 85/56	Nov 52/25
Mar 52/25	June 81/52	Sept 76/47	Dec 44/17

FACTS ABOUT COLORADO

Residents claim that old cliché about the weather—if you don't like it, wait an hour—started in Colorado. The state is known for its ability to go from clear skies to thunderstorms, tornadoes, and flash floods and back before you've had time to complain about any of it. Temperatures can drop thirty degrees in a matter of hours, and just when you thought it was Indian summer in October, a blizzard can dump 3 feet of snow in two days' time. It never hurts to keep an eye on the sky, especially when traveling in the mountains.

COLORADO FOOTHILLS

Front Range

When you first come upon the seventy-million-year-old amphi-theatre at **Red Rocks Park,** west of Denver, the primeval scene takes your breath away. Huge reddish sandstone formations jut upward and outward. Each is higher than Niagara Falls. The view conjures up dinosaurs, sea serpents, and flying reptiles; indeed, tracks of those long-extinct creatures remain embedded in nearby rock, along with valuable fossil fragments. The saturated colors rival those of the Grand Canyon, and the tortured geology is evidence of earth-shattering, monolith-building cataclysms, retreating ancestral oceans, violent upwelling, and centuries of water erosion. Geographers once considered this site one of the Seven Wonders of the World.

Long before the first settlers arrived, the Ute tribe favored the area for camping. The U.S. Geographical Survey showed up eager for surveys in 1868. By 1906 financier John Brisben Walker had acquired the land, claiming the acoustics of these rocks would be perfect for an amphitheater. Walker eventually donated the land to the community, and in 1927 it was incorporated into the Denver Mountain Parks System.

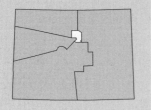

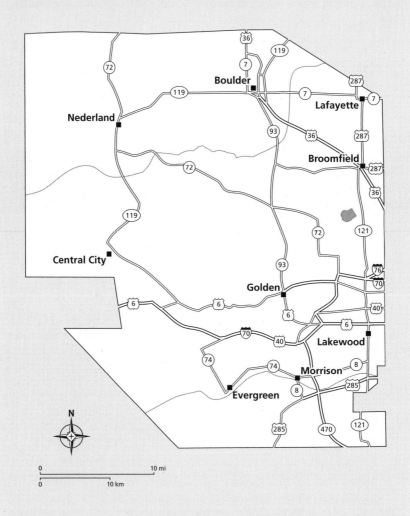

Construction started a few years later, followed in 1941 with dedication of the tiered outdoor area. The local symphony came, producing perfect sound and aesthetic inspiration against a magnificent backdrop panorama of Denver and the plains far below. Triumphant ballet performance and celebrated orchestras wowed audiences. Over the years improvements were made to the stage and seating.

However, the cost of bringing large groups of classical musicians and opera companies proved to be financially draining. What's more, performers sometimes fought with winds that would tear away the orchestra's notes or with sudden five-minute rains that would drench the singers.

Since 1961 classical music has rarely been heard at the amphitheatre. In 1964 the Beatles arrived, and for an admission price of $6.60, rock and roll came to Red Rocks. From the 1970s forward to today, the summer season is packed with an assortment of rock, pop, blues, folk, jazz, and country western stars—often with sellouts of the 9,000 seats. The stage is now covered,

AUTHOR'S FAVORITES IN THE COLORADO FOOTHILLS

Beaver Brook Trail,
(303) 697-4545
www.trails.com

Buffalo Bill Grave and Museum,
(303) 526-0747
www.buffalobill.org

Central City Opera House,
(800) 851-8175
http://new.centralcityopera.org

Eldorado Canyon,
(303) 494-3943
http://parks.state.co.us

Glacier Homemade Ice Cream,
(303) 440-6542
www.glaciericecream.com

Lookout Mountain Nature Center and Preserve,
(720) 497-7600
http://jeffco.us/openspace

Matthews/Winters Park,
(303) 271-5925
http://jeffco.us/openspace

Mt. Falcon Park,
(303) 271-5925
www.co.jefferson.co.us/openspace/

Pearl St. Mall in Boulder,
(303) 442-2911
www.bouldercoloradousa.com/

Red Rocks Park and Amphitheatre,
www.redrocksonline.com

Waterton Canyon,
(303) 628-6189
http://recreation/strontia.html

and tickets can be expensive, but the magical setting brings fans regardless of price.

Red Rocks is truly one of the world's great open air stages. Many famous groups return year after year, claiming this venue among their favorite places to perform. For music lovers, sitting down to a summer show at Red Rocks as the sun sets and stars sparkle overhead is one of life's perfect moments.

At all other times, admission is free to Red Rocks. Many locals come here during the day for a vigorous workout running or walking up and down the amphitheatre stairs. An Easter Sunrise Service has been a strong Denver tradition for several decades. A 30,000-square-foot underground ***Red Rocks Visitor Center*** at the top of the amphitheatre features an excellent exhibit of the venue, with geological history and a chronological list of every performance over the last 50 years. Featuring sweeping views from terraces, elevator access for people with disabilities, and new restrooms, the Visitor Center is open to the public free of charge year-round. Also included are a meeting center (call 303-697-6047 for details) and a restaurant.

Hiking trails in the park surrounding the amphitheatre offer hours of exercise or just quiet contemplation among the birdlife, browsing deer, and ancient geology. Mere minutes from the Denver suburbs, the splendor of Red Rocks can feel like another world.

Red Rocks, located at 16352 County Rd. 93 in Morrison, is easy to reach via numerous routes. From Denver you can take West Alameda Avenue west, drive U.S. Highway 285 west to County Road 470 to Morrison Road, or follow Interstate 70 west and watch for the marked exit. The total distance varies between 14 and 17 miles, depending on your route. Hours are 5 a.m. to 11 p.m. daily; admission is free. For more information go to www.redrocks online.com.

You can see the amphitheater from the hiking trails of ***Mount Falcon Park,*** a protected sanctuary in the foothills just above Red Rocks. In the early 1900s, John Brisben Walker, financier, entrepreneur, and visionary, built a mansion on a promontory high above the surrounding hills. His next project was to be a Summer White House. Walker's fortunes ultimately waned. The Summer White House was never built, and the financier's own castle-like home was struck by lightning and burned in 1918. The stone walls, fireplaces, and chimneys remain—an interesting destination for hikers.

The Mount Falcon area is surrounded by mountains, and in the distance you can spot Mt. Evans (elevation 14,264 feet) and the Continental Divide. Other vistas of the 2,130-acre park include the Colorado plains and, with a little imagination, Kansas.

The park is surprisingly serene; it is so vast that walkers and mountain bikers and the occasional horseback rider easily spread out. No motorcycles are permitted, and cars are restricted to two parking lots. The well-marked foot trails are often shaded by conifer forests. In winter, cross-country skiers enjoy the park in winter at no charge.

Picnic tables invite families, and there are meadows for kite-fliers and butterfly fans. Lovers find privacy among the daisies, the scrub oak, and the spruce. Here, at 7,750 feet above sea level, a light breeze blows often. Summers are cooler here than in Denver far below. Far from traffic, you hear only the light Colorado wind in the pines.

trivia

Long ago, a vast inland sea, which contained sediments that gradually built up on its floor, covered the Colorado area. After the sea receded, the sediments hardened and the forces of geology and erosion went to work over the next few million years to sculpt the formations you see at Red Rocks today.

Mount Falcon Park is accessible via Highway 8 to Morrison (turn west on Forest Avenue and north on Vine Avenue) or via US 285 and the Indian Hills exit (stay on Parmalee Gulch Road for 5 miles to Picutis Road, and then follow signs to the parking area). Be prepared for a brief dusty road to the park entrance. For more information contact Jefferson County Open Space at (303) 271-5925; www.co.jefferson.co.us/openspace/.

Mount Falcon Park and Red Rocks feel far from the city, but they are only twenty minutes west of Denver. Just south of Red Rocks, *Morrison Road* winds through the foothills toward higher country. It's a popular route into the mountains, but along the way there are jewels to be discovered.

TOP ANNUAL EVENTS IN BOULDER

Bolder Boulder 10K race,
May;
(303) 444-7223
www.bolderboulder.com

Colorado Music Festival,
Boulder Chautauqua Park;
June through August;
(303) 449-1397
www.coloradomusicfest.org

Colorado Shakespeare Festival,
CU–Boulder; July through August;
(303) 492-0554
www.coloradoshakes.org

Boulder Climbing Series,
Boulder Rock Club;
October through March;
(303) 449-0202
www.boulderrock.com

One such jewel is the town of **Morrison.** On any given weekday neighbors meet on the street corners to catch up on local news. Bicyclists ride the paths along Bear Creek and stop at a cafe for lunch. Visitors browse eclectic boutiques and people-watch the steady stream of locals, tourists, and on weekends, bikers. Indeed, at times, Morrison is very Norman Rockwellesque.

But along with a pleasant atmosphere, this community offers a treasure trove of antiques that will please collectors and browsers alike. Old western memorabilia, crafts, and unusual one-of-a-kind items pack tiny stores. Drop by *Lacey Gate Antiques,* 116 Stone St.; *La Boutique des Boudreaux,* 309 Bear Creek Ave.; (303) 697-8661; or *El Mercado,* 120 Bear Creek Ave.; (303) 697-8361.

Whatever your pleasure—buying, selling, or window shopping—Morrison is a pleasant place to spend an hour or two and enjoy lunch or an ice-cream cone. For more information call (303) 697-8749; or write P.O. Box 95, Morrison 80465.

A five-minute uphill drive from Morrison will take you to the much photographed locale of *The Fort,* which is a replica of Bent's Fort, an 1834 early Colorado fur-trading post. The thick, picturesque adobe building contains a small shop that sells authentic Indian jewelry and other items. But The Fort is best known as an award-winning restaurant, popular among locals for impressing out-of-town guests. The walls are covered with western oil paintings and original etchings celebrating the West. The cuisine features foods of the American West, both old and contemporary, with appetizers such as roast bison marrow bones, delicate buffalo tongues, and Rocky Mountain "oysters" (bull testicles). Entree selections include Elk Chop St. Vrain, prime rib of buffalo, Tlingit-style cedar-plank salmon, and grilled quail, accompanied by an

Tracks in Time

A visit to the Morrison area would not be complete without a stop at the outdoor museum known as *Dinosaur Ridge.* View more than 300 dinosaur footprints, all preserved in the sandstone of the Dakota Formation on the east side of the hogback. This National Natural Landmark is open for free viewing year-round, with interpretive signs providing information about the tracks and other fossils found in the area. Visitors can also arrange for a guided tour with the visitor center ($3 per person) or call ahead to find out about the next Dinosaur Discovery Day, held through the warm months, when part of West Alameda Parkway is closed to traffic and visitors can enjoy free guided tours. For more information, call (303) 697-3466 or write Friends of Dinosaur Ridge, 16831 West Alameda Parkway, Morrison 80465; www.dinoridge.org.

extensive wine list and original desserts. The Fort is located at US 285 and Highway 8. The restaurant is open for dinner Monday through Friday from 5:30 to 9:30 p.m., Saturday from 5 to 10 p.m., and Sunday from 5 to 9 p.m. For reservations call (303) 697-4771; www.thefort.com.

Close to Denver, **Matthews/Winters Park** and the adjacent **Hogback** are popular for wildlife viewing, hiking, and mountain biking. The trails range from easy to moderately difficult. The park is a mixture of undulating grasslands, trails, and fields of silver-green sage, purple thistles, wild roses, and wild plums. Trails run through rabbit brush and tall dill, and a short walk away from the parking lot the highway noise fades, replaced by birdsong and serenity.

trivia

Colorado's Front Range has an average of 300 days of sunshine per year—second only to Miami, Florida.

The Hogback with its twisted geology dramatically separates the mountains and the plains. On the eastern face is the Dinosaur Ridge Visitors Center. Red Rocks Park is nearby. Serious bikers can cross the road from the park and find a variety of paths.

The park lies astride the entrance to Mt. Vernon Canyon, which is one of the early routes to the gold fields of Central City and South Park. The big year here was 1859. Stagecoaches and wagons rolled through, and the nearby town of Mt. Vernon had a 150-horse corral. For awhile Mt. Vernon became a stage stop. An inn, a saloon, and a schoolhouse were built, used, and abandoned. Once boasting forty-four registered voters, the town of Mt. Vernon lost its place in history after the railroads arrived.

Sunflowers, chokecherries, and willows now lean over the gravestones and crosses of long-gone pioneers: One marker reads I.I. DEAN, DIED AUGUST 12, 1860, AGED 31 YEARS, I AM AT REST. Not far from the few square gravestones, the crosses and picnic tables sit under leafy trees near Mt. Vernon Creek.

Weekends and evenings are the busiest times, and the small parking lot fills quickly. For more information contact Jefferson County Open Space at (303) 271-5925; www.co.jefferson.co.us/openspace/.

The public parking area is located off Highway 26, just south of I–70, and lies within the Mt. Vernon town site. All Jefferson County Open Space parks are closed from one hour after sunset until one hour before sunrise unless otherwise noted by signage at individual parks.

To the west of Morrison, approximately 30 miles west of Denver on US 285, is the sign for **Meyer Ranch Park.** Here are 397 quiet acres with miles of well-maintained hiking trails winding through aspen groves and pine forests.

Through the spring and summer, the meadows are home to Colorado's state flower, the columbine, shooting stars, lady slippers, and the purple Indian paintbrush. The trail names fit the surrounding scenery: Owl's Perch, Lodge Pole, and Sunny Aspen.

In winter the park becomes a popular sledding and tubing destination. Motorized vehicles are not permitted here at any time, and dogs belong on a leash. The Meyer Ranch Park area has a history of homesteading, haying, and grazing. According to local legend, during the late 1880s the animals of the P. T. Barnum circus wintered here. The handsome Victorian-style Meyer home—still occupied by the Meyers—stands proudly across the highway. For more information about the park, call Jefferson County Open Space at (303) 271-5925; http://jeffco.us/openspace.

The same US 285 will take you to a truly offbeat family destination that even many Denverites don't know about. Around 25 minutes from the city is **Tiny Town,** a Lilliputian village and miniature railway.

Tiny Town appeals to children and anyone interested in miniature re-creations. Imagine about a hundred toy-size, handcrafted buildings to peek into, and sometimes even crawl into, and you get the picture. This town has old miniature log cabins, a fire station, a post office, a water tower, a flourmill, a bank, stables, a school-house, a rooming house, farms, ranches, barns, windmills, mines, and miners' shacks. There's even a miniature train ride around the entire Tiny Town village loop.

The attraction is run on a not-for-profit basis by the Tiny Town Foundation, which donates a portion of its annual proceeds to local charities. The distance from Denver is about 12 miles via US 285, turning south at South Turkey Creek Road. Bring a picnic and be prepared to pay $5 for adults and $3 for children ages two to twelve. Children younger than two get in free. There is a $1 train fare per person. Open every day from Memorial Day weekend through Labor Day 10 a.m. to 5 p.m. Open weekends in May and September 10 a.m. to 5 p.m. For more information call (303) 697-6829; www .tinytownrailroad.com.

Continuing on US 285 heading southwest away from Denver, the road is sometimes narrow and curvy, so it's easy to miss the entrance to **Glen-Isle** resort, a cozy, unusual retreat for vacationers. These humble log cabins and a well-worn lodge are largely hidden from view by bushes and trees off the highway between Grant and Bailey. This unpretentious holiday settlement dates back to 1900 and is a popular retreat for families, couples, and singles who want to cook and who appreciate the silence of a 160-acre forest. The forest is honeycombed with footpaths for hikers; horse trails are nearby, too. A National Historic Site, Glen-Isle is nicely old-fashioned; don't be surprised if you don't find a television set. For folks who don't want to cook, a dining room offers homey food. Prices are reasonable for these basic but comfortable accommodations. Lodge open June through mid-September, cabins open all year. For more information call (303) 838-5461; www.coloradodirectory.com/glenisleresort.

trivia

Golden's Armory Building, built in 1913, is the largest cobblestone building in the country. Workers hauled 3,300 wagonloads of stream-worn boulders from nearby Clear Creek and quartz from Golden Gate Canyon to construct the building, which is located at Thirteenth and Arapahoe in Golden.

Just west of Denver, the plains of eastern Colorado end and the foothills of the Rockies begin. Nestled in a long valley with the jagged foothills rising on both sides, **Golden** is a historic town and home to the Colorado School of Mines.

Golden greets its visitors with a sign arched across Main Street that reads: HOWDY FOLKS! WELCOME TO GOLDEN, WHERE THE WEST LIVES. The concept of the West is among the most basic cornerstones of American folklore and legend. Its connotations extend well into the realms of history, geography, morality, and philosophy. To the traveler visiting the western states, it's an almost mythical sense of place blending with the past. Golden, with its ten museums—a record for a town of its size—does not disappoint in either category.

The Golden story began back in 1859, when a man named Tom Golden set up a hunting camp with a few men. Soon some representatives of the Boston Company passed by on a wagon train, looking for a suitable place to establish a trading and supply base for the prospectors who were flooding the mining areas to the west. They liked the site and stayed.

Golden grew rapidly. Within a year it had a population of 700. By 1862 it became the territorial capital but lost this honor five years later to Denver. There was sporadic gold excitement in the immediate area but no big gold findings. Even today people still occasionally pan Clear Creek just west of town, but it's more for the sight of gold in their pan than for any profit. Golden's early economy was built on trading. It was the major supply center for mining operations at Black Hawk, Central City, Idaho Springs, and other communities.

With the decline of mining, new economic bases emerged. Golden's present economy is based in part on two institutions, both of which have brought it international recognition: the Colorado School of Mines, for a century the leading school in the world devoted to mining and minerals, and Coors Brewery, one of the largest in the country.

trivia

Golden once rivaled Denver; it was the capital of the Colorado Territory from 1862 to 1867.

To the west of Golden you'll find range after range of mountains, each higher than the last. These mountains serve the practical purpose of limiting the size to which Golden can grow—it currently has about 18,000 inhabitants. Unlike with other Front Range cities, the Rockies have protected Golden from becoming part of a growing urban sprawl.

A good first stop when exploring the town is the **Golden Visitors Center,** located at 1010 Washington Ave. adjacent to historic downtown, for an overview of what to do while you're in town. Grab a cup of coffee there and surf through the informational touch-screen kiosk. The center, run by the Greater Golden Chamber of Commerce, is open Monday through Friday from 8:30 a.m. to 5 p.m.; Saturday and Sunday from 10 a.m. to 4 p.m. For more information call (303) 279-3113 or write 1010 Washington Ave., Golden 80402; www .goldencochamber.org.

Consider a trip to nearby **Heritage Square** to get a sense of Golden's history. This rustic artisan and entertainment village was built on the 1860 town site of Apex, another mining boomtown. It has metalsmiths, jewelers, candy makers, tree-lined, lamp-lighted streets and more, including horseback rides; an alpine slide and water slide; a narrow-gauge train trip; a large family dinner theater; and plenty of free parking. Take exit 259 off I–70 and go north 1 mile. Open daily 10 a.m. to 9 p.m. (summer); 10 a.m. to 9 p.m. Monday through Saturday and noon to 9 p.m. on Sunday (fall, winter, and spring). For more information call (303) 279-2789; www.heritagesquare .info.

The **Colorado School of Mines** has an interesting, kid-friendly museum that fits the theme of the school. The **Geology Museum,** on the corner of

Golden Adventures

Seekers of thrilling family fun will want to check out Heritage Square's **Alpine Action.** After riding a chairlift nearly 500 vertical feet up the mountainside, visitors can cruise downhill for half a mile on one of two tracks, aboard a toboggan that fits on the tracks of the alpine slide. Those who can't get enough of heights can leap from a 70-foot tower—attached to a bungee cord, of course! Or they can try the go-carts, bumper boats, and other amusement rides. Contact Alpine Action, Heritage Square, Golden 80401; (303) 279-1661; www.heritagesquare.info.

Sixteenth and Maple on campus, is almost an art gallery. Murals by Irwin Hoffman depict many periods in the development and history of mining. See minerals from around the world, Colorado's mining history, fossils, Colorado gem trails, and more. Regular hours are 9 a.m. to 4 p.m. Monday through Saturday and 1 to 4 p.m. Sunday; closed all CSM holidays and on Sunday during summer. Admission is free. Contact Colorado School of Mines, Department of Geology and Geological Engineering; (303) 273-3823; www.mines.edu/Academic/geology/museum.

Train buffs and anyone interested in old transportation and machinery will want to drop by the *Colorado Railroad Museum,* which displays many ancient, narrow-gauge locomotives and even a small depot. The narrow-gauge railroads of Colorado made it possible for miners and other fortune seekers to access the mineral riches of the Rocky Mountains. These tracks also allowed the wealth to be carried out and sent across the country. The history of railroads in Colorado is preserved in the fifteen-acre Colorado Railroad Museum. Here you will see the original rolling stock, including locomotives. A rail spur allows the facility to "steam up" different engines throughout the year.

The building itself, a masonry replica of an 1880 depot, houses some 50,000 photographs and artifacts. The basement contains one of the state's largest HO-scale model railroad exhibits, open to the public on the first Thursday of each month. It recreates some of Colorado's old rail lines, such as the one in Cripple Creek. Famous relics of the museum include the Rio Grande Southern 1931 Galloping Goose No. 2 and the steel observation car used on the Santa Fe Super Chief, the Navajo. A bookstore sells more than 1,000 specialized titles and magazines, tapes, gifts, and mementos, while the Robert W. Richardson Library, a reference library, holds more than 10,000 railroad-specific publications.

Open every day except Thanksgiving, Christmas, and New Year's Day. Hours are 9 a.m. to 5 p.m., September through May; 9 a.m. to 6 p.m., June through August. The museum, library, and gift shop stay open until 9 p.m. on Thursday. Admission is $8 for adults, $7

trivia

Golden is where Jolly Rancher candy was first produced, back in 1949.

for seniors, and $5 for children two to sixteen (children under two free); family admission (two adults and children under sixteen) is $18. Contact the Colorado Railroad Museum by writing to P.O. Box 10, Golden 80402, or call (800) 365-6263 or (303) 279-4591; www.crrm.org.

Golden in its early days was the true West, home to pioneers who left the civilized east in search of a new life. They were risk-taking, self-reliant doers on the path toward something better. These days Golden folks embody this spirit of the west with their love of the outdoors, and an abundance of campers, backpackers, cyclists, and off-road enthusiasts. For many here, life is more about "doing" than sitting back and watching.

Given the town's outdoorsy reputation, it should come as no surprise that Golden is home to the 37,000-square foot **American Mountaineering Center,** located at 710 Tenth St. This center is the headquarters for the century-old American Alpine Club, the Colorado Mountain Club, the Outward Bound Wilderness, the Colorado Fourteeners Initiative, and the nonprofit organization Climbing for Life, which uses rock climbing to have a positive impact on at-risk youth in the Denver metro area. Stop by the center for a visit to the **Henry S. Hall Jr. American Alpine Club Library.** The library, with more than 25,000 volumes specific to rock climbing and mountaineering, is open to the public for research (only club members can check out books). Hours are Tuesday and Thursday, 10 a.m. to 7 p.m., and Wednesday and Friday, 10 a.m. to 6 p.m. For more information call (303) 384-0112; www.americanalpineclub.org. A new museum, the **Bradford Washburn Museum,** is the only one in the country devoted to the culture and spirit of mountaineering, houses numerous climbing exhibits and artifacts from the United States and around the world. Admission is $6.50 for adults, $4.50 for children. For more information, (303) 996-2755; www.bwamm.org.

After a day of touring the museums and riding the alpine slide, or biking and hiking the nearby trails, how about a cold one? How about several free cold ones? The famous **Coors Brewery,** the world's largest single-site brewery, offers free, self-guided tours on a first-come, first served basis. No reservations are taken. Plan to spend at least 90 minutes on the tour, which includes a close-up look at the malting, brewing, and packaging process. Afterward, visitors gather for a short tasting session in the hospitality room to sip limited servings of Coors products. You must be 21 or over to sample beer; minors can enjoy nonalcoholic drinks.

The brewery is located at Twelfth Street and Ford Street in Golden. Hours are Thursday through Monday, 10 a.m. to 4 p.m., Sunday 12 p.m. to 4 p.m. Closed holidays. For more information call (866) 812-2337; www.miller coors.com.

Before you leave Golden, ask yourself what could possibly epitomize the West more than the place where Buffalo Bill is buried? Buffalo Bill was a unique character of the frontier. And the museum that bears his name, 12 miles west of Denver on Golden's Lookout Mountain, has a uniquely western quality. Here are the mementos that bring a fascinating man to life: the paintings and posters that show him in full regalia on his white horse, with flowing white hair and beard, and a cowboy hat jaunty on his head. You can see his clothes, saddles, old weapons, a mounted buffalo, and numerous other artifacts at the ***Buffalo Bill Grave and Museum.*** More than half a million visitors come annually to see the artifacts and photographs that retrace his careers as a buffalo hunter, Indian fighter, army scout, and entertainer.

Born as William F. Cody, Buffalo Bill led an extraordinary life. As a long-time Pony Express rider, he was pursued by Indians, escaping (as he wrote), "by laying flat on the back of my fast steed. I made a 24-mile straight run on one horse." On another occasion he rode 320 miles in some twenty-one hours to deliver the mail. (En route he exhausted twenty horses for the journey.) He had few rivals as a hunter and was said to have shot 4,280 bison in a 1½-year period. His slogan: "Never missed and never will / always aims and shoots to kill."

The buffalo shooting had a purpose, of course; the meat was needed to feed some 1,200 men who were laying track for the railroad. And though William Cody had his battles with the Indians, he later learned the Sioux language and befriended the Cheyenne, among other tribes.

William Cody may have had his best years as a circus rider, actor, and showman, gaining fame all over the world. The first "Buffalo Bill's Wild West" show opened in 1883. The extravaganza toured for nearly three decades, spreading myths and legends of the American West around the globe. Almost a hundred mounted Sioux Indians chased wagon trains and a stagecoach; Annie Oakley and Johnny Baker amazed audiences with their marksmanship; eighty-three cowboys rode bucking broncos, thereby formalizing a cowboy sport into rodeo; and the entire Battle of Little Big Horn was re-created. Spectators could see live elk and deer from Colorado. There were horse races and even a bison hunt complete with a charging herd.

At its height Buffalo Bill's show employed more than 600 performers. In one year he traveled 10,000 miles, performing in 132 cities in 190 days. (He was particularly popular in Europe.) Cody's flamboyant style and rifle-holding figure symbolized the Wild West in many European capitals. Buffalo Bill gave a command performance for Queen Victoria at Windsor Castle and amused Kaiser Wilhelm II in Berlin.

No fewer than 557 dime novels were written about Cody during his lifetime. His face beamed out from hundreds of thousands of posters. At his peak he was one of the most famous men in the world. Even today the distinctive goatee and silver hair continue to make him as recognizable as the kings, generals, and presidents who may have honored him.

Cody made one of the first movie Westerns ever produced. Although near the end of his career, he also lived to see the start of the tourist industry as he opened the first hotel near Yellowstone National Park. Toward the end of his life, he turned into an entrepreneur and author. He gave most of his life's savings away to various good causes. His money ran out; his fame did not.

When Buffalo Bill died, President Woodrow Wilson wired his condolences. Former president Teddy Roosevelt called Cody "an American of Americans." The Colorado legislature passed a special resolution ordering that his body lie in state under the gold-plated rotunda of the State Capitol in Denver. Nearly 25,000 people turned out to pay their last respects and walk in his funeral on Memorial Day, June 3, 1917.

Buffalo Bill's grave is a few steps from the museum atop Lookout Mountain, with a good view of Denver and the plains. Anyone can come and see the burial place. It is marked by white pebbles. The simple legend reads: WILLIAM F. CODY 1846-1917.

The museum stands in a quiet conifer forest. First opened in 1919, it has been restored and improved over the years. The Pahaska Tepee Gift Shop sells original western artwork and western-themed toys, and serves food—including buffalo—in its large coffee shop.

Museum hours are 9 a.m. to 4 p.m. Tuesday through Sunday, November 1 through April 30; closed Christmas; open 9 a.m. to 5 p.m., May 1 through October 31. Call (303) 526-0747 or write to 987½ Lookout Mountain Rd., Golden 80401; www.buffalobill.org. Admission is $4 for adults, $3 for seniors over sixty-five, and $1 for children six to fifteen (children under six free). For the most scenic drive, take U.S. Highway 6 west of Denver to Golden, turn left on Nineteenth Street, and proceed uphill via Lookout Mountain Road, also called Lariat Trail due to its winding loops all the way up Lookout Mountain.

Whether or not the museum is your final destination, no visit to Golden would be complete without a trip up Lookout Mountain. The drive twists and turns up hairpin curves, narrow roads, rewarding travelers with spectacular

Home on the Range

The city of Denver has continuously maintained a herd of bison since 1914 at Genesee Park, just down the hill from the Buffalo Bill Grave and Museum. The buffalo roam free in their natural habitat and are best seen in fall, winter, and early spring when park officials feed them daily. Take I-70 west to exit 254 (Genesee Park). The bulls and cows can be seen on either side of the highway—a tunnel under the road allows the animals safe passage.

Flying over Golden and Lookout Mountain

On warm weekday afternoons and during weekends, the sky just west of Golden is the playground for daredevil hang gliders. The steep slopes of Lookout Mountain combine with steady updrafts to create the perfect location for launching hang gliders and riding the thermals for minutes, and sometimes an hour or more. Whenever cars fill the small roadside parking lot just before the Lookout Mountain Road, there's a good chance hang gliders will be soaring overhead.

views of Golden and Denver. At night the city below sparkles bright beneath the radiance of a thousand stars.

As you continue south on Lookout Mountain Road after leaving Buffalo Bill's grave, a sign on Colorow Road will direct you to turn right toward the ***Lookout Mountain Nature Center and Preserve.*** Situated on 110 acres of a fenced nature preserve, the center has a Discovery Corner, Observation Room, plant and animal displays, and a self-guiding nature trail (all wheelchair accessible). Admission is free. Nature Center hours are 10 a.m. to 4 p.m. Tuesday through Sunday; the facility is closed Monday and holidays. The preserve is open 8 a.m. to sunset daily. Also offered are nature classes that range from "Tales of the Trail" to "Foxes in the City!" to night tours where you'll discover constellations and nocturnal animal activity. Most sessions require preregistration. The Nature Center is located at 910 Colorow Rd., just off Lookout Mountain Road, Golden. Call (720) 497-7600; www.co.jefferson .co.us/openspace/.

Of the many trails that explore the foothills outside Denver, one has been traveled for centuries. ***Beaver Brook Trail,*** curving around Lookout Mountain, was first used by the Cheyenne and Arapaho Indians as a lookout. It is one of the state's most interesting paths, yielding views of the gorges below, dipping and climbing through a varied landscape of leaf trees and dramatic Douglas fir. Hillsides of yucca, aster, and wild rose bloom in summer. Although you're close to Denver, the trail quickly leads you away from civilization.

The Beaver Brook Trail includes scrambling across several small boulder fields, making it a challenging hike. The trail, a little more than 14 miles out and back, remains blissfully quiet during the week. Weekends are busy but those starting early will find solitude. If you hike up here in June and July, you'll be surrounded by lots of color. On the trail you may also spot the state flower, the blue Rocky Mountain columbine, as well as deer and abundant birdlife.

Mother Cabrini Shrine

On a 900-acre hilltop on Lookout Mountain sits the Mother Cabrini Shrine. There is no charge to enter the famous little chapel, which was built in 1954 and devoted to Saint Frances Xavier Cabrini. The setting includes lovely fields, surrounding forests, and enough steps to make hikers happy. For more information call (303) 526-0758; www.den-cabrini-shrine.org.

Wildflowers bloom later at the higher elevations, so by the time plants have already wilted around Golden (elevation 5,675 feet), flowers on the Beaver Brook Trail are just beginning to unfold. The higher you climb, the later the growth, the smaller the flower, and the cooler the air.

Small Colorado plants appear and disappear with the seasons, go underground, or take many years to mature. Certain wildflowers can sleep peacefully under the thickest snow cover, biding their time until spring. In summer the mountain flowers on the Beaver Brook Trail are as profuse as any in the region.

The Beaver Brook Trail is an easy drive from Denver. Follow US 6 into Golden, turn left at the first traffic light (Nineteenth Street), then drive up Lookout Road for 3 miles. Before you get to Buffalo Bill's grave, look for a sign on your right. Admission is free, and the trail is open one hour before sunrise until one hour after sunset year-round. For more information contact Jefferson County Open Space at (303) 697-4545; www.co.jefferson.co.us/openspace/.

Around 30 miles west of Denver up I–70 is a remnant of the Ice Age. *St. Mary's Glacier* is actually an ice field, covering a steep year-round snow bowl of about ten acres. In summer, when Denver swelters in a 95°F heat wave, it's about 45°F on the glacier, and people come to ski and snowboard here in July and August. Other visitors to the famous snowfield bring platters or tire tubes or even race downhill on shovels. Hikers, campers, and backpackers can be spotted at the 11,000-foot level as they scramble uphill past the last scrub pines. A few tourists come to sit on rocks and soak up the Colorado sun.

The ever-present snow and ice make St. Mary's Glacier a refreshing warm-weather trip, luring city dwellers as soon as the hiking trail opens each spring. After exiting I–70, the road follows a creek flanked by stands of conifers and aspen trees. After about 8 miles the road steepens and leads into a series of challenging curves and serpentines. Then the valley widens and the forest thickens. During snowmelt you see several rushing waterfalls, and at around

10,400 feet the parking lot appears. Hike up the rocky jeep trail or follow the uphill footpaths through kinnikinnik (evergreen groundcover), past the many fallen trees that are returning nutrients to the soil as they decompose. On weekends you'll share the trail with plenty of hikers.

After half an hour of hiking you reach a cold lake, topped by the glacier. Don't be fooled by the harmless appearance. Mountain dwellers know the glacier's record; almost every year someone who skis too fast or careens downhill on a shovel gets bruised, bloodied, or even killed. On rare occasions cross-country skiers are buried by an avalanche. In winter, the ill-prepared and under-clothed can get frostbitten at higher elevations. Prudent visitors know that the mountains are unforgiving and come prepared.

From I–70 just past Idaho Springs, take exit 238, known as Fall River Road. A 12-mile drive brings you to the parking lot and the trailhead to St. Mary's Glacier.

Richest Square Mile on Earth

At one point in history, **Central City** vied with Leadville for Colorado's mining bonanzas. They called Central City the Richest Square Mile on Earth. In all, some $75 million in gold was found there. Although the rich veins are long gone, tourists can still do a bit of gold panning in nearby creeks. Surrounding the town are the bleached mountainsides, the old abandoned mounds of earth, and the mines from another era.

Sloping, winding **Eureka St.** has been kept up. The redbrick buildings look as well preserved as those of Denver's restored Larimer Square. Central City's pharmacy and several other stores display their oldest relics in the windows.

For an overview of the area's history, visit the **Gilpin History Museum,** located at 228 High St. Housed in a brick building built in 1870 and used as a school until the 1960s, this two-story museum includes a replica of a classic Main Street of the past. The Gilpin History Museum is open 11 a.m. to 4 p.m. daily, Memorial Day through Labor Day. For another window back into days gone by, visit the **Thomas House Museum** at 209 Eureka St. This Greek Revival frame house was built in 1874 around the entrance to a mine. The Thomas House Museum is open 11 a.m. to 4 p.m. Friday through Sunday from Memorial Day through Labor Day. Entrance to each museum costs $5, or you can pay $8 for entrance to both. For more information call (303) 582-5283; www.gilpinhistory.org.

The Gilpin History Museum, the Thomas House Museum, and the well-appointed Central City Opera House contrast dramatically with the miners'

allaboard!

The first train from Denver to Black Hawk rolled through on December 15, 1872. It took another six years for the line to extend to Central City. Regardless of the railroad's success, writer-explorer Isabella Bird once complained that she had never seen such "churlishness and incivility as in the officials of that railroad." She wrote of her disapproval in her excellent 1875 book about her adventures, *A Lady's Life in the Rocky Mountains*. Back then, the train traveled a 200-foot-per-mile grade through Clear Creek Canyon. Black rock walls rose more than a thousand feet on either side. You can still see those ominous walls if you travel Highway 6 through the area; it follows the same route as the railroad did.

dwellings. The latter are small, modest cubes scattered across the pale gold, ochre, and russet slopes.

The first frame houses sprang up during the 1860s, along with the mine dumps. Gold was being discovered not just in the river but in the mountain too. In 1859 a man named John Gregory had walked from Denver to 8,500-foot-high Central City, a trip of some 35 miles with an elevation gain of more than 3,000 feet. Gregory soon dug up a fortune. The word raced as fast as the spring waters of Clear Creek. Horace Greeley, a New York editor, heard about Gregory Gulch and traveled west to take a personal look. Greeley reported: "As yet the entire population of the valley, which cannot number less than four thousand, sleep in tents or under pine boughs, cooking and eating in the open air."

A mass of prospectors swarmed into the hillsides. Most never struck it rich, but some had a grand time. A theater was built. Sarah Bernhardt and Edwin Booth came to perform. The **Teller House Hotel** rose in 1872, attracting the finest artisans.

Large, carved bedsteads, marble-topped commodes, and tall rosewood and walnut highboys were ferried across the prairies and up the rough roads by teams of oxen and mules and on wood-burning trains. The fine hotel hosted famous people; President Ulysses S. Grant, Walt Whitman, Oscar Wilde, Baron de Rothschild, and assorted European noblemen and their wives all slept in Central City.

In 1874 most of the community burned down, but gold rebuilt it. Fewer than four years later there was a new opera house, which still stands. Built in 1878 by Welsh and Cornish miners, the **Central City Opera House,** located on Eureka Street, is home to the fifth-oldest opera company in the nation. This restored Victorian opera house holds an annual summer festival that draws patrons from nearly every state. Performances range from its popular one-act opera *The Face on the Barroom Floor,* which recounts the local lore behind the painting on the Teller House Bar floor, to classic operas such as Giuseppe

Verdi's *La Traviata.* Central City Opera House invites opera buffs to sit back and relax in one of its 550 comfortable seats while taking in performances by known stars and future divas.

For show dates (performances are in summer), prices, and times, write to Central City Opera at 400 South Colorado Blvd., Suite 530, Denver 80246 or call (303) 292-6500 or (800) 851-8175; htpp://new.centralcityopera.org.

Opening night remains a prominent Colorado social event. Cars and busloads of operagoers from nearby cities climb the road along Clear Creek Canyon, the same route taken by John Gregory more than one hundred years ago.

trivia

Sherill Milne and Beverly Sills both got their operatic starts in Central City.

These days gamblers also swarm to the area, since gaming was approved some years ago for Central City and Black Hawk. New casinos have replaced many historic buildings and shops. Where parking was once hard to find it is now almost impossible, but shuttle services run from Golden and other areas in Denver on a regular basis.

If you want to try your luck, stop at these Central City establishments: Doc Holliday, Famous Bonanza, and Fortune Valley. Down the road in Black Hawk, try Bullwackers and Colorado Central Station.

Central City is about an hour's drive from Denver via US 6 and Colorado Highway 119. For more information, contact the Central City Marketing Office at (303) 582-5251; P.O. Box 249, Central City 80427; www.centralcitycolorado .com.

Rock Canyons and Boulders

As you drive toward ***Boulder,*** the towering Flatirons, huge slabs of metamorphic sandstone thrust up by the same geologic forces that gave birth to the Rocky Mountains, dominate your view to the west. Now the city's trademark, the Flatirons—some of which reach heights of more than 1,000 feet—offer ample opportunities for rock climbers of all abilities. These monoliths also appeal to hikers and trail runners due to the abundance of trails through the meadows and hills surrounding the Flatirons. Forming the abrupt border between the plains and the Rocky Mountains, this stunning rock formation is a perfect destination for walking, wildflower watching, or sitting with friends and enjoying a warm Colorado afternoon. Located 22 miles northwest of Denver, Boulder is easily reached in about half an hour via the Boulder Turnpike, U.S. Highway 36.

Arguably in possession of the highest population of rock climbers per capita of any city or town in the United States, Boulder enjoys its status as one of the centers of U.S. rock climbing. This reputation becomes even clearer when you drive up nearby Boulder Canyon or Eldorado Canyon to watch the climbers clinging to the steep rock faces. Dozens of world-class climbing areas within several hours' drive, combined with two of the best indoor climbing facilities in the country right in Boulder, only add to the city's appeal.

trivia

Boulder is the only U.S. community that uses its own city-owned glacier, Arapahoe Glacier, for its water supply.

Rock climbing's popularity has grown tremendously since the early 1990s. Boulder's reputation as a climbing mecca spread quickly, attracting both experienced climbers and those eager to try for their first ascent.

Eldorado Canyon is one of the birthplaces of rock climbing in the United States. Gorgeous sandstone cliffs soar above the canyon floor in shades of red speckled with greenish and golden-hued lichen that appears to take on its own luminescence when viewed in the right light. Formed of the same type of hardened sandstone that makes up the Flatirons—known as the Fountain Formation—the world-class walls of Eldorado Canyon enjoy international prestige within the rock-climbing community.

Hundreds of established routes await rock climbers of all abilities on the canyon walls, but none should be taken lightly. "Eldo," as climbers affectionately refer to the place, is known for its stiff grades, polished rock (especially on popular climbs), and sometimes scant protection. All of these factors mean that climbers should take caution when they first start out climbing in the canyon, perhaps choosing an easier route to allow themselves time to grow accustomed to the area.

trivia

President Dwight Eisenhower and his wife, Mamie, spent their honeymoon in Eldorado Canyon.

Once a bastion for some of the state's hardest routes, Eldorado Canyon's heyday as far as pure difficulty for climbing moves has passed, but that doesn't relegate its challenges to second-tier status by any means. Exposure—that sensation you get when you can truly feel just how high above the canyon floor you are—is the name of the game on classic routes like the Naked Edge, the Yellow Spur, and even Bastille Crack. Easily identified as the crack that divides the Bastille formation (the crag that sits on the left of the auto road as soon as you start to drive up

Traditional vs. Sport Climbing

Most of the rock climbing done in Eldorado Canyon falls under the definition of traditional climbing, meaning that climbers place and remove virtually all the pieces of protection that they utilize on any given climb. These days, "sport climbing" has taken off in a variety of locations, including Boulder Canyon. In sport climbing, climbers hook devices called quickdraws into preplaced expansion bolts that are relatively permanent fixtures to the rock face, meaning that the bolts remain in the rock for the use of future parties.

the canyon), it is an ever-popular classic; more likely than not you will see someone climbing it any given day, at any given time.

If scaling the walls isn't your idea of fun, Eldorado Canyon has plenty of other options. Tourists flock to the canyon in at least as many numbers as rock climbers, often clogging the narrow road up the canyon as they stop to gawk at tiny figures dangling from the walls high above. At the end of the canyon's road lies a lovely streamside picnic area with tables and barbecue grills, perfect for a family outing. Numerous hiking trails allow non-climbers to keep their feet on the ground while exploring the canyon's deeper realms. Kayakers and anglers delight in South Boulder Creek, which burbles its way down the canyon for most of the year, freezing over during winter months.

Mountain bikers get a solid workout as they slog their way up the unrelenting **Rattlesnake Gulch Trail,** a strenuous but short trail that challenges the rider with 1,200 feet of elevation gain in 2 miles along some tight, technical single track. To find the trail, turn left on the Fowler Trail after passing through the first parking area in Eldorado Canyon State Park.

To reach Eldorado Canyon State Park, 25 miles northwest of Denver, take the Boulder Turnpike to the Superior exit; turn south at the light and then turn right onto Highway 170 which will take you to Eldorado Springs. From Boulder, head south on Highway 93 and then take a right (west) on Highway 170 (Eldorado Springs Drive). The visitor center is located 1 mile up the canyon.

Eldorado Canyon State Park is open from dawn to dusk year-round. A $6-per-vehicle charge is required for entry from October through April 30; from May 1 through September 30 a vehicle pass costs $7 per car. For more

trivia

Tightrope walker and all-around daredevil Ivy Baldwin made 86 journeys across Eldorado Canyon on a tightrope suspended 582 feet above the ground. He made his last walk (and survived!) in 1948, at the ripe young age of 82.

information write 9 Kneale Rd., Eldorado Springs 80025, or call (303) 494-3943; http://parks.state.co.us.

Another popular canyon destination is **Eldorado Springs** at the entrance to the canyon. This tiny, eclectic town not only serves as a gateway to the park but also is home to the Eldorado Springs Pool at the historic Eldorado Springs Resort, which makes for a great place to cool off during hot summer months.

Once a major tourist destination known as the "Coney Island of the West," more than 60,000 guests flocked to the **Eldorado Springs Resort** every summer during the early 1900s. The pool, built in 1906 and then advertised as the largest pool in the country, is filled to the brim with artesian water from the springs. Open from 10 a.m. to 6 p.m. daily from the Saturday before Memorial Day through Labor Day. Admission is $8 for adults, $5 for children five to twelve and seniors; children under five free. Call (303) 499-1316 for more information; www.eldoradosprings.com.

To find out more about the history of rock climbing, as well as mountaineering and skiing, stop by **Neptune Mountaineering** on your way into Boulder. There you can explore owner Gary Neptune's impressive collection of climbing and skiing artifacts while you stock up on hydration packs, hiking boots, and energy bars. Make sure you grab an event schedule—Neptune Mountaineering hosts frequent audio-visual presentations, bringing some of the most famous names in the adventure sports and climbing community to Boulder. Usually held on Thursday nights, the slide shows are generally low in cost and high in fun.

The store (633 South Broadway, Suite A) is located on the upper level of the Table Mesa Shopping Center at the corner of Broadway and Table Mesa in Boulder. From Eldorado Springs, take Highway 93 north (it turns into Broadway). Open Monday through Friday, 10 a.m. to 8 p.m.; and Saturday and Sunday, 10 a.m. to 6 p.m. For more information call (303) 499-8866 or check the Web site at www.neptunemountaineering.com.

After stopping at Neptune's, continue along Broadway to Baseline Road, turning west to head up **Flagstaff Mountain,** the perfect place to mingle with rock climbers while taking in some beautiful scenery. Bouldering—a type of rock climbing that involves short, intense movements up the sides of the rocks, with the climber normally staying low to the ground—is a popular pastime on Flagstaff, and for good reason. Plenty of high-quality boulders dapple the flanks of Flagstaff, serving up myriad boulder challenges that both delight and frustrate the numerous rock climbers who flock to test their skills on the sharp, rough sandstone. Pull out at any of a number of locations along the road and follow the paths back to the boulders where you'll likely find some climbers who have come to test their skills for an afternoon. Continue strolling along one of the mountain's marked trails, or just grab a seat on one of the surrounding smaller boulders and relax in the shade of ponderosa pines while you watch the fun. The jagged ridge of the First Flatiron pokes out above the trees to the south, and obstructed views of the city of Boulder can be seen to the east.

For more information on Flagstaff Mountain contact the City of Boulder Open Space and Mountain Parks Department, P.O. Box 791, Boulder 80306; (303) 441-3440; www.ci.boulder. co.us/openspace. Open year-round, 5 a.m. to 11 p.m. (midnight for Panorama Point parking lot). Daily permits can be purchased for $3 from any of the six well-marked, self-service stations located along Flagstaff Road.

trivia

The pure, 76° water of Eldorado Springs flows at a constant rate of 200 gallons per minute. Bottled at the source, Eldorado Springs drinking water is available for purchase at grocery stores around the state.

For a treat, make dinner reservations at the ***Flagstaff House Restaurant,*** one of Boulder's finer dining establishments. Nestled on the side of Flagstaff Mountain, this lovely restaurant is sure to delight even the most discriminating food lover. Expect to shell out a bundle (think $50 to $75 per person before wine) for gourmet New American cuisine complete with impeccable service, occasional complimentary appetizers from the chef, and a terrific wine list, not to mention the sweeping views of Boulder. The Flagstaff House Restaurant (1138 Flagstaff Rd.; 303-442-4640) is on the right as you drive up the mountain. Visit them on the Web at www.flagstaffhouse.com.

After dinner, walk off your meal with your date by taking a romantic moonlit stroll at ***Panorama Point*** (1 mile up Flagstaff Road from the base of the mountain) or at one of the many other overlooks that line Flagstaff Road. If you're still feeling guilty about your marvelous dinner the next morning, you can always come back and bike up Flagstaff Road; it's one of the most popular workouts for local bikers of both breeds: mountain and road.

The tree-lined campus of the University of Colorado at Boulder (known to locals as simply "CU") warrants a visit, particularly in the summer when the university stages its annual ***Colorado Shakespeare Festival.*** During the season, you'll notice banners proclaiming the performances—and telling you to keep quiet—along Broadway as you head toward downtown Boulder. The festival performs several Shakespeare plays in July and August. National auditions attract actors from all over. Contact the festival organizers at (303)

492-0554 or write Colorado Shakespeare Festival, 277 UCB, Boulder, 80309; www.coloradoshakes.org.

Macky Auditorium Concert Hall, also on the CU campus, hosts performances by the Boulder Philharmonic, the College of Music, visiting musicians participating in the Artists Series, and concerts by nationally known groups. For information call (303) 492-8423; www.colorado.edu/macky.

trivia

CU-Boulder's mascot is a live buffalo named "Ralphie." Five Ralphies—all females—have trotted around the football field since the original Ralphie made her debut in 1966.

Boulder also hosts the *Colorado Music Festival* from June through August. Visiting performers and composers lend their talents and energy to the festival. Reservations are required. Call (303) 449-1397 or write to 900 Baseline Rd., Cottage 100 (at Chautauqua) Boulder 80302 for details; www.coloradomusicfest.org.

Hopefully you haven't tired of rock formations yet—Boulder still has more to offer in this department. Turn west from town for a drive up *Boulder Canyon,* with a stop at beautiful *Boulder Falls.* Tall, granite outcroppings line Highway 119 as it wends its way up toward the rustic town of Nederland and the Peak-to-Peak Highway. Find the canyon via Broadway (Highway 93) in Boulder. Head west on Canyon Boulevard (Highway 119)—you can't miss it. Stop at the pullout 11 miles up the canyon on your left to park, and then cross the street for a short walk back to the falls. Free; open from dawn to dusk. Contact City of Boulder, Open Space and Mountain Parks Department, P.O. Box 791, Boulder 80306; (303) 441-3440; www.ci.boulder.co.us/openspace.

Boulder Creek Path

From Eben G. Fine Park at the base of Boulder Canyon to Fifty-fifth Street on the east side of town, the 7 milelong wooded Boulder Creek Path winds its way along the creek, passing through some of the prettiest scenery in town. You can walk it, run it, bike it, bird it, push a baby stroller, or just pause and enjoy the surroundings. You'll never have to stop at intersections, since underpasses provide escape from traffic. And there's plenty to see along the way: Xeriscape gardens, fishing ponds for kids, wildflowers, and stately old trees. A network of other paths connect with this main artery, allowing for easy access to virtually all areas of Boulder. West of town, the path follows Boulder Creek up Boulder Canyon for a ways, turning to dirt before it ends.

Boulder Hiking

The *Mesa Trail,* one of Colorado's most scenic introductions to year-round hiking and trail running is easily accessible. From Denver, drive the Boulder Turnpike (US 36) until you get to the Superior exit; Highway 170 will take you toward Eldorado Springs. Slow down until you notice the picnic tables and a small parking area on the right. The Mesa Trail is well marked. Cross a little bridge and soon zigzag through a landscape of sumac bushes, ferns, and sedges. The uphills are gentle enough, leading into impressive pine forests, with views of the Flatirons. The Mesa Trail winds up in Boulder's Chautauqua Park. In winter the trail is popular with cross country skiers.

You'll probably catch glimpses of rock climbers on the formations as you drive up the canyon, weather permitting. In winter you're more likely to see people with crampons (metal-toothed attachments) on their boots and ice axes in their hands hacking their way up frozen waterfalls and sheets of ice—Boulder Canyon attracts ice climbers, too. But with its classic rock climbs, both traditional and sport, the canyon most likely sees far more climbing traffic from those who like to feel the rock instead of ice beneath their fingers and under their feet in warmer weather. After all, some claim that the canyon's famous Country Club Crack (5.11a) was the hardest rock climb in the country for a period of time!

Seeing all this rock climbing around Boulder might spark your interest in trying out rock climbing yourself—but don't head out there uninformed. Though rock climbing is a relatively safe sport, you should receive proper instruction and learn the safety basics before trying it out on your own. Rock climbing also requires specialized equipment that can take a big bite out of your wallet. To get a thorough understanding of ropes and gear, novices take lessons or get an experienced climber to show them the ropes, so to speak. Boulder has a number of local schools and workshops that teach safe climbing.

trivia

Boulder has no shortage of trails to explore: The city's Open Space and Mountain Parks Department maintains 120 miles of trails.

One of the best places to learn rock climbing in Boulder is ***Boulder Rock School.*** Affiliated with ***Boulder Rock Club,*** the AMGA-accredited school offers a wide range of classes for all ages and ability levels. The school teaches a four-session class called Indoor Climbing 120 for $176. After these lessons, the novice climber should be able to go to any gym around the country and pass the belay test, the rope safety skills test required by all climbing gyms.

Pretty much anybody can take a beginning climbing class—rippling abs or bulging biceps are not prerequisites. Especially at the more moderate levels of the sport, technique, balance, and flexibility count just as much as, if not more than, sheer strength.

More adventurous novices can also try an outdoor lesson. Most guiding services, Boulder Rock School included, offer beginning climbing courses, with the option for private instruction (more expensive). As with indoor classes, the school provides all the necessary climbing equipment, allowing the student to sample rock climbing without making any monetary investment beyond the price of the class.

Contact the Boulder Rock Club/Boulder Rock School for details by calling (303) 447-2804 or (800) 836-4008; www.totalclimbing.com. The facility is located at 2829 Mapleton Ave. Take US 36 into Boulder, and then head east on Mapleton. The club is on the north side of the street. Call for class schedules and to reserve a space.

For a tamer introduction to Boulder's famous monoliths, head up to pretty **Chautauqua Park.** This popular park has large, grassy meadows perfect for picnics and views of town. Hiking trails meander into the woods and up to the Flatirons. It's the location for the Colorado Music Festival, weddings, and summer film and music events. Follow Baseline Drive west from Broadway to 900 W. Baseline Rd.

One of the best places to feel the eclectic, funky mood of Boulder is on a stroll along the pedestrian **Pearl Street Mall.** Take Broadway north from

South Boulder Creek Trail

Rain or shine, summer and winter, one of the most popular walkways in Boulder is the South Boulder Creek Trail. Located east of the main part of town, the trail doesn't tackle any of Boulder's hilly terrain but rather offers a nice, flat, 3½-mile dirt path alongside South Boulder Creek. This route winds through trees and grasslands, offering interpretive signs along the way as well as the opportunity to see wildlife, from coyotes to entire prairie dog towns. Each season brings a different mood to the trail. In fall the trees burst into glorious shades of orange and yellow, while winter finds them stark and bare and the trail is covered with snow. With spring comes budding greenery, songbirds, and the fragrant scent of new growth. In summer the walk bursts with life. From Broadway in Boulder, head east on Baseline, passing Foothills Parkway. The trailhead, with plenty of parking, is on the right side of the street. Located on City of Boulder Open Space.

the Canyon Boulevard intersection; the mall crosses Broadway a few blocks up. Locals and visitors mingle among boutiques, bookstores, and restaurants, many of which feature outdoor patios. Find a bench and enjoy some of the most colorful people-watching in the state. Musicians, jugglers, magicians, and other street performers entertain, especially on weekends and during the summer. Many are quite good. The mall has been closed to auto traffic since the 1970s.

If you have a sudden, uncontrollable craving for ice cream, head straight to locally-based *Glacier Homemade Ice Cream & Gelato.* They have three locations: 3133 28th St. one block north of Valmont, (303) 440-6542; 4760 Baseline Rd., (303) 499-4760; and 1350 College Ave. by the university, (303) 442-4400; www.glaciericecream.com. Each store serves up to 80 flavors, all of which are made fresh in the store using premium ingredients. Popular flavors include coffee caramel crunch, death by chocolate, pralines 'n' cream, and bing cherry. The menu includes sorbets, banana splits, creamy gelato, smoothies, root beer floats, hot fudge sundaes and more, proof that this is "not just an ice-cream store."

Places to Stay in the Colorado Foothills

(All area codes 303 unless noted otherwise)

The rating scale for hotels is based on double occupancy and is as follows:
Inexpensive:
Less than $75 per night
Moderate:
$75 to $100 per night
Expensive:
$101 to $150 per night
Deluxe:
More than $150 per night

BAILEY

Glen-Isle Resort,
838-5461;
www.coloradodirectory
.com/glenisleresort
Inexpensive to expensive

BOULDER

Alps Boulder Canyon Inn,
38619 Boulder Canyon Dr.;
444-5445 or
(800) 414-2577
(outside Colorado)
www.alpsinn.com
Expensive to deluxe

Boulder Mountain Lodge,
91 Fourmile Canyon Dr.;
444-0882
www.thebouldermountain
lodge.com
Moderate to expensive

The Bradley Boulder Inn,
2040 Sixteenth St.;
545-5200
www.thebradleyboulder
.com
Deluxe

Briar Rose Bed-and-Breakfast Inn,
2151 Arapahoe Ave.;
442-3007 or
(888) 786-8440
www.briarrosebb.com
Expensive

Rodeway Inn & Suites,
555 Thirtieth St.;
444-3330
www.boulderbrokerinn.com
Expensive

OTHER ATTRACTIONS WORTH SEEING IN THE COLORADO FOOTHILLS

BOULDER

Boulder Museum of History,
(303) 449-3464
www.boulderhistorymuseum.org

University of Colorado,
(303) 492-1411
www.colorado.edu

CENTRAL CITY

Coeur d'Alene Mine,
(303) 582-5283
www.gilpinhistory.org

GOLDEN

Coors Brewing Company,
(303) 277-2337
www.coors.com

Golden Gate Canyon State Park,
(303) 582-3707
http://parks.state.co.us

Courtyard by Marriott,
4710 Pearl East Circle;
440-4700
www.mariott.com
Expensive

Hotel Boulderado,
2115 Thirteenth St.;
442-4344 or
(800) 433-4344
www.boulderado.com
Deluxe

Boulder Twin Lake Inn,
6485 Twin Lakes Rd.;
530-2939 or
(800) 322-2939
www.twinlakesinn.com
Moderate to expensive

CENTRAL CITY

Fortune Valley Hotel/ Casino,
321 Gregory St.;
582-0800
Moderate

GOLDEN

La Quinta,
3301 Youngfield
Service Rd.;
279-5565
Inexpensive to moderate

Table Mountain Inn,
1310 Washington Ave.;
277-9898 or
(800) 762-9898
www.tablemountaininn
.com
Moderate to deluxe

Places to Eat in the Colorado Foothills

(All area codes 303)

The rating scale for restaurants is as follows:
Inexpensive:
Most entrees less than $10
Moderate:
Most entrees $10 to $15
Expensive:
Most entrees $16 to $20
Deluxe:
Most entrees more than $20

BLACK HAWK/ CENTRAL CITY

Millie's Restaurant,
120 Main St.; Central City;
582-5914
www.famousbonanza.com
Inexpensive

BOULDER

Cafe Gondolier,
1738 Pearl St.;
443-5015
www.gondolieronpearl.com
Moderate to expensive

Boulder Dushanbe Teahouse,
1770 Thirteenth St.;
442-4993
www.boulderteahouse.com
Moderate

Flagstaff House,
1138 Flagstaff Rd.;
442-4640
www.flagstaffhouse.com
Deluxe

Illegal Pete's,
1447 Pearl St.;
440-3955
www.illegalpetes.com
Inexpensive

The Kitchen,
1039 Pearl St.;
544-5973
www.thekitchencafe.com
Expensive

Mediterranean Cafe,
1002 Walnut St.;
444-5335
www.themedboulder.com
Moderate to expensive

Q's,
2115 13th St.;
442-4880
www.qsboulder.com
Deluxe

Royal Peacock,
5290 Arapahoe Ave.;
447-1409
www.royalpeacocklounge
.com
Expensive

Sunflower,
1701 Pearl St.;
440-0220
www.sunflowerboulder
.com
Expensive to deluxe

GOLDEN

Ali Baba Grill,
109 Rubey Dr.;
279-2228
www.alibabagrill.com
Inexpensive to moderate

Bridgewater Grill,
800 Eleventh St.;
279-2010
www.bridgewatergrill.com
Expensive

Chart House,
25908 Genessee Trail Rd.;
526-9813
www.chart-house.com
Deluxe

SELECTED COLORADO FOOTHILLS GENERAL INFORMATION RESOURCES

BOULDER

Boulder Convention and Visitors Bureau,
2440 Pearl St., 80302;
(303) 442-2911 or (800) 444-0447
www.bouldercoloradousa.com

CENTRAL CITY/BLACK HAWK

Central City–Black Hawk Chamber of Commerce,
281 Church St.,
Central City, 80427;
(303) 582-5077

Gilpin County,
203 Eureka St.,
P.O. Box 366,
Central City, 80427;
(303) 582-5214
www.ccionline.org/counties/gilpin.html

GOLDEN

Greater Golden Chamber of Commerce,
1010 Washington Ave.,
Golden, 80402;
(303) 279-3113
www.goldencochamber.org

Cody Inn,
866 Lookout Mountain Rd.;
526-0232
www.codyinn.com
Moderate to expensive

Sherpa House Restaurant,
1518 Washington Ave.;
278-7939
Moderate to expensive

Table Mountain Inn,
1310 Washington Ave.;
277-9898
www.tablemountaininn
.com
Expensive

MORRISON

The Fort,
19192 Hwy. 8;
697-4771
www.thefort.com
Deluxe

NORTHWESTERN MOUNTAINS

Rocky Mountain National Park Territory

If you come to **Estes Park** during the high summer season—and want to be above the melee—you might consider the short uphill drive to the **Stanley Hotel and Conference Center.** It stands above the busy town like a white castle. The one-hundred-room Stanley reminds you of those old Swiss Grand Hotels—aristocratic, flawlessly kept up, frequently restored, a monument to good taste and good manners.

The hotel is all stately white columns, Victorian furniture, fireplaces crackling in the lobby, rooms with impeccable white linen, polished cherrywood furniture, and antique dressers. The handwrought leaded-glass windows, the spotless tablecloths in the elegant dining room, and the comfortable bar add to a feeling of being on vacation. Miles of walks surround the hostelry, which is at an elevation of 7,500 feet.

The historic hotel was built by the inventor of the Stanley Steamer automobile. Back in 1905, doctors gave F. O. Stanley, who had tuberculosis, only a few months to live. Stanley

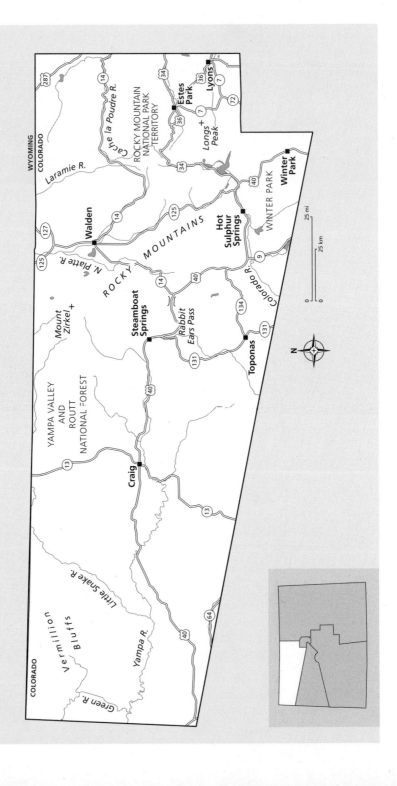

gathered his wife, her maid, and his controversial Steamer and left Massachusetts, heading for the Colorado Rockies. Stanley lived another 37 years, to the age of 91. His palatial hotel opened in 1909, and the "all-electric" hotel charged $8 a day, gourmet meals included. Celebrities such as Theodore Roosevelt, John Philip Sousa, and Molly Brown came, adding to the grandeur. More recently, novelist Stephen King found inspiration for his book *The Shining* while staying at the hotel.

The hotel still hosts guests with deluxe accommodations. Non-guests can enjoy the restaurant and cafe, admire the architecture and the views, and stroll the grounds. Contact Stanley Hotel at 333 Wonderview Ave., Estes Park 80517; or call (970) 586-3371 or (800) 976-1377; www.stanleyhotel.com.

The town of ***Estes Park*** (elev. 7522 feet) is the eastern and most popular gateway to Rocky Mountain National Park. For those not camping in the park, the town offers a variety of hotels, motels, and cabins. The main thoroughfare through town is lined with shops catering to tourists. During July and August traffic slows to a crawl. Those passing through on the way to the National

AUTHOR'S FAVORITES IN THE NORTHWESTERN MOUNTAINS

C Lazy U Ranch,
(970) 887-3344
www.clazyu.com

Devil's Thumb Ranch for Cross Country Skiing,
P.O. Box 750, Tabernash;
(800) 933-4339
www.devilsthumbranch.com

Grand Lake,
(970) 627-3402 or (800) 531-1019
www.grandlakechamber.com

Ice Cream at Myauchi's Snack Shack,
Grand Lake by the beach

Rocky Mountain National Park,
(970) 586-1206
www.nps.gov/romo

Stanley Hotel for lunch,
(970) 586-3371 or (800) 976-1377
www.stanleyhotel.com

Strawberry Park Hot Springs,
Steamboat Springs;
(970) 879-0342
www.strawberryhotsprings.com

Trail Ridge Road,
(Rocky Mountain National Park between Grand Lake and Estes Park)
(970) 586-1206
www.nps.gov/romo

Vista Verde Ranch,
(800) 526-7433 or (970) 879-3858
www.vistaverde.com

Winter Park,
(800) 903-7275 or (970) 726-4118
www.winterpark-info.com

trivia

The Stanley Hotel earned some of its more recent notoriety as the setting that inspired Stephen King's novel, *The Shining*. King wrote roughly half of the manuscript for the novel while staying in room 217 at the hotel. He returned to the Stanley Hotel in 1997 to make the ABC miniseries version of *The Shining* (the motion picture was filmed elsewhere).

Park should look for the sign just inside the town limits for the bypass road that avoids the traffic.

Despite the touristy downtown scene, many thousands of visitors enjoy Estes Park each summer. Shoppers have fun browsing for Native American crafts and jewelry, outdoor gear, and western wear. Kids ride go-carts, play miniature golf, or speed down a giant slide. Fishing and golf are close by. And there's a full calendar of music, theater, and entertainment events throughout the summer. Just keep in mind that you will be sharing the town with plenty of others. To avoid the crowds, plan your visit for late spring or fall.

Estes Park is 65 miles northwest of Denver and easy to reach via the Boulder Turnpike and U.S. Highway 36 through Lyons. For more information contact the Estes Park Chamber Resort Association, 500 Big Thompson Ave., Estes Park 80517; (970) 586-4431 or (800) 443-7837; www.estesparkcvb.com, www.estes-park.com.

Most people who come to Estes Park do so with another destination in mind. The east entrance to **Rocky Mountain National Park** is just a few miles beyond the town. Leave behind the noise and congestion of Estes Park, step into the natural grandeur of the park with its high peaks, meadows, and rivers, and you will see the reason you came here. With almost no commercial activity inside the park, the landscape looks much as it did when Mr. Stanley first arrived more than 100 years ago.

With 415 square miles of park, there's no shortage of acreage to explore. The park has more than a hundred peaks over 11,000 feet. The highest is Longs Peak at 14,259 feet. Surrounding those mountains is a vast wonderland of lakes, waterfalls, streams and rivers, meadows, forests, and tundra.

The best way to explore the park is to leave your car and walk some of the 355 miles of hiking trails. Trails ranging in difficulty from easy to extreme lead to remote valleys, sprawling meadows, and granite peaks. Several popular ones are short, level paths to beautiful lakes and waterfalls. Some trails to consider: Nymph, Dream, and Emerald Lakes; Ouzel Falls; Adams Falls; Bear Lake; Lulu City; Deer Mountain.

Frequent nature presentations and guided walks sponsored by the park are a great way to get kids interested in their surroundings. Backpackers obtain

TOP ANNUAL EVENTS IN THE NORTHWESTERN MOUNTAINS

Winter Carnival,
Grand Lake; Jan or Feb;
(970) 627-3402 or (800) 531-1019
www.grandlakechamber.com

Cowboy Roundup Days,
Steamboat Springs; July 4 weekend;
(970) 879-0880
www.steamboatchamber.com

Rooftop Rodeo,
Estes Park; mid-July;
(970) 586-6104
www.estesnet.com/events/rooftop
rodeo.htm

RockyGrass Bluegrass Festival,
Lyons; late July;
(303) 823-0848 or (800) 624-2422
www.bluegrass.com/rockygrass

Longs Peak Scottish Irish Festival,
weekend after Labor Day;
(800) 90-ESTES or (970) 586-6308
www.scotfest.com

permits and disappear into the mountains for days at a time. The streams and lakes offer trout fishing. For many, sitting next to a meadow or river and watching the afternoon go by is reward enough.

In summer, wildlife watchers may spot deer, elk, sheep, beaver, coyotes, pikas, and many bird species. Afternoon lightning and thunderstorms are not uncommon, cooling the air with rain before they blow to the east. In winter, bundle up and choose from dozens of cross-country skiing and snowshoeing destinations.

For many, autumn is the best time of all, with its seemingly endless string of clear, warm days. The evenings turn crisp and the nights are chilly, so bring an overcoat. After Labor Day you'll find less competition for campground spaces, lodging, restaurant tables, and traffic lanes.

Estes Park: The Best Views

The *Estes Park Aerial Tramway,* west on US 34 to Moraine Park Road, carries passengers to the 8,896-foot summit of Prospect Mountain for an unmatched look at the community and surrounding mountains. Sit on one of two suspended cabins and view the Continental Divide, and then picnic at the summit. For more information call (970) 586-3675; www.estestram.com.

Grand County Fishing

Grand County has some of the largest bodies of water in the state: natural Grand Lake and manmade reservoirs Lake Granby and Shadow Mountain Lake. They are home to rainbow, brook, mackinaw, brown, and cutthroat trout. The area is also popular for winter ice fishing. Area streams are also well-known for fly fishing. Try Willow Creek, Fraser River, and Colorado River in the area west of Granby for brook, rainbow, and brown trout.

Visitors in the fall get two additional bonuses: Aspen turn golden, and elk gather in the meadows to assemble and defend harems, and bugle their high-pitched calls. Both events begin in September and last well into October, with exact dates varying slightly from year to year. For many Coloradans, coming to the park to hear the elk and watch the fall colors is an annual tradition. The Park Visitor Center can provide forecasts in early fall on foliage and elk activity.

One of the park highlights is the drive along spectacular *Trail Ridge Road* (U.S. Highway 34), the highest continuously paved highway in the United States. Climbing 4,000 feet from Estes Park, the road winds along for 48 miles before dropping down to Grand Lake. Eleven miles of the road are above tree line in an arctic tundra environment, with the high point at 12,183 feet. Up here the air is thin and the ultraviolet rays are strong. It's a fragile world of tiny plants and flowers, alive in summer with birds and small mammals.

Like most important Colorado highways, Trail Ridge has a long history. The first human travelers along this route were Utes and other Native American tribes, who followed the already marked trails of wild animals. Miners used it in the 1880s. In 1929 Congress approved the highway, and in 1935 the road was finally completed.

Multiple parking areas along the way are the starting points for exploring the area. To truly experience this unique ecosystem, leave the car and set out on one of the designated trails. Keep an eye on the weather to avoid lightning storms; the first half of the day is generally less prone to storms. Stay on trails to avoid damaging the fragile foliage underfoot.

The season is short for a drive on the road, though. Deep snows and snowdrifts cover Trail Ridge all winter and spring. The road is open from around Memorial Day until the first heavy snowfall, usually in mid-October.

More than three million people visit the park each year. As a result, sites in the five campgrounds fill up fast. If you're camping, make reservations in advance. Without reservations from July through Labor Day, arrive by early afternoon for the best chances for a site. There are private campgrounds around Estes Park but they also fill up quickly.

The best way to avoid crowds is to visit before Memorial Day or after Labor Day, when children are in school. Renting a room or cabin around Estes Park may also be easier than getting a drop-in campsite in the park during these peak months.

The park entrance fee is $20 for a private vehicle, good for seven days. The Rocky Mountain Annual Pass at $35 is good for a year. Travelers age sixty-two and older can purchase the Golden Age Passport—a lifetime pass to all national parks for a onetime $10 charge.

You have four options for getting to the park from Denver. One of two quickest routes is driving through Boulder and Lyons (use US 36); from Boulder it's about 34 miles to Estes Park and the east gate to the national park. The other is to travel some 70 miles north from Denver on Interstate 25 north to Highway 66, then west on 66 until it joins US 36 to Estes Park.

You can also come on the spectacular Peak-to-Peak Highway (Highways 119, 72, and 7) from Black Hawk. The drive is especially enjoyable in late fall when aspen trees burst into gold. Plan on 2 to 3 hours, depending on sightseeing stops, to reach the national park via this route. For a more leisurely course, head west from Denver on Interstate 70, cross Berthoud Pass via U.S. Highway 40, and then get to Rocky Mountain National Park via Grand Lake. You can do a loop by returning to Denver using one of the previous two routes. For more information contact Rocky Mountain National Park, 1000 Hwy. 36, Estes Park 80517, (970) 586-1206; www.nps.gov/romo.

After spending the day on Trail Ridge Road, you can continue west and drop into a wide river valley with meadows and thick stands of pine, spruce, and aspen. After exiting through the park's west entrance, you will

Break the Ice: Ice Climbing near Estes Park

The *Colorado Mountain School* (CMS), the sole concessionaire permitted to guide rock and ice climbs in Rocky Mountain National Park, offers classes out of their Estes Park location. Wintertime is the perfect season to test yourself on the park's frozen waterfalls under the watchful eyes of one of CMS's expert guides. From introductory one-day courses to an intensive, multiday advanced course, CMS has classes appropriate for all skill levels. Contact CMS at 341 Moraine Ave., Estes Park 80517; (303) 447-2804 or (800) 836-4008; www.totalclimbing.com.

Coping with the Altitude

Most out-of-state visitors need a day or two to become accustomed to the altitude, especially those coming from near sea level. Colorado's resorts and ski lifts are from 8,000 to 12,000 feet up. Some skiers arriving from lower elevations fly to Vail and immediately storm the slopes. The abrupt altitude change can result in headaches, fatigue, and nausea. Sleep may not come easily those first nights in the mountains. The solution? Take it easy the first day or two. Stay hydrated by drinking plenty of water. Cut back on or even avoid alcohol at first. And keep the ibuprofen close by.

come to the town of ***Grand Lake,*** which skirts the shores of Grand Lake itself. This unusually blue lake—the largest natural lake in the state—will be dotted with sailboats in August, its marinas filled with yachts. At an elevation of almost 8,400 feet above sea level, Grand Lake boasts the "World's Highest Yacht Club." The high surrounding peaks stand over a stunning, Swiss-like scene.

The first people to visit here many centuries ago were Paleo-Indians, crossing the high mountain passes in search of game. In the 1800s, Arapahoe, Sioux, and Cheyenne began venturing here, resulting in fierce conflicts with Utes who lived throughout the area. Trappers, traders, and explorers trickled in, and in 1875 gold, silver, copper and lead discoveries touched off a mining boom. Ten years later the boom went bust, and population dropped from 600 to 80 year-round residents.

But the beauty of the area was not forgotten. Tourists, ranchers, and sportsmen began coming to the lake, and when Rocky Mountain National Park was designated in 1915, the future of Grand Lake as a tourist destination was firmly sealed.

Today Grand Lake can serve as an overnight getaway or the base for a week of exploring the area. The lake is a major landlocked sailing destination with frequent regattas. During the summer marinas rent kayaks, canoes, rowboats, paddleboats, and motorboats. Lakes and nearby streams give anglers numerous places to wet a line. Stables offer horseback rides along mountain trails.

With mountains on all sides, there's no shortage of hiking trails. The East Inlet Trail leads to a spectacular set of cascading falls, continuing into a

trivia

The 1,000-foot east face of Longs Peak, a vertical granite cliff known as the Diamond, attracts rock climbers from all over the world.

mountain valley with a river and large meadows. Just inside the west park entrance are a variety of hikes to choose from, including the trail to Lulu City, an abandoned mining town with only a few foundations remaining from a once-thriving settlement.

But Grand Lake is more than outdoor pursuits. The town is an idyllic setting to spend a lazy summer day just wandering. The last six blocks of Grand Avenue, the town's main street, are filled with boutiques, restaurants, and shops. The beach area has plenty of benches and grassy areas to sprawl with a good book. Stop by the **Kauff-man House Museum** for fascinating peek into the past. Exhibits, photos, books, and descriptions of life over the last century help bring to life the history of a region that was anything but dull. Volunteer docents answer questions and share information about the collection of antiques and memorabilia. The museum is open from 11 a.m. to 5 p.m. daily from Memorial Day to Labor Day. It's located in a log house on the hill overlooking the lake, just above the beach.

> # trivia
>
> Rocky Mountain National Park's annual budget is about $10 million—which may seem like a lot, until you consider that the park has nearly 3.4 million visitors each year!

After a day spent outdoors, return to Grand Lake to choose from a handful of restaurants. At Sagebrush BBQ and Grill, a basket of peanuts arrives as soon as you're seated. Follow the crowd and toss your discarded shells on the floor. Several ice-cream parlors offer cool, creamy desserts, but locals claim the best is the homemade ice cream at little Myauchi's Snack Shack across the street from the beach. Village Hub Coffee Shop has a homey atmosphere and well-made drinks. For an incredible weekend breakfast buffet, visit Fat Cat Cafe, where British owner Sally wants you to feel "comfortable, cozy, and well fed." You will.

In winter the handsome, wooden summer homes along the lake are abandoned. The souvenir shops along the boardwalk close down; only a few saloons, a tiny grocery, and the pharmacy stay open. Trail Ridge Road is closed. At the same time, the cross-country ski possibilities are plentiful. The Rocky Mountain National Park entrance is only a mile away, and you see Nordic skiers even on the golf course. Noisy snowmobile enthusiasts show up with their machines. Most winter tourists stay in nearby Granby; those not on a budget head to the C Lazy U Ranch.

Grand Lake in winter is popular for riding snowmobiles. But the roaring engines and blue exhaust fumes quickly shatter the deep stillness that winter brings to the Rockies. One place to escape the snowmobiles is the **Grand**

Lake Touring Center (415 CR 48, Grand Lake 80447; 970-627-8008; www .grandlakeski.com). From the intersection of Highway 40 and Highway 34 go east on 34 16 miles to Country Road 48 and turn left at the sign marked Golf Course Road. Yes, under all that snow is a golf course! The Ski Touring Center is set in beautiful terrain, and the 35 kilometers of trails are immaculately kept up. Some of the runs are surprisingly steep—especially for a golf course!—but other trails are gentle enough for beginners. The center is open daily through the winter from 9 a.m. to 4 p.m. For more information contact Grand Lake Area Chamber of Commerce, P.O. Box 429, Grand Lake 80447; (970) 627-3402 or (800) 531-1019; www.grandlakechamber.com.

For a memorable retreat from the outside world, try the *C Lazy U Guest Ranch* in the Willow Creek Valley. This is no ordinary dude ranch. Private and secluded, the 8,000-acre ranch offers endless outdoor activities and gourmet-western cuisine. In summer and fall, choose from horseback riding (with a personal horse during your stay), fishing, hiking, mountain biking, yoga, tennis, swimming, and trap shooting. Winter means downhill skiing over at Winter Park, cross country skiing, ice skating, sledding, horseback riding, and warming up in the heated outdoor pool or hot tub. Beyond the reach of cell phones, this luxurious ranch is a perfect place to unwind, relax, and be pampered.

Rates are high and commensurate with the ranch's amenities and all-inclusive package. C Lazy U is open June 1 through March 1 for destination travel; March 1 through May 31 for group retreats. Take I–70 to exit 232, then along US 40 to Highway 125. You'll see the sign. For more information and to make reservations, contact C Lazy U Ranch, 3640 Colorado Hwy. 125, Box 379, Granby 80446; (970) 887-3344; www.clazyu.com.

A ten-mile drive west from Granby along US 40 toward Kremmling will take you to *Hot Sulphur Springs Resort.* Once used by the Ute Indians as a place for bathing and healing, the resort has been in operation for 140 years. Facilities include twenty-two pools and private baths, and a summer swimming pool. Anyone staying at the resort gets free use of the outdoor pools. Massage, body treatments, and facials are available. For those not staying at the resort, guests 12 and older can soak in the outdoor pools for $17.50 a day; the price is $11.50 for kids age 6-11 (four pools) and free for children age five or younger (four pools). Open every day from 8 a.m. to 10 p.m. Reservations are recommended for all services; call for details. Hot Sulphur Springs Resort, 5609 County Rd. 20, Hot Sulphur Springs 80451; (970) 725-3306 or (800) 510-6235; www.hotsulphursprings.com.

Another guest ranch offering a true Colorado experience is ***Devil's Thumb Ranch Resort.*** Located about 10 minutes drive north of Winter Park, this upscale resort has a new lodge, cabins in the woods, and fine dining. Guests enjoy horseback riding, mountain biking, trout fishing, and exploring 5,000 acres of meadows, forests, and streams. In winter the ranch opens their Nordic center with 100+ km of groomed trails for some of the best cross country skiing in the state. From Winter Park, take US 40 past Fraser. About 2 miles after Fraser, turn right on Highway 83. The road forks a short distance after this; turn onto the right hand fork and follow it for 3 miles. For more information, Devil's Thumb Ranch Resort, 3530 County Rd. 83, P.O. Box 750, Tabernash 80478; (800) 933-4339; www.devilsthumbranch.com.

Winter Park

Winter Park is one of Colorado's most beloved ski resorts, and for good reason: great runs for all skill levels, consistent snowfall, and close proximity to Denver. And if you don't feel like driving, take the ski train from Denver's Union Station and get dropped off at the base of the resort, just a short walk from the lifts.

But just like elsewhere in the state, Winter Park is a year-around destination. In summer and fall the ski slopes and surrounding mountains transform into a playground for mountain bikers, with over 600 miles of marked and mapped trails, from single tracks to back country roads. Hikers, fishing enthusiasts, and lovers of the outdoors find plenty to do the surrounding national forests. Festivals and special events fill the calendar during the warm months. Colorado's longest alpine slide is here. In town, a variety of unique restaurants keep locals and visitors well-fed. Kids are welcome everywhere, and there's easily enough to keep visitors busy for several days.

Two of the Winter Park Resort lifts that move skiers up the mountain all winter haul a different load in summer: mountain bikers and their bikes. Miles of trails include jumps, obstacles, and fast downhill runs, along with more leisurely rides. For information and directions to other bike routes in the area, drop by one of several area bike shops or the Chamber of Commerce and get a free Winter Park/Fraser mountain biking trail guide.

Yes, biking is big here. The area is becoming a mecca for riders, and several important competitions are held here each summer. Two events are especially fun for spectators. ***Crankworx Colorado*** freestyle mountain bike competition (www.crankworxcolorado.com) is a four-day festival of jumps, big-air tricks, downhill races, and stunts. ***The Fat Tire Classic,*** (www.nscd .org/fattireclassic) is a fundraising event sponsored by the American Red Cross. It includes a family-friendly course, technically-challenging rides, and a great party at the end. The Winter Park-Fraser Valley Chamber of Commerce Web site at www.playwinterpark.com lists dates for these and other local events such as the Winter Park Jazz Festival, Art Affair, and Fraser River Days.

The main drag through town is a series of strip malls and shopping complexes that's not especially conducive to strolling. But it's worth browsing to find places like B Jammin' in Cooper Creek Square, for fun family souvenirs, and Ski Depot Sports (78717 U.S. Hwy. 40) for outdoor gear.

A hearty, healthy breakfast is a wise prelude to an active day in the mountains. Carver's Bakery Cafe behind Cooper's Creek Square, Rise and Shine Cafe downtown next to the Conoco station, and Mountain Rose Cafe next to the post office are all local favorites. For a friendly local coffeehouse, try Rocky Mountain Roastery along the main drag. Lunch and dinner offer a range of choices including Mexican, German, Japanese, Italian, and Colorado Cuisine.

Winter Park Resort, with 142 runs, has the fourth largest terrain area of any ski resort in Colorado. Neighboring Mary Jane ski area is known for its ski moguls, and if you want to learn how to master moguls, there's no better place. There's no celebrity parade here, and not much in the way of wild nightlife. But the amount of snow here and the varied terrain make this a Colorado favorite year after year.

Winter Park: Rail Trips

For seventy years the Ski Train has taken skiers from Denver to Winter Park. Starting at Denver's Union Station, it climbs into the Rockies and ends at the resort's ski slopes. Beginning in late December, the Winter Ski Train departs on weekends from Denver at 7:15 a.m. and leaves Winter Park to return to Denver at 6:30 p.m. Thursday and Friday departures begin later in the ski season. The summer train runs on Saturdays, leaving Denver at 9 a.m. and returning to Denver at 5:30 p.m. The two and a half hour adventure covers 56 miles, travels through 29 tunnels, and climbs almost 4,000 feet. You will travel through scenery that can't be seen any other way. For more information call (303) 296-4754; www.skitrain.com.

Grand Adventure Balloon Tours

Passing through Winter Park in the summer and looking for a fun adventure? Try a hot air balloon flight. The tour takes you and your companions soaring up above the treetops with aerial views of the surrounding mountainous terrain. For reservations and information, contact *Grand Adventure Balloon Tours,* P.O. Box 1124, Winter Park 80482; (970) 887-1340; www.grandadventureballoon.com.

For $48, non-skiers can take a two-hour ride to the summit in a heated vehicle called a snowcat, stopping at the top for a hot chocolate and photos before heading back down the mountain. Cross country skiing and snow shoeing are available at Devil's Thumb Ranch; www.devilsthumbranch.com; (970) 726-5632, *Snow Mountain Ranch/YMCA,* www.ymcarockies.org, or along many of the area's trails. Nighttime sleigh rides through a quiet winter landscape are available through Devil's Thumb Ranch and *Dashing Through the Snow,* (970) 726-0900 or (888) 384-6773.

To avoid the hassle of renting a car, many visitors take advantage of *Home James Transportation Services,* with their frequent shuttle vans that run from Denver International Airport (DIA) directly to lodging properties in Winter Park. The cost is $60 for adults, with discounts for groups of three or more. Children ages 2 to 11 are $40. Contact them at P.O. Box 279, Winter Park, CO 80482; (800) 359-7503; www.homejamestransportation.com.

In decent weather the 67-mile drive from Denver to Winter Park will take less than two hours. Go west on I–70, then north on US 40 over Berthoud Pass. Winter Park Resort opens in November and closes in April. Resort hours are 9 a.m. to 4 p.m. Monday through Friday and 8:30 a.m. to 4 p.m. Saturday, Sunday, and holidays. For more information on summer and winter activities contact Winter Park/Fraser Valley Chamber of Commerce, (800) 903-7275; www.playwinterpark.com, or Winter Park Resort, (303) 316-1564; www.skiwinterpark.com.

trivia

Winter Park's Mary Jane area offers 143 trails on three mountains for more advanced skiers, including the mountain known as Mary Jane itself, which has been voted the best mogul mountain in North America.

Colorado's Winter Park Ski Resort offers the *National Sports Center for the Disabled (NSCD),* the world's largest teaching program for physically challenged skiers. More than a thousand volunteers and a staff of fifty-four participate in it. Each ski season, nearly 30,000 lessons are given here. The NSCD

Playground for Cross-Country Skiers

After a ten-minute drive north from Winter Park, near Tabernash you come to the turnoff for the year-round *Snow Mountain Ranch/YMCA* of the Rockies. Thanks to more than 100 km of cross-country skiing, the ranch in winter has become one of Colorado's most popular Nordic ski centers. The setting is quiet and remote: no shops, restaurants, or movies in the vicinity, no television in the rooms; and for dinner you line up for simple, wholesome meals. Apart from cross-country skiing, you can try snowshoeing, swimming in an indoor pool, and in summer, a wide variety of outdoor activities and family programs. For more information contact YMCA of the Rockies, P.O. Box 169, Winter Park 80482; (970) 887-2152 or (303) 443-4743; www .ymcarockies.org.

provides services for people with almost any disability. More information on the program can be obtained by writing or calling National Sports Center for the Disabled, P.O. Box 1290, Winter Park 80482; (970) 726-1540 or (303) 316-1540; www.nscd.org.

Yampa Valley and Routt National Forest

In 1875 James Crawford, the first white settler of **Steamboat Springs,** arrived here from Missouri with two wagons, his family, his horses, and a few head of cattle. He was attracted to the area by a newspaper article. The author of the piece described his view from the top of the Park Mountain Range as "a wilderness of mountain peaks and beautiful valleys, dark forests and silvery streams—a deserted land except for immense herds of elk and deer and buffalo which had not yet learned by experience to shun the presence of man."

The Yampa Valley's idyllic setting and mild climate made the eventual "presence of man" inevitable. Even before Crawford built his log cabin along the west bank of Soda Creek, the Yampa Valley had sheltered Ute Indians and, later, French and English fur trappers.

Cattle ranchers found Steamboat's emerald-green slopes ideal for fattening their herds en route to market. Hot and cold running water in the forms of three creeks, numerous hot springs, and the flow of the Yampa River lured more and more settlers to the valley.

Recreational skiing first came here in the early 1900s, when Norwegian Carl Howelsen introduced the sports of ski jumping and ski racing to the community.

Today Colorado's northernmost ski town is a delightful blend of western ranch culture and outdoor adventure where tourists come for a taste of mountain life. Along with fleece and skiwear, you will see plenty of jeans, Stetsons, cowboy boots, and saddles. Skiing is a strong tradition in Steamboat. The town has produced numerous world-class skiers, and many Olympians first cut their ski teeth here.

In summer, the fields outside town are ripe with hay. Horses graze in sprawling meadows. The Yampa River flows through the valley, and mountains rise on all sides. Tourists come to browse the shops along Lincoln Avenue, float down the Yampa on inner tubes, ride the gondola for some high altitude hiking, and fish area streams and lakes. Dude ranches offer guests horseback riding and the experience of a working ranch. Especially in summer, the town is a tranquil blend of rural Colorado and relaxing tourist destination.

Like other Colorado ski towns, Steamboat has no dearth of kitschy tourist stores. Tucked between the fast food joints and T-shirt shops, or hidden down quiet back streets, are little gems waiting to be discovered. Try Off The Beaten Path bookstore at 68 Nineth St. for a morning latte and a browse through local photo books. Sweet Pea Market, housed in an old pole barn along the river at 735 Yampa St., offers fresh produce, homemade pies, and a coffee bar with free Wi-Fi. Historic F.M. Light and Sons has been at

Winter in Steamboat Springs

With 165 trails over almost 3,000 acres of terrain, giant **Steamboat Ski Area** has something for everyone. Its northern location is blessed with some of the highest annual snowfall in the state. Plenty of lifts, short lines, a prestigious ski school, and a top-notch ski patrol all add to the resorts' quality. Free mountain tours are offered daily at 10:30 a.m. starting outside the upper gondola terminal at the top of Vagabond. Choose from runs like Tomahawk, Buddy's Run, Stampede, Giggle Gulch, Last Chance, High Noon, Calf Roper, and Chutes.

Four Nordic centers, Steamboat Touring Center, Howelsen Hill, Steamboat Lake, and Lake Catamount, cater to cross country skiers. In addition, many public lands are open and free to the public, such as the popular Rabbit Ears Pass area.

With national forests on all sides, Steamboat abounds with free snowshoeing opportunities. At the ski resort, Steamboat's Ambassadors offer guided snowshoe tours daily at 1 p.m. Tours depart from the Information Center in Gondola Square and wind along a one-mile loop from the top of Steamboat Gondola, with sweeping views of Yampa Valley and the Flat Top Mountains. Call (970) 871-5444 to sign up in advance. Participants will need a Gondola foot pass.

830 Lincoln Ave. for more than 100 years, outfitting customers in authentic Western wear.

But you didn't come to Steamboat just for shopping. Perhaps the most unique way to explore the valley is to rent an inner tube from one of several shops in town and float down the Yampa River. The trip takes 45–60 minutes depending on stops, allowing floaters to meander lazily downstream. Local guidelines require "tubers" to start below Fletcher Park, which has a parking lot and easy access to the river. Take-out is around the Thirteenth Street Bridge, Several commercial outfits offer tubes and shuttle service back to your car. Although the water is tame, this is a natural river with an unpredictable flow. Life jackets or helmets are suggested, especially for weak swimmers and children. Local tubing rules include no littering, glass, or dogs, and respecting the marked quiet zones along three residential areas. Go early in the day to avoid the crowds and afternoon thunderstorms.

Howelsen Hill ski jump is famous worldwide among the ski jumping community. It's long, steep jump has launched many world records. But you don't have to wait for winter to watch jumpers racing down the steep run. When the snow melts, a porcelain surface on the jump gives young skiers a place to practice during the warm months. They lift off at the end of the jump and soar impossible distances before alighting in the grass below. They practice throughout the week and on weekends. The jump is located across the Yampa River next to the rodeo arena. Ask for directions around town.

trivia

Ten national ski-jumping records have been set on Howelsen Hill.

For a combination sightseeing ride and hike/bike, take the gondola ride up Mt. Werner at the ski resort. Within minutes the town and valley to the west shrink to a tiny panorama far below. Eliminate the croaking ravens, drop some cows on the hillsides and squint just a bit, and this could be the Swiss Alps. At the top, biking and hiking trails fan out in every direction and you can explore the surrounding alpine landscape before returning on the gondola, or heading down the mountain on foot or bike. The gondola will take your bike along with you.

Yes, Steamboat does have springs. A walking tour downtown will take you past ten hot springs, easily identified by their pungent smell. In town you can visit Old Town Hot Springs (www.steamboathotsprings.org) with eight hot spring-fed pools, two waterslides, massage, and a fitness center. For a rustic hot springs experience, check out **Strawberry Park Natural Hot Springs** (www.strawberryhotsprings.com), located about 7 miles outside of downtown Steamboat Springs. With three main pools varying in temperature and gorgeous stonework, this special place warrants a visit. The unpaved upper part of the road can be challenging if wet or snowy. Ask in town for directions. Hours are 10 a.m. to 10:30 p.m. (admission until 9:30 p.m.) Sunday through Thursday, and 10 a.m. to midnight (admission until 10:30 p.m.) Friday and Saturday. Admission to the pools is $10 for adults, $5 for teenagers, $3 for children three to twelve. (Children younger than three are free.) After dark, only adults are admitted and clothing is optional.

trivia

Steamboat Springs received its name in the early 1800s from French trappers, who mistakenly thought that they heard the chugging steam engine of a steamboat. In fact, they were hearing a natural mineral spring.

When it comes to quirky mountain town festivals and events, Steamboat Springs doesn't disappoint. Several times each winter, spectacular torch-lit parades stream down the ski slopes at the Torchlight Parades & Fireworks. The *Cowboy Downhill* each January is the result of placing 70 professional rodeo cowboys and cowgirls, many with questionable skiing skills, on skis and snowboards instead of horses and bulls. Locals and visitors cheer on their favorites, who are dressed in chaps and cowboy hats during slalom races, roping and saddling in the snow, and a wacky cowboy stampede race at the end. The Annual Winter Carnival, approaching its 100th year, celebrates winter with ski jumping, slaloms, a tubing party, the Diamond Hitch parade, madcap street events for kids on snow-covered Lincoln Avenue, and a brilliant fireworks display at Howelsen Hill with the famous Lighted Man.

The Cardboard Class, Steamboat's traditional rite of spring, features homemade crafts constructed from cardboard, glue, string, and duct tape racing down the face of Headwall run to a hysterical finish. Information for these and other events can be found at www.steamboat.com.

Steamboat's most colorful weekend is a festival of vibrant colors and art. The annual Hot Air Balloon Rodeo combines with the Annual Art in the Park as a staple of summertime in Steamboat. Early in the morning more than 40 hot air balloons rise and drift across the valley. Later on, West Lincoln Park hosts Steamboat's biggest arts and crafts festival.

For a less wacky, more authentic western event, the Steamboat Springs Pro Rodeo Series (www.steamboatprorodeo.com) runs on Friday and Saturday evenings most weekends during the summer from June through Labor Day. Some of the best cowboys from Colorado and Wyoming compete in bull riding, team roping, steer roping, barrel racing, and bareback riding. Come early for the barbecue and live entertainment.

The Saturday Farmers' Market on Sixth Street between Lincoln and Oak brings locals in search of buffalo meat, organic peaches, gourmet bakery breads, sheep cheese, barbecue pork sandwiches, and other edible specialties and local handicrafts. The market is open from 8 a.m. to 2 p.m., beginning in June and running through August.

trivia

More Olympians—69 at last count—have emerged from Steamboat Springs than from any other town in the United States. The reason? World-class skiing and an almost endless supply of the area's famous Champagne Powder.

Steamboat Springs is also home to one of the country's best automobile driving schools. But don't expect to learn how to parallel park here. The ***Bridgestone Winter Driving School*** is patterned after similar facilities at European ski resorts. In operation since 1983, the school is open from mid-December through early March. The track is a snow- and ice-covered course with enough turns, loops, and straights to satisfy anyone who envisions being a race-car driver.

But this is not play. You often share your class with law enforcement officers and ambulance personnel. Although these people are professional drivers, they recognize the need for practice, and many return every year. But every skill level is welcome.

The school's three tracks are designed for safety and forgiving of mistakes. In case of a spinout—and there will be spinouts!—the snow walls catch the car and hold it safely with no injury to driver or machine.

After the one-day class, you will feel confident in your ability to avoid collisions due to ice- and snow-covered roads. Six levels of instruction are available in half-day and full-day sessions to match your winter driving skills. Costs start at $270 for a half-day of instruction. For more information contact the Bridgestone Winter Driving School at (800) 949-7543; www.winterdrive.com.

Steamboat Springs is closer to Denver (around 156 miles) than Aspen (approximately 200 miles). From Denver, the three-hour drive follows I–70 west to the Silverthorne exit (exit 205). Head north on Highway 9 to Kremmling, and then west on US 40, which takes you over Rabbit Ears Pass and into Steamboat. Arrival by air is also possible; daily direct flights land at Yampa Valley Regional Airport, near Hayden, which is 22 miles from the ski area. For information on year-round Steamboat Springs, contact Steamboat Springs Chamber Resort Association, P.O. Box 774408, Steamboat Springs 80477; (970)

trivia

Steamboat boasts more than 100 natural hot springs.

Steamboat Water Sports

The Steamboat area is renowned for its variety of water sports options, including river floats, churning whitewater rafting, kayaking, canoeing, tubing, sailing, fly fishing, and more.

Anglers will love **Steamboat Lake State Park,** which allows fly, lure, and bait fishing for its cutthroat and rainbow trout year-round. Camping, water skiing, swimming, and boating is available. Take US 40 west through Steamboat Springs for 2 miles, and then turn north on County Road 129 and go another 26 miles. Cost is $6 for a vehicle day pass; $14-$18 per night for camping. For information call (970) 879-3922; www.parks.state.co.us.

To the south of town, Stagecoach Reservoir offers fishing, boating, water skiing, camping, biking, and in the winter, cross country skiing and ice fishing. Go 4 miles east of Steamboat on US 40, then south on Colorado 131 for 5 miles to Routt County Road 14. Drive 7 miles south on County Road 14 to the park entrance. A daily pass is $6; camping is $8-$18 per night. For information call (970) 736-2436; www.parks.state.co.us.

Fishing licenses may be purchased from most sporting goods and convenience stores in Colorado. A one-day license costs $9 and a five-day license costs $21 for residents. An annual fishing license costs $26 for residents and $56 for nonresidents.

Whitewater rafting is great on the nearby Yampa and Elk Rivers during the summer. There are a number of guiding services available. In Steamboat Springs contact the **Steamboat Rafting Company** at (970) 879-6699. Kayakers, too, will find plenty of paddling options. **Contact Mountain Sports Kayak School,** (970) 879-8794.

879-0880; www.steamboatchamber.com. For ski resort information, contact Steamboat Ski & Resort Corporation, 2305 Mt. Werner Circle, Steamboat 80487; (970) 879-6111 or (877) 237-2628; www.steamboat.com.

The *Vista Verde Guest & Ski Ranch* sits at the end of a rugged road, 30 miles north of Steamboat Springs. Another stand-out among Colorado dude ranches, it's among the best choices in the state for a family or couples vacation. More than 500 acres of ranch to explore, and thousands more in the surrounding Routt National Forest, mean riders, cyclists, and hikers have an almost unlimited choice of trails. Apart from horseback riding, this dude ranch offers supervised hiking, cycling, fly fishing, white-water rafting, and even rock-climbing instruction. In winter, you can cross-country ski, backcountry ski, sled, snowshoe, and ride horses. Enthusiastic

trivia

One of North America's largest elk herds ranges near Steamboat Springs.

staff make sure there's never an idle moment, unless of course you prefer to read a book, soak in your private hot tub, or just find a quiet meadow and enjoy the secluded surroundings. For more information contact Vista Verde Guest & Ski Ranch, Inc., P.O. Box 770465, Steamboat Springs 80477; (800) 526-7433, (970) 879-3858; www.vistaverde.com.

Continuing west on US 40 past Craig and Maybell, you will eventually reach the out-of-the-way *Dinosaur National Monument,* which straddles the Utah border. You get to it via the small town of Blue Mountain, or via Dinosaur, another small town.

The main visitor center with its dramatic display of dinosaur skeletons is unfortunately closed at time of publication. The building was declared structurally unfit and will remain closed pending rebuilding plans. But the surrounding area, once a real-life Jurassic Park (without the Hollywood actors, of course), is dinosaur fossil bone country. Even without the visitor center, it's hard to ignore this magnificent landscape of giant sandstone cliffs, gray-green sage, juniper, and piñon pine. And the spectacular Yampa River is never far away. A temporary visitor center for the monument is open with limited fossil displays. A variety of hikes and two self-guided driving tours take visitors deeper into this unusual park. For more information contact Dinosaur National Monument, 4545 East Hwy. 40, Dinosaur 81610; (970) 374-3000; www.nps.gov/dino. An entry fee ($10 per vehicle) is charged from Memorial Day through Labor Day only in Utah at the Dinosaur Quarry entrance.

Back Road to Steamboat Springs

Far from the interstate, State Highway 14 winds through some of the most diverse geography in the state. At 150 miles long, it's not the quickest way to Steamboat Springs, but for wide open spaces and long sightlines, it can't be beat. This is a route meant for meandering. Beginning in Fort Collins, enter Poudre Canyon and follow the Cache La Poudre River toward 10,276 foot Cameron Pass. Drop down the mountain into North Park, a sprawling glacial basin. This is moose country, and the valley's largest town, Walden (pop. 750) proclaims itself the moose-viewing capital of Colorado. Continue through mile after mile of lovely, lonely high-plains emptiness, where abandoned cabins squat in the sage, wind whistling through their gaping windows and sagging doorframes. At the western edge of North Park, Highway 14 meets Highway 40 and Muddy Pass. Continue up to Rabbit Ears Pass at 9426 feet, and begin the long downhill coast into Steamboat Springs.

Downhill All the Way

No, it's not about skiing, but about the annual *Steamboat Springs Marathon,* which takes place in early June. Starting out at an elevation of 8,128 feet and finishing at 6,728 feet, the marathon really is mostly downhill, but don't let that fool you. Though *Runner's World* magazine cited this course as one of the "10 Most Scenic Marathons of the Year" and one of the "Top Ten Destination Marathons in North America," it's still quite a challenge. Spectators stand along Lincoln Avenue or at the finish line at the courthouse lawn. The marathon is limited to 500 runners and it fills early. For more information call (970) 879-0880 or visit www.running series.com.

Places to Stay in the Northwestern Mountains

The rating scale for hotels is based on double occupancy and is as follows:
Inexpensive:
Less than $75 per night
Moderate:
$75 to $100 per night
Expensive:
$101 to $150 per night
Deluxe:
More than $150 per night

ESTES PARK

Holiday Inn,
101 South Saint Vrain Ave.;
(970) 586-2332 or
(800) 315-2621
www.ichotelgroup.com
Inexpensive to expensive

Ponderosa Lodge,
1820 Fall River Rd.;
(970) 586-4233 or
(800) 628-0512
www.pondersoa-lodge
.com
Moderate to expensive

The Stanley Hotel,
333 East Wonderview Ave.;
(970) 586-3371 or
(800) 976-1377
www.stanleyhotel.com
Deluxe

YMCA of the Rockies,
Estes Park Center;
2515 Tunnel Rd.;
(970) 586-3341 or
(303) 448-1616
www.ymcarockies.org
Inexpensive to moderate

GRANBY

Bar Lazy J Guest Ranch,
447 County Rd. 3, Parshall;
(970) 725-3437
www.barlazyj.com
Deluxe

C Lazy U Ranch,
3640 Colorado Hwy. 125;
(970) 887-3344
www.clazyu.com
Deluxe

Devil's Thumb Ranch,
P.O. Box 750;
3530 County Rd. 83;
Tabernash 80478;
(800) 933-4339 or
(970) 726-5632
www.devilsthumbranch
.com
Moderate to expensive

Drowsy Water Ranch,
P.O. Box 147;
Granby, 80446-0147
(970) 725-3456
www.drowsywater.com
Deluxe

Inn at Silver Creek,
62927 U.S. Highway 40;
(970) 887-4080 or
(888) 878-3077
www.silvercreekgranby
.com
Expensive

Trail Riders Motel,
215 E. Agate Ave.;
(970) 887-3738
Moderate

GRAND LAKE

**Daven Haven Lodge
Cabins,**
604 Marina Dr.;
(970) 627-8144
www.davenhavenlodge
.com
Expensive to deluxe

**Gateway Inn,
200 W. Portal Rd.;**
(970) 627-2400
www.gatewayinn.com
Expensive

**The Inn at Grand Lake,
1103 Grand Ave.;**
(800) 722-2585 or
(970) 627-9234
www.innatgrandlake.com
Expensive

The Rapids Lodge,
209 Rapids Lane;
(970) 627-3707
www.rapidslodge.com
Expensive

**Western Riviera Motel
and Cabins,**
419 Garfield St.;
(970) 627-3580
www.westernriviera.com
Moderate to expensive

OTHER ATTRACTIONS WORTH SEEING IN THE NORTHWESTERN MOUNTAINS

ESTES PARK

Big Thompson Canyon,
(970) 498-1100
www.fs.fed.us/r2/arnf/

**Cascade Creek Miniature Golf and
Ride-A-Kart,**
(970) 586-6495
www.rideakart.com

Enos Mills Cabin Museum Center,
(970) 586-4706
www.home.earthlink.net/~enosmillscbn/
index.htm

Estes Park Area Historical Museum,
(970) 586-6256
www.estesnet.com/museum

GRANBY

Arapaho National Forest,
(970) 498-1100
www.fs.fed.us/r2/arnf

SolVista Golf & Ski Ranch,
(800) 757-7669
www.solvista.com

GRAND LAKE

Kaufman House Museum,
407 Pitkin, 80447
www.kauffmanhouse.org

STEAMBOAT SPRINGS

Haymaker Golf Course,
(970) 870-1846
www.haymakergolf.com

Howelsen Ice Arena (ice skating),
(970) 879-0341
www.steamboatsprings.net

Routt National Forest,
(307) 745-2300 or (970) 879-1870
www.fs.fed.us/r2/mbr

Tread of Pioneers Museum,
(970) 879-2214
www.yampavalley.info

WINTER PARK

Children's Center,
(ski center for children),
(970) 726-1551
www.winterparkresort.com/activities/
familyresortactivities.html

Winding River Resort,
(RV, tent, cabins and lodge rooms)
Road 491 outside Grand Lake;
(970) 627-3215
www.windingriverresort.com
Moderate to expensive

KREMMLING

Base Camp Cabins,
(located on the Colorado River)
214 Park Ave.;
(970) 724-9559
www.gofishcabins.com/
Moderate to expensive

Latigo Ranch,
(970) 724-9008;
www.latigotrails.com
Expensive to deluxe (all-inclusive)

STEAMBOAT SPRINGS

Alpine Rose Bed-and-Breakfast,
724 Grand St.;
(970) 879-1528 or
(888) 879-1528
www.alpinerosesteamboat.com
Expensive

Alpiner Lodge,
424 Lincoln Ave.;
(970) 879-1430 or
(800) 340-9169
www.alpinerlodge.info
Inexpensive to expensive

Bear Claw Condominiums,
2420 Ski Trail Lane, 80487;
(970) 879-6100
Moderate to expensive

Ptarmigan Inn,
2304 Apres Ski Way;
(970) 879-1730 or
(800) 538-7519
Inexpensive to deluxe

Rabbit Ears Motel,
210 Lincoln Ave.;
(970) 879-1150 or
(800) 828-7702
www.rabbitearsmotel.com
Expensive

Scandinavian Lodge,
2883 Burgess Creek Rd.;
(800) 233-8102
www.steamboat-springs.com/lodge.php
Moderate to deluxe

Vista Verde Guest & Ski Ranch,
3100 County Rd. 64;
P.O. Box 770465, 80477;
(800) 526-7433 or
(970) 879-3858
www.vistaverde.com
Deluxe

WINTER PARK

Alpine Resort Properties,
P.O. Box 66, 80482;
(800) 797-2750 or
(970) 726-8822
www.alpineresortproperties.com
Moderate to deluxe

Beaver Village Condominiums,
P.O. Box 349, 80482;
(800) 824-8438 or
(970) 726-8813
www.beavercondos.com
Moderate to deluxe

Destinations West,
120 Zerex St. Fraser;
(970) 726-8881 or
(800) 545-9378
www.mtnlodging.com
Moderate to deluxe

Rocky Mountain Inn & Hostel,
15 Country Road 72
(866) 467-8351
www.therockymountaininn.com
Moderate to expensive

Snow Mountain Ranch,
P.O. Box 169;
(970) 887-2152
www.ymcarockies.org
Expensive

The Vintage Hotel,
100 Winter Park Dr.;
(800) 472-7017
www.vintagehotel.com
Moderate to deluxe

The Vintage Resort,
100 Winter Park Rd.;
(970) 726-8801 or
(800) 472-7017
www.vintagehotel.com
Moderate to deluxe

Wild Horse Inn,
1536 County Rd. 83, Fraser;
(970) 726-0456
www.wildhorseinncolorado.com
Deluxe

Winter Park Central Reservations,
(condos, homes, hotel);
(800) 979-0332
www.winterparkresort.com
Moderate to deluxe

SELECTED NORTHWESTERN MOUNTAINS GENERAL INFORMATION RESOURCES

ESTES PARK

Estes Park Chamber Resort Association,
500 Big Thompson Ave., 80517;
(970) 586-4431 or (800) 378-3708
www.estesparkresort.com

KREMMLING

Kremmling Area Chamber of Commerce,
203 Park Ave., 80459;
(877) 573-6654
www.kremmlingchamber.com

GRANBY

Greater Granby Area Chamber of Commerce,
365 E. Agate #B;
P.O. Box 35, 80446;
(970) 887-2311 or (800) 325-1661
www.granbychamber.com

STEAMBOAT SPRINGS

Steamboat Springs Chamber Resort Association,
125 Anglers Dr.;
P.O. Box 774408, 80477;
(970) 879-0880
www.steamboatchamber.com

GRAND LAKE

Grand Lake Area Chamber of Commerce,
P.O. Box 429, 80447;
(970) 627-3402 or (800) 531-1019
www.grandlakechamber.com

WINTER PARK

Winter Park/Fraser Valley Chamber of Commerce,
P.O. Box 3236, 80482;
(800) 903-7275 or (970) 726-4118
www.winterpark-info.com

YMCA of the Rockies,
Snow Mountain Ranch,
P.O. Box 169;
(970) 887-2152 or
(303) 443-4743
www.ymcarockies.org
Inexpensive to moderate

Zephyr Mountain Lodge,
201 Zephyr Way;
(970) 726-8400 or
(877) 754-8400
www.zephyrmountainlodge
.com
Deluxe

Places to Eat in the Northwestern Mountains

The rating scale for restaurants is as follows:
Inexpensive:
Most entrees less than $10
Moderate:
Most entrees $10 to $15
Expensive:
Most entrees $16 to $20
Deluxe:
Most entrees more than $20

ESTES PARK

Mama Rose's,
(Italian)
338 East Elkhorn Ave.;
(970) 586-3330
www.mamarosesrestaurant
.com
Moderate to expensive

Nicky's,
(Greek, Italian; near park entrance)
1350 Fall River Rd. West;
(970) 586-5376
www.nickysresort.com
Inexpensive

Timberline Family Restaurant,
(American food; kids' menu)
451 South St. Vrain Ave.;
(970) 586-9840
Moderate to expensive

Twin Owls Steakhouse at Black Canyon Inn,
(continental),
800 MacGregor Ave.;
(970) 586-9344
Expensive to deluxe

GRANBY

Grand River Coffee,
100 E. Agate Ave.;
(970) 887-0469
Inexpensive

Ian's Mountain Bakery,
358 E. Agate Ave.;
(970) 887-1176
Inexpensive to moderate

Java Lava,
200 W. Agate Ave.;
(970) 887-9810
Inexpensive

Longbranch Restaurant,
(German-American; eclectic menu)
185 East Agate;
(970) 887-2209
Inexpensive to moderate

GRAND LAKE

Caroline's Cuisine,
(French, steak, continental)
9921 US Hwy. 34;
(970) 627-9404
www.sodaspringsranch
.com/carolines.htm
Deluxe

Fat Cat Cafe,
(breakfast/lunch, huge weekend buffet)
916 Grand Ave.;
(970) 627-0900
Inexpensive

Pancho and Lefty's,
(Mexican and American)
1120 Grand Ave.;
(970) 627-8773
Moderate

Rapids Lodge Restaurant,
(Colorado cuisine, fine dining)
209 Rapids Lane;
(970) 627-3707
www.rapidslodge.com/
restaurant.htm
Deluxe

Sagebrush Barbecue and Grill,
(BBQ, comfort food)
1101 Grand Ave.;
(970) 627-1404
Moderate

Terrace Inn,
(salmon, steak, duck, contemporary)
813 Grand Ave.;
(970) 627-3000
www.grandlaketerraceinn
.com
Expensive

Village Hub Coffee Shop,
(Coffee, tea, light cuisine, comfy atmosphere)
830 Grand Ave.;
(970) 627-5095
www.thevillagehub.net
Inexpensive

STEAMBOAT SPRINGS

Antares,
(eclectic, continental)
57½ Eighth St.;
(970) 879-9939
www.steamboat-dining
.com
Deluxe

Cafe Diva,
(unique, eclectic menu)
1855 Ski Time Square Dr.;
(970) 871-0508
www.cafediva.com
Expensive

Creekside Cafe & Grill,
(hearty breakfast and lunch)
131 Eleventh St.;
(970) 879-4925
www.creekside-cafe.com
Moderate

La Montana,
(Tex-mex)
2500 Village Dr. #102;
(970) 879-5800
www.steamboat-dining
.com
Moderate to expensive

Mazzola's Italian Restaurant,
917 Lincoln Ave.;
(970) 879-2405
www.mazzolas.com
Moderate

Off The Beaten Path Book Store, Coffee House & Bakery Café,
68 9th St.;
(970) 879-6830 or
(800) 898-6830
www.steamboatbooks.com
Inexpensive

Ore House at Pine Grove,
(steak, seafood, game)
1465 Pine Grove Rd.;
(970) 879-1190
www.orehouseatthepine
grove.com
Expensive to deluxe

The Shack Cafe,
(breakfast and lunch)
740 Lincoln Ave.;
(970) 879-9975
www.steamboat-dining
.com
Inexpensive to moderate

WINTER PARK

Carlos and Maria's,
(Mexican)
Cooper Creek Square;
(970) 726-9674
Moderate

Carver's Bakery Cafe,
983 Vasquez Rd.;
(970) 726-8202
www.carversbakery.com
Inexpensive to moderate

Deno's Mountain Bistro,
78911 Hwy. 50;
(970) 726-5332
www.denosmountainbistro
.com
Expensive to deluxe

Dezeley's at Gasthaus Eichler,
(European, continental)
78786 US 40;
(970) 726-5133
www.gasthauseichler.com/
restaurant.html
Expensive to deluxe

Fontenots Fresh Seafood and Grill,
78336 Hwy. 40;
(970) 726-4021
www.fontenotswp.com
Moderate to expensive

Hernando's Pizza and Pasta Pub,
78199 Hwy. 40;
(970) 726-5409
www.hernandospizzapub
.com
Moderate

**Mountain Rose Cafe,
78542 Hwy. 40;**
(970) 726-1374
www.mountainrosecafe
.com
Inexpensive to moderate

**Rise and Shine Cafe,
78437 Hwy. 40;**
(970) 726-5530
Inexpensive to moderate

Tabernash Tavern,
72287 U.S. Hwy 40;
970.726.4430
Moderate to expensive

Untamed Steakhouse,
(steak, seafood)
78491 US 40;
(970) 726-1111
www.untamedsteakhouse
.com
Moderate to expensive

CENTRAL MOUNTAINS

Beyond the Front Range

Most travelers in a hurry to cross Colorado take Interstate 70, the wide, fairly straight thoroughfare that cuts east-west across the upper third of the state. Yes, it's the quick route between Grand Junction and Denver, and as far as highway scenery goes, it's probably one of the prettiest drives in the country. But those rushing through will miss out on the central mountains that contain some of the state's highlights.

Although the region deserves weeks of exploring to do it justice, many of the places of interest on the eastern side can be seen during a day trip from Denver. Each fall, when aspen begin changing and entire mountains turn a shimmering gold, locals around the state hit the roads and trails to appreciate the fleeting magic of this brilliant display. Everyone has his or her favorite route, but one of the more popular ones is a loop trip: Denver, Idaho Springs, Silver Plume, Breckenridge, Fairplay, Denver. The trip can be done in a day, or easily stretched into two or more days with stops along the way. But don't wait for September and October to take this drive; no matter when you go, it's a

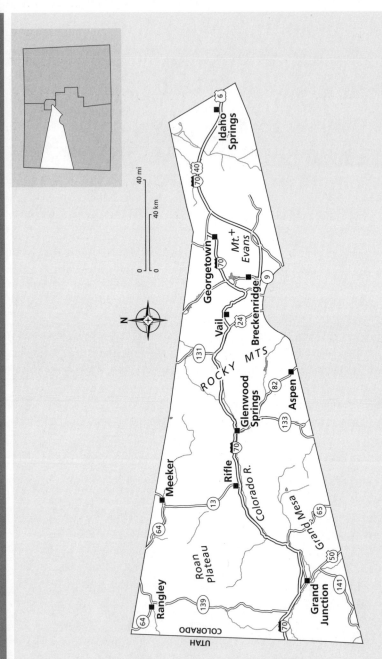

40 mi
40 km

N

UTAH
COLORADO

6
Idaho Springs
70 40
70 40
Georgetown
70
Mt.+ Evans
9
24
Vail
Breckenridge
131
ROCKY MTS
82
Glenwood Springs
Aspen
133
70
Rifle
Colorado R.
13
65
Meeker
Grand Mesa
64
Roan Plateau
50
Rangley
139
141
Grand Junction
70
64

diverse sampling of small mountain towns, western geography, and stunning scenery.

Beginning in Denver, head west on I–70 toward the mountain community of Idaho Springs (altitude 7,540 feet). Those wanting to explore the eastern side of the Mount Evans Wilderness can turn south here, climbing up into the high country above the tree line. Continue west past Georgetown, the historic mining town of beautifully preserved Victorian homes that's worth a visit on its own. This is also the access point to the western side of Mount Evans and dramatic Guanella Pass at over 10,000 feet.

As you continue along I–70, the mountains rise steeply and the valley turns narrow. Spruce, fir, and aspen blanket the mountains. Shortly before the Eisenhower Memorial Tunnel—weather permitting, of course—turn off on U.S. Highway 6 at the sign for *Loveland Pass* and head up to the Continental Divide (11,990 feet). The views are unbeatable from up here, so stop and take in the alpine panoramas. Afterward, cruise down the mountain past Keystone ski resort to Dillon Reservoir.

AUTHOR'S FAVORITES IN THE CENTRAL MOUNTAINS

Colorado National Monument,
(970) 858-3617
www.nps.gov/colm

Georgetown,
(303) 569-2840
www.historicgeorgetown.org

Glenwood Canyon,
(970) 945-6589
www.glenwoodchamber.com

Gore Range/Pass,
(970) 638-4516
www.fs.fed.us/r2/mbr/about/districts/yampa.shtml

Grand Valley Wineries,
(970) 464-5867 or (303) 399-7586
www.grandvalleywine.com

Lake Dillon Recreational Area,
(970) 468-5100
www.dillonmarina.com

Mount Evans,
(303) 567-3000
www.mtevans.com

Museum of Western Colorado's Cross Orchards Living History Museum,
(970) 434-9814
www.wcmuseum.org/crossorchards.htm

Palisade Orchard Tours,
(970) 464-7458
www.palisadecoc.com

Rifle Falls State Park,
(970) 625-1607
www.parks.state.co.us

Safe Travel in Colorado

Colorado is renowned for its afternoon thunderstorms which proliferate during the summer months but are possible year-round. For this reason, outdoor activities—particularly those involving a long time away from safe shelter—should be undertaken only with careful planning and attention to time. If you do find yourself caught in a thunderstorm, take refuge in a car (with the windows up) or a substantial building—not a shallow cave or rock outcropping. If no safe shelter is available, seek a low-lying area or trench with shrubs or trees of similar stature. Avoid lone trees, open spaces, higher ground, water, and contact with two different objects (such as rock and ground). Also maintain a 15-foot distance from others. Crouch low to the ground with both of your feet together and cover your ears. For more safety tips, visit the National Lightning Safety Institute's Web site at www.lightningsafety.com.

Flash flooding can pose a real danger in narrow canyons, even on days that begin with clear skies and sunny weather. Be sure to check weather reports for thunderstorm predictions and always have a backup plan.

Drinking water from lakes, rivers, and streams is not exactly the same wilderness treat it once was. Unless you want to find out just how nasty a bout of giardiasis can be—think diarrhea, stomach cramps, and a visit to the doctor—avoid drinking water from lakes, streams, or rivers unless you purify it first. Bring adequate drinking water (minimum of two liters per person per day), and for backcountry trips, a water purification filter, which can be purchased from most sporting-goods stores. You can also purify water by boiling it for at least twenty minutes to kill all disease-causing organisms.

The reservoir area is popular with boaters, fishermen, and cyclists, and the osprey that nest annually along the lake. Linger here and stretch your legs, or follow the signs to Frisco, staying on the road around the lake. After Frisco, swing left onto Highway 9 and head down the valley to Breckenridge.

This former mining community is in the middle of another bonanza. In 1859 it was gold. Now it's skiing, vacation homes, and mountain life. Stay the night to enjoy the restaurants and shops, or continue driving through thick forests past beaver ponds to ***Hoosier Pass.*** You're surrounded by 14,000 foot peaks—Quandary Peak, Mt. Lincoln, Mt. Sherman—as you drop down into Placer Valley, leaving the subalpine terrain and returning to forests and streams.

At the town of Fairplay, turn north on U.S. Highway 285 through South Park. Keep an eye out for antelope in the surrounding grasslands and approach the steep incline toward Kenosha Pass. Dropping into the valley along the South Platte River, the road twists through a valley of pastures and grazing horses before coming to the tiny settlement of Grant. From there you climb up Crow Hill, then pass communities whose names signify Colorado: Pine Junction, Deer Creek, Conifer, Indian Hills, Aspen Park. From there it's a quick drop out of the foothills back to Denver, where you began your circle tour 175 miles ago.

Idaho Springs is a short drive west on I–70 from Denver and the area makes an interesting half-day trip. Stroll along the short main street and browse the shops, some of which are in historic buildings from the mining days. Take a walking tour with the Historical Society of Idaho Springs (303-567-4382) to learn more about the history and mining past of the area. Two museums, the

TOP ANNUAL EVENTS IN THE CENTRAL MOUNTAINS

Wintersköl Carnival,
Aspen; mid-Jan;
(970) 925-1940 or (800) 670-0792
www.aspenchamber.org

Fruita Fat Tire Festival,
late Apr;
(970) 858-3894
www.fruitamountainbike.com/festival

Aspen Music Festival,
June through Aug;
(970) 925-9042
www.aspenmusicfestival.com

Breckenridge Music Festival,
June through Aug;
(970) 453-9142 or (800) 753-9142
www.breckenridgemusicfestival.com

Grand Junction Farmers' Market Festival,
Thurs throughout summer;
(970) 245-9697
www.visitdowntowngj.org

Breckenridge Film Festival,
June;
(970) 453-6200
www.breckfilmfest.com

Strawberry Days,
Glenwood Springs; mid-June;
(970) 945-6589
www.strawberrydaysfestival.com

Gold Rush Days Festival,
Idaho Springs; mid-summer;
(303) 567-4660

Peach Festival,
Palisade; mid-Aug;
(970) 464-7458
www.palisadecoc.com/

Colorado Mountain Winefest,
Palisade; mid-Sept;
(800) 704-3667
www.coloradowinefest.com

Beaver Creek Oktoberfest,
Vail; mid-Sept;
(970) 845-9090
www.beavercreek.snow.com

Annual Fall Art Festival,
Glenwood Springs;
last week in Sept;
(970) 945-2414
www.glenwoodchamber.com

Little-Known Facts about Idaho Springs

Some of Colorado's earliest gold strikes took place here in 1859.

The Ute Indians were the first to discover and use its famous hot springs.

When it was completed after 17 years in 1915, Argo Tunnel was the world's longest mining tunnel. The 5-mile-long tunnel once ran all the way to Central City, another gold-rush town. Unfortunately, only a portion of the tunnel remains, and it is not open to the public.

The highway that runs to the summit of Mount Evans from Idaho Springs is the highest paved driving road in North America.

Heritage Museum and Visitor Center (open daily; 2060 Miner St.; 303-567-4382) and the Underhill Museum (June–Sept; 1416 Miner St.) offer interesting tidbits, artifacts, and memorabilia about the area's colorful past.

If you decide to spend the night, keep in mind that the local motels, while not fancy, are among the lowest-priced in Colorado. A quick drive down Colorado Boulevard will give you a dozen or so to choose from. If you reach the area around lunch or dinner time, Idaho Springs's *BeauJo's Pizza* is well-known in Colorado for its varieties and its "pizza by the pound." You can build your own pizza here as well (1517 Miner St.; 303-567-4376; www.beaujos .com). Open Sunday through Thursday from 11 a.m. to 9 p.m. and Friday and Saturday from 11 a.m. to 9:30 p.m.

Another excellent dining choice is *Two Brothers Deli.* For fast, quality sandwiches, breakfast wraps and specials, soup, salad, smoothies, hot drinks, and free wireless, this is a smart stop before or after hiking, skiing, or exploring the town. Located at 1424 Miner St.; (303) 567-2439; www.twobrothersdeli .com. Open daily 6:30 a.m.–6 p.m.

The gold rush may be long over, but at the *Phoenix Gold Mine,* located at the west end of Idaho Springs, anyone can try his hand at what brought thousands of men to Colorado back in the 1800s . . . gold panning!

This is the only working gold mine in Colorado that is open to the public. Take a tour guided by actual miners. Better yet, dig your own samples—you even get to keep what you find! Gold panning costs $8 per person, which is included in the price if you take a tour. Walking tours with panning cost $5 for children under twelve, $15 for adults, and $8 for seniors. Tours cost only $10. Open from 10 a.m. to 5 p.m. daily May–October, 10 a.m. to 4 p.m. November–April. NOTE: The temperature in the mine is only 42° to 54° F, so you'll need to dress accordingly.

To get to the Phoenix Gold Mine, take I–70 eastbound to exit 239, and then take Stanley Road southwest to Trail Creek Road. For more information call (303) 567-0422 or write P.O. Box 3236, Idaho Springs 80452; www.phoenix goldmine.com.

Most of Colorado's highest places can only be attained by a long, arduous hike. The rewards are worth the effort: sweeping views of the Rockies for miles in all directions, alpine wildflowers, and the shrill whistle of marmots and pikas. But for those not desiring a high-altitude workout, there are several places around the state where you can enjoy these grand views with little more effort than steady pressure on the gas pedal and both hands on the steering wheel.

The road to 14,264-foot-high ***Mount Evans*** is the highest paved auto road in the United States. Starting at 8,700 feet in Idaho Springs, it winds steadily upward, rising through spruce and pine forests. As you go higher the views only get better. You will pass through several ecological zones, an ancient bristlecone pine forest, and alpine lakes before reaching the summit. Keep at eye out for mountain goats and bighorn sheep that are often seen near the summit. And be prepared for cold weather at the top. It can be 90 degrees in Denver and 40 degrees on top of the mountain. The vista from the viewing platform is one of Colorado's premier scenic overlooks.

The road to the top of Mount Evans usually opens in May and stays open until the first significant snowfall of the year—meaning that if you want to tackle the peak in winter, you'll need to plan accordingly by packing snowshoes or cross-country skis and having the necessary wilderness skills to do so safely.

Once the road has been opened for the season, it is accessible twenty-four hours a day. Cost is $10 for a three-day vehicle pass, on sale at the entrance station. There is also a mechanical collection station that accepts cash ($1, $5, $10 bills) and credit cards; it will issue you a valid pass.

Any sunny summer day will do to make your drive up to the summit, but weekdays are preferable if you want to avoid the crowds. In addition, visiting very early or very late in the day increases your chances of seeing the many animals that call Mount Evans home.

If you're starting your journey in Denver, you can choose to approach the mountain via Bergen Park and return via Idaho Springs, or vice versa. Expect to see stunning Colorado scenery along the way, including large, fertile meadows, dense lodgepole pine forests, aspen trees, ponderosa pine, Douglas fir, and thick bushes of wild raspberries, as well as the occasional chipmunk or squirrel.

Placid ***Echo Lake*** makes for a nice stopping point en route to the summit. Park and stretch your legs, and perhaps enjoy a picnic lunch, do some fishing, or join hikers on one of several trails heading into the woods. If you're visiting after Thanksgiving, expect to see a vast frozen expanse—the lake freezes completely, and you can skate across it on cross-country skis, reaching numerous trails that yield great views. But even in summer it gets cool up here, so dress warmly and bring extra layers. Theoretically, for every 1,000 feet of elevation gain in the Rockies, you can compare your journey to traveling 200 miles north. Of course, this means you get to experience the cooler air in each zone on the way up, not to mention the shifting vegetation.

Above Echo Lake, a beautiful and complex world lies at your feet. Follow trails through alpine tundra, stooping to study the small grasses, sedges, herbs, and the almost microscopic plants with their tiny flowers. These plants grow close to the ground in order to withstand the harsh conditions at this altitude.

At one point on the way up you will see posted signs for the bristlecone forest hunkered on both sides of the road. If you take a close look at the twisted forms of these ancient trees, you can read the story of their struggle for survival in this unforgiving setting. Each dwarfed bristlecone and leaning Douglas fir in this area shows the signs of withstanding blizzards and summer storms as well as coping with blazing sunlight followed by rains. This wild weather destroys most exposed buds and conifer seeds, limiting the trees' reproduction. Some trees are bent and twisted from the relentless wind, while others are bleached from the sun or blackened and split by lightning strikes. At timberline, the already small array of trees becomes even sparser, with only single, isolated soldiers standing to face the elements.

Above timberline, in Colorado's alpine life zone, the fauna changes, too. Marmots often show themselves sunning on warm boulders. Well-camouflaged ptarmigan can be spotted browsing among the grasses or leading their brood of chicks across the tundra. Tiny pikas scurry between rocks as they gather grasses for the long winter. Mountain goats are frequently seen up here, and once in a while you'll spot a bighorn sheep. Don't feed any animals; they stay much healthier with a natural diet.

Mount Evans's upper reaches are also dotted with lakes. At 11,700 feet, you'll spot Lincoln Lake; it's 800 feet below the highway. Then at 12,830 feet, Summit Lake awaits, complete with a short trail overlooking the picturesque Chicago Lakes, some 1,400 feet below. The Forest Service warns parents not to let their children run around in this area due to the sudden drop-offs—the highway has few guardrails.

Finally, complete the journey by pulling into the parking lot at 14,130 feet. Get out of your car and hike that last 134-foot gain in altitude to the summit via a ¼-mile hike along a trail. Catch your breath—the air is much thinner up here than it is on the plains, so visitors from the flatlands should walk slowly and take in the scenery. And if the thin air doesn't take away your breath, the views surely will.

Start your tour to Mount Evans on I–70. Take exit 240 in Idaho Springs onto the Mount Evans Highway (Highway 103). After Echo Lake, pay your fee and head onto Highway 5, which will take you to the summit. For a change of pace on the way back, continue west along Highway 103 to Bergen Park, and then take Highway 74 and I–70 to Denver. The distances are moderate— it's only 28 miles from Idaho Springs to the summit of Mount Evans. For more information call the Clear Creek Ranger Station at (303) 567-3000 or write to the CCRD Visitor Information Center, P.O. Box 3307, Idaho Springs 80452; www.mountevans.com.

Idaho Springs is home to the ***Edgar Experimental Mine,*** where students and faculty from the Golden-based Colorado School of Mines try their hands at traditional mining methods and put to use the most recent technological advances. Open to the public for tours throughout the year from Monday through Friday, 8 a.m. to 4 p.m. Admission is $10 for adults, $6 for seniors, and $6 for children ages six to sixteen. Call ahead to reserve a tour: (303) 567-2911

Loveland in Wintertime— or All Year Long

Loveland Ski Area—which is nowhere near the city by the same name—has always been a favorite ski spot for Denverites. And for good reason. A big plus is Loveland's proximity—just 55 miles from Denver via I–70. There are no passes to cross and no Eisenhower Tunnels, either (which Loveland publicists call "a big bore").

Snowboarding is big here, and the ski area has excellent instructors. If you've been a skier your whole life, try snowboarding. It's definitely a different experience from skiing, and worth it to discover the distinction. Many Colorado skiers start snowboarding and never return to skiing.

The ski center shuts down in late spring when the snow melts, and since Loveland Ski Area does not have hotels or offer condominiums, that's it for winter sports. In summer the slopes fill up with mountain flowers and hikers out to enjoy the high country.

To arrange snowboarding lessons or for more information contact Loveland Ski Area, P.O. Box 899, Georgetown 80444; (303) 571-5580 or (800) 736-3754; www.skilove land.com. Loveland Ski Area is open from November through April; lift ticket prices run from $15 to $56.

or rkcooper@mines.edu; www.mining.mines.edu/edgar_mine.htm. Or write to 3658th Ave., P.O. Box 1184, Idaho Springs 80452.

In autumn the wind whistles through the well-kept streets of ***Georgetown,*** rattling the windows of its many Victorian houses. The winter snows pile up high here, and spring is slow to come at an elevation of 8,500 feet. The mountains rise so steeply on all four sides of Georgetown that even the summers are cool; the sun shines for only a few hours a day.

Yet, this community 45 miles west of Denver has more ambience, more sightseeing, and more genuine concern for preserving its past than most other Colorado cities. The city officials have spent six-figure sums to rebuild and preserve the pink-brick houses, the old-time saloons, and the museums that conjure up the nineteenth century of gold and silver riches. The antiques shops, silversmiths, and weavers are among the best in the state. The craft shops are unique and worth browsing in, and often offer much better deals than those of Vail, Aspen, and other ski resorts to the west.

Unlike Vail, which rose from a cow pasture, Georgetown is a historic community. And residents are proud of it. On a clear spring day in 1859, two prospecting brothers, George and David Griffith, struggled their way up Clear Creek searching for minerals. Unsuccessful at the other mining camps in Colorado, the two prospectors reached out for new, untried land, and this time they had luck—they found gold.

After their discovery the Griffith brothers did a highly unusual thing for gold or silver seekers of the time—instead of just digging up the mountain and leaving with their wealth, they brought their entire family out from Kentucky to live permanently in their valley. The tiny settlement they founded became known as George's Town, and although no more significant strikes were made, it grew steadily for five years.

Then in 1864 assays showed an extremely high silver content. The boom was on. Over the next thirty years, the mines in and around the town produced more than $200 million worth of silver. The town became known as the Silver Queen of the Mountains—and in 1868 it was renamed Georgetown.

By 1880 some 10,000 people made the city their home. Fortunes and reputations flourished. Elaborate mansions were built. Hotels served fine cuisine in gilt rooms with elegant furniture. An opera house brought Broadway productions and favorite classical operas to the wealthy.

All this came to an abrupt end when the silver panic of 1893 hit, with silver prices dropping to almost nothing. Almost overnight, mines, mills, and livelihoods vanished. The town became a ghost of its past glory.

Georgetown languished this way for more than six decades. As more people moved to the state, tourism followed, and interstate highways transported millions of travelers to the high mountains. People discovered the beautiful old Victorian homes and set about restoring them to their former grace. Unlike other Colorado mining towns, Georgetown was never totally destroyed by fire, so today it has more than 200 carefully preserved historic buildings.

Luckily for Georgetown, forward-thinking residents and town officials passed a historic preservation ordinance many years ago. The local historical society actively watches over its Victorian treasures to ensure they will be around for many years. One of Georgetown's landmarks is the French-style *Hotel de Paris Museum,* full of Tiffany fixtures, lace curtains, and hand-carved furniture. Open from Memorial Day through Labor Day 10 a.m. to 4:30 p.m., and on weekends from September to December noon to 4 p.m. Adults are $4, seniors $3, students $3. Call (303) 569-2311; www.hoteldeparis museum.org.

trivia

Two historic Georgetown homes, the Bowman-White House and the Hamill House, exemplify the city's Victorian style. See the Web site www.historicgeorgetown.org.

Georgetown is a perfect town for parking and wandering. Walk in any direction and discover dozens of well-preserved homes well over a century old. The small business district has a mix of antiques shops, art galleries, a bookstore, and several restaurants. During the first two December weekends, a well-known Christmas market with small booths and outdoor stalls is a popular place for holiday shopping.

Georgetown is a good base for travelers who plan to explore the Continental Divide in summer or ski country in winter. It's also the best starting point for the spectacular drive to 11,669-foot *Guanella Pass.* Passing through forests of aspen, fir, and spruce at lower elevations, the road climbs up a glaciated valley past meadows and cascading creeks. Camping, hiking, fishing, fall aspen foliage, and winter cross-country skiing and snowshoeing are some of the attractions. At the pass, tundra and willow thickets replace the forest, and in summer tiny wildflowers add color to the landscape. Look for ptarmigan in all seasons, white in winter and mottled brown in summer.

Mt. Bierstadt, one of Colorado's "Fourteeners," is the large mountain looming to the east. The trail to the summit starts from the parking lot. Other trails lead hikers across the tundra.

trivia

A mysterious Frenchman named Louis Dupuy originally ran the Hotel de Paris; some Georgetown people say he left a large family in France.

Georgetown Fishing

The lakes in this area are often crowded during the summer, with the exception of **Silver Dollar Lake.** A somewhat steep jaunt on foot leads off the beaten path to the lake, which yields good catches and offers peace and quiet. From Georgetown, head 8½ miles south on Guanella Pass Road. Turn right at the Silver Dollar Lake sign.

Passenger cars can easily traverse the well-graded road, but it will be too narrow in places for RVs. Remember to bring warm clothes; the weather at the pass is often much colder than in Georgetown. Contact (303) 567-4660; www .georgetowncolorado.com/guanella.htm.

Georgetown is about an hour west of Denver via I–70. For information about Georgetown, write to the Downtown Georgetown Community Center, 613 Sixth St., P.O. Box 444, Georgetown 80444; (303) 569-2888 or (800) 472-8230; www.historicgeorgetown.org.

Want to experience a bit of the Colorado West? Then plan a vacation at one of Colorado's dude ranches.

Imagine riding horseback with family and friends through an aspen grove to a sunny meadow full of wildflowers. Along the way you pass weathered settler's cabins with caved in roofs and sagging door frames, the wood bleached and cracked by a century in the sun. The trail leads across brooks, through willow thickets, and then slowly down a steep, rocky slope. The riders move with care, savoring the moment as they hang on firmly. A light warm breeze blows through the pines. Alone with their thoughts, far away from high-rises and freeways, they find rhythm in the creak of the leather saddles and the clicking of the hooves. Arriving at a sunny forest clearing, everyone finds a log to sit on. Coffee steams. The cowboys fry up eggs and sausage. It's morning in the Rockies.

Ask dude ranch visitors what's so special about staying in one of these places. They'll mention the informality, the quiet seclusion, the good food, and the friendliness of the place. With an average of twenty to about eighty guests, it's easy to become acquainted with the staff and guests. The mood is calm and relaxed. But there's also plenty to do: horseback riding, fishing, hiking, mountain biking, and just relaxing with a good book are a few of the many options. You can stay as busy as you like, or you can do nothing at all. Either way, you'll be well taken care of.

The names say a lot: C Lazy U Ranch, Tumbling River Ranch, Drowsy Water Ranch, **Peaceful Valley Ranch.** They are just a few of the many endearing places set in romantic, isolated Colorado locations. Some of them still breed cattle or horses. A Colorado dude-ranch vacation is one of the most satisfying, genuine holidays available today. The air is clean, days are warm, evenings cool, and the mountain scenery is absolutely spectacular. Most dude ranches are family-oriented, with separate programs especially for kids.

Accommodations range from rustic to deluxe. Colorado has some forty dude ranches, generally located in the scenic mountain regions. These are small, self-contained worlds that feel far from city life. There are lots of horse trails for novices, guided breakfast rides, ghost-town trips, and even six-day rides into the wilderness. Some dude ranches arrange river-rafting trips, or you can rent a jeep. Archery, boating, rock climbing, fishing, and even golf are possibilities. And there are usually hot tubs and plenty of soft lounge chairs.

How much does a dude-ranch vacation cost? Less than you'd expect. A week at an average guest ranch costs considerably less than a Caribbean cruise for the family. Everything is included: meals, activities, and accommodations.

The ***Peaceful Valley Ranch*** near Lyons is known for its summer evening entertainment including square-dancing. This ranch has a special teen program, trips to ghost towns, and even English riding instruction. Lyons is easy to reach from Denver via the Boulder Turnpike; then continue on Highway 7 and Highway 72. For more information contact the ranch at 475 Peaceful Valley Rd., Lyons; (303) 747-2881 or (800) 955-6343; www.peacefulvalley.com. Open year-round.

The ***Tumbling River Ranch*** in Grant seems hewn out of native rock and local wood. At night you can hear the tumbling river outside your window. The ranch stands at 9,200 feet, and each evening the stars shine brighter than any city sky. The ranch features not only trail riding but also a handsome outdoor heated pool. The food is excellent, and there are enough activities to keep you busy all summer.

Grant is a short trip southwest from Denver via US 285. For more information contact Tumbling River Ranch, P.O. Box 30, Grant 80448; (303) 838-5981 or (800) 654-8770; www.tumblingriver.com. Open from June 1 through September 30.

To explore the many dude ranch choices across the state, contact the Colorado Dude and Guest Ranch Association, P.O. Box D, Shawnee, 80425; (303) 758-1386; www.coloradoranch.com.

Driving east on Highway 70, after you've climbed out of steep Glenwood Canyon and dropped down from Vail Pass into Summit County, you'll see a large lake on your right. If you're coming west from Denver, you'll cross the Continental Divide at 11,158 feet and after a quick drop into Summit County, the road straightens out, and there it is—***Lake Dillon.***

No matter which direction you're coming from, this lake is hard to miss. With its 26-mile shoreline, the water on a summer day is often a deep blue, dotted by white sails, and alive with small motorboats, canoes, and kayaks skimming the surface. Anglers fish from shore for rainbow trout. Osprey nest here each year. Bike paths run the length of the lake, continuing all the way to Breckenridge ten miles away.

Mountains surrounding the lake are the domain of climbers, hikers, and horseback riders. Streams are everywhere: Blue River, Snake River, Ten Mile Creek. Almost all the water spills into the reservoir, flowing toward Denver, through the unseen Roberts Tunnel, not far from Dillon. Highway traffic along I-70 moves fast along the north side of the lake, and if you're in a hurry, you may miss the sign for Dillon and continue toward Denver, 78 miles to the east.

Once you pull off the highway and drive into town, you leave the road noise behind. Dillon is a convenient base for exploring Lake Dillon and the surrounding mountains, and the ski destinations of Breckenridge, Copper, and Keystone are a short drive away. But unlike other Colorado mountain towns, there are no old buildings here. No dilapidated miner's cabins, no Victorian houses. The hotels, condos, restaurants, sports stores, and boutiques are all newer structures. The lakeside setting seems perfect for an early settlement, but oddly, there is no trace of the historical past here.

Dillon did not always sit at the edge of the lake. In fact, until the 1960s, there was no Lake Dillon. The story of Dillon is one of development, water rights, and changing times.

The old town, originally situated to the east, was named after an early prospector. The area saw off-and-on gold mining, a little railroading, lumber trading, and much ranching. The first post office opened here in 1883. With the advent of the car came garages and service stations. Roads improved, and more tourists showed up "to breathe the exhilarating Rocky Mountain air," as one advertisement put it. A longtime resident remembers the Dillon of the 1930s: "Ranchers picked up their mail here," he says, "and it was a place for a beer on Saturday night."

trivia

In the early 1960s, the original town of Dillon—the whole town!—was moved in order to make way for the Dillon Lake reservoir.

But on the other side of the mountains, Denver was growing, and it desperately needed more water. All through the forties and early fifties, the Denver Water Department bought up lands and ranches with water rights. Then, in 1955, Dillon residents were told about the coming storage reservoir. It would flood their town.

After many meetings and complex legal work, the machinery ground into high gear. Dillon had to move. Some people left for warmer climates; others settled in nearby villages. But the young, sports-minded citizens decided to create a new Dillon on a hill of pine and evergreen. Here was a chance for a model town.

Down in the valley the old community was dismantled stick by stick. Because the water supply had to be pure, all buildings had to go. Some were cut in half and hauled elsewhere by trucks. Others had to be burned down. The Water Board uprooted telephone lines, removed old pipes, buried the last rusty tin cans. Even the peaceful graveyard, with its rococo stones and metal crosses, had to be shifted to higher ground. The school was moved, and the church found a new home in the reborn Dillon.

Slowly the dam rose until it stood 231 feet high at some points and was capable of backing up 257,000 acre-feet of water. The Harold Roberts Tunnel, more than 23 miles long and costing $50 million, was completed to connect the reservoir with rivers flowing into Denver. Water from thawing snows and the mountain streams steadily accumulated in the reservoir behind the dam.

One August day, the waters rushed over the top and through the "glory hole" spillway into the outlet tunnel. By then nothing was left of the old Dillon town site. The roads that led to it now lay under about 150 feet of water. The old Dillon was no more.

Among the trees to the west stands the new Dillon. The town officials and the city planners conceived it well. Buildings can be no higher than 30 feet, providing unobstructed views of the lake. Dillon's signs are subdued, modest, and inviting. There is little neon. Only natural materials—the stone and wood of the Rockies, plus glass—are permitted for the houses. The wood may be stained but not painted. The lots and homes have to keep their distance, for utmost peace. And timber was cut sparingly, for conservation's sake.

Development continues in Dillon and around the 3,300-acre lake. New shopping areas and businesses appear regularly. The city is currently dealing with the pine beetle infestation that is affecting the entire western United States, and many trees are being removed to control the spread of the beetles. So far the town and the lakefront remain an enjoyable place to rent a canoe, ride a bike, or walk around and enjoy the local shops and eateries.

The **_Dillon Marina_** hosts a number of fun community events, including regattas throughout the summer. For details call (970) 468-5100; visit www.dillonmarina.com or write P.O. Box 1825, Dillon 80435. Free Saturday night concerts take place throughout the summer at the Lake Dillon Amphitheatre; call (970) 262-3400 for details. For more information about events and attractions in Dillon during your stay, call (970) 468-2403; visit www.townofdillon.com; or write Town Office, 275 Lake Dillon Dr., Dillon 80435.

Denver is a mere seventy minutes from Lake Dillon thanks to the time-saving *Eisenhower Tunnel,* which is a story in its own right.

For a hundred years, since the days when railroads were first reaching across the continent, men had worked and dreamed of tunneling through the Continental Divide here at its narrowest point. "Nearly impossible!" a geologist said when a Colorado financier first suggested a long tunnel through the Continental Divide during the 1930s.

"Unpredictable rock!" other geologists warned in 1941. The drilling of a pilot bore already gave a clue to the unstable rock strata of this area. Steel linings buckled in the exploratory shaft. But plans were drawn and the work began in 1968. For five years tunnel builders, sometimes as many as 1,100 men at a time, battled the mountain some 58 miles west of Denver. Lack of money, politics, explosions, fires, and, most of all, geological problems all thwarted the builders. A tunnel engineer later summed it up better than anyone else. "We were going by the book," he said. "But the damned mountain couldn't read!"

> ## trivia
>
> The utility bill for the Eisenhower Tunnel runs about $70,000 a month—each tunnel (one for east-bound and one for westbound traffic) has 2,000 light fixtures, and each light fixture contains an eight-foot bulb!

Fortunately, the 8,941-foot-long Eisenhower Tunnel was eventually drilled despite the obstacles. The tunnel makes travel possible in all seasons, and saves the motorist 10 miles over the twisting and turning highway that crosses Loveland Pass. Since the tunnel opened in 1973, drivers need no longer expose themselves to the fierce storms and howling winds of the pass. No more jackknifed trucks, stranded cars, or vehicles swept off the highway ledges by avalanches, rock slides, or icy curves taken too fast. One of North America's best-known mountain passes was finally tamed.

The Eisenhower Tunnel is 58 miles west of Denver via I–70. Visit www .dot.state.co.us/Eisenhower/description.asp for more information.

Year-Round Vacation Areas

Breckenridge is the perfect Colorado frontier town—one of the few that was rebuilt and is now well preserved and thriving.

In 1859, a group of fourteen prospectors discovered gold in the Breckenridge area. A town was quickly built by miners who were hopeful that they would strike it rich. One such miner, Tom Groves, walked away a big winner when he discovered "Tom's Baby," a 136-ounce gold nugget. But, like all areas rich in minerals, the mines eventually played out. Breckenridge citizens wouldn't give up, and they found another moneymaker when Summit County's first ski area opened in 1961.

Breckenridge has a western charm that especially delights European visitors. Here are the earmarks of the old Gold Rush West: fairytale Victorian houses with columns, crenellations, and gingerbread trim; the clapboard structures of the miners, beautifully repainted; and store windows filled with antiques. Travelers from the Midwest and East feel the same way; they're walking through a colorful piece of American history. The ski slopes are still named for the old mines in the area: Gold King, Wellington, Bonanza, Cashier, Silverthorn—these were the names that excited the gold hunters more than a century ago.

Breckenridge is actually one of Colorado's oldest towns. In August 1859 the first gold seekers came streaming across the Continental Divide to pan gold in the waters of the Blue River. More than $30 million in gold was taken out of the district during its heyday. Later, a silver lode started a second boom. By 1861 some 5,000 people lived in and around Breckenridge. Summit County then extended as far as the Utah line and was one of seventeen counties composing the Colorado Territory. It has since been whittled down to 600 square miles. Then, as now, Breckenridge was the county seat.

As with other mountain mining towns in Colorado, the precious minerals ran out and mining came to a halt. In the early 1960s, Breckenridge became a year-round resort, at the same time maintaining its century-old status as a former mining community. Development may have brought condos and shopping centers, but it hasn't destroyed the town's historical district. Take a walk along the six-block stretch of Main

trivia

Gold was first panned in Breckenridge's Blue River in 1859.

Street through the old town for a glimpse back in time. Old storefronts and original brick and wood buildings continue to serve a purpose, housing restaurants, shops, and boutiques.

But there's more. Walk east a couple of blocks from Main Street on Lincoln or Washington or Adams Avenues, and wander the grid of quiet back streets. Many dozens of old homes sit back among the trees, lovingly restored reminders of the glory mining days of old Breckenridge. Grassy yards, flower gardens, and hummingbirds thrive, and after strolling through this lovely area you may just be tempted to drop by a real estate office or two.

Summer and fall are busy seasons in Breckenridge. Coloradoans and out-of-state visitors come here to stay for a few days, renting rooms in nearby condos and lodges. This is a great base for exploring the area south toward Hoosier Pass and beyond to Fairplay. The Blue River runs through town, and several riverfront plaza areas are perfect for sitting under a tree and people-watching. Stop by Clint's Bakery and Coffee at 131 S. Main for excellent drinks, baked goods, breakfast and lunch items. Or drop by Crepes a la Cart, the outdoor crepes stand at 307 S. Main St. They open at 11 a.m. offering a wide variety of savory lunch and dinner crepes, and decadent dessert crepes. There's often a line; meet other travelers and swap stories until your crepe arrives.

Breckenridge in winter is another Colorado favorite. More than 2,300 acres of skiable terrain on 155 trails offer something for every ski level. Snowboarding, snowshoeing, tobogganing, and nearby ice fishing are all part of the cold-weather scene here. Contact the Breckenridge Ski Resort, 1599-C Summit County Rd. 3, (970) 453-5000 or (800) 789-7669; www.breckenridge.snow.com.

Breckenridge is located 88 miles west of Denver via I–70 and Highway 9. For more information call the Breckenridge Resort Chamber (311 South Ridge Rd.) at (970) 453-2913 or (888) 251-2417; www.gobreck.com.

Mining—an important part of Colorado's past—is alive and well and can be glimpsed at the *Country Boy Mine,* 2 miles from downtown Breckenridge. This working mine is one of the few that offers travelers a journey into some of the same places that hard-rock miners went more than one hundred years ago when the mine was established. At the Country Boy Mine you can don a hard hat and venture 1,000 feet underground, seeing, feeling, and hearing what actual miners experienced. After the tour you can try your hand at gold panning in Eureka Creek or take a hay ride past the authentic mine buildings. Sleigh rides are offered in winter. In Breckenridge turn left/east on Wellington Road and follow it to a final fork. Turn right, and then drive a mile east on French Gulch Road. Admission costs $16 for anyone thirteen and older, $11 for children four to twelve, children three and younger free. Open year-round. Call (970) 453-4405 for hours; www.countryboymine.com.

Where else but in Colorado would you expect to find an extensive ski museum? Founded in 1976, the *Colorado Ski Museum* in *Vail* reaches back to the old miners of the nineteenth century who raced in the Rockies surrounding their camps, competing against one another on long wooden boards while holding a long staff in one fist for braking. The museum contains a magnificent, enlarged 1859 etching of Snowshoe Thompson, the Norwegian

trivia

Breckenridge features several ghost towns worth checking out: Lincoln City, Swandyke, Dyersville, and others.

Breckenridge Horseback Riding

Tired of walking? **Breckenridge Stables** offers ninety-minute rides along the Breckenridge Trail, which passes some of Colorado's finest scenery. Reserve all rides at least one day in advance. Ride prices are $55 for ninety minutes, with children age six or younger paying $25 for any ride. Call (970) 453-4438 or write P.O. Box 6686, Breckenridge 80454; www.breckstables.com.

who skied from camp to camp in severe blizzards. He delivered mail, candy, and medicines to the marooned miners.

Here are the photos and artifacts of skiing clergymen like Father John Lewis Dyer, who brought the gospel to Colorado's historic gold towns, as well as the stories of sheepherders and trappers who braved the snows in the nineteenth century on 9-foot enormous wooden contraptions with crude leather straps holding their boots. Mementos of the first long-ago jumpers will fascinate viewers; photos show them taking off from knolls or flying through the air, equipment sometimes falling off high above ground.

Do you want to learn more about the first ski lifts? The Colorado Ski Museum displays the drive mechanism, pictures of the first rope tows, and photos of funny "grippers," which latched onto the moving ropes. The localized history of chairlifts, gondolas (including a gondola rescue), ski patrol toboggans, the first U.S. Army Snow Tanks, and the first ski area snow-packing and grading gear can all be seen here. Any student of ski equipment can learn much about the development of skis, bindings, boots, poles, even the first ski suits, knickerbockers, parkas, or the women's fashions of still earlier days when ladies skied in ankle-length black skirts.

The history of Colorado's famous Tenth Mountain Division is well illustrated; an entire room is devoted to the Mountain Troopers and their initial camps and wartime exploits. A viewing area shows ski videos. Exhibits on avalanche control, up-to-date ski racing, and the history of upscale, pricey Vail, it's all here in the very center of Vail. Admission is free. Open daily from 10 a.m. to 6 p.m. Colorado Ski Museum, 231 South Frontage Rd. East, P.O. Box 1976, Vail 81657; (970) 476-1876; www.skimuseum.net.

Within walking distance of the ski museum—but nicely concealed by a thick grove of fir trees—you'll find the beautifully designed *Town of Vail Public Library.* It was built in 1972 with native Colorado stone and woods and a grass lawn roof. A massive fireplace is lit all year. Picture windows look out into the little forest and onto the footpath that meanders along Gore Creek to Vail Village. With more than 55,000 volumes, including many

Ski Vail—Hut to Hut

For an off-the-beaten-path ski experience, try Vail's backcountry hut-to-hut skiing. The Tenth Mountain Division Hut Association was formed in 1980 to build a back-country ski hut system in the high mountains between Aspen, Leadville, and Vail.

Now you can reserve the huts for a fee as a take-off for day adventures or to ski from hut to hut. These shelters are within the White River and San Isabel National Forests, so stunning vistas are guaranteed. The adventure isn't for everyone, however; the Forest Service advises that the trails require at least intermediate ability. The Hut Association also requires that someone in each group be proficient in backcountry skills, such as avalanche awareness and compass reading.

The huts include wood burning stoves, propane burners, cooking and eating utensils, kitchen supplies, and mattresses and pillows.

NOTE: With average elevations of 11,000 feet, you need to prepare for high altitude.

Reservations are required; call (970) 925-5775 or write Tenth Mountain Division Hut Association, 1280 Ute Ave., Suite 21, Aspen 81611; www.huts.org.

mountain books, the building is a cozy escape when rain or snow is falling outside.

Library hours are 10 a.m. to 8 p.m. Monday through Thursday, and 11 a.m. to 6 p.m. Friday through Sunday. For more information write 292 West Meadow Dr., Vail 81657 or call (970) 479-2185; www.vaillibrary.com.

Two hours west of Denver lie some of the state's most impressive mountains—the *Gore Range.* In Vail itself you'll see the Gore Creek, especially in summer. Gore Mountain, Gore Wilderness—who in the world was Gore? No, it's not a former vice president. George Gore was one of the more interesting visitors who ever roamed through Colorado. The best place to get acquainted with him might be north of Vail on Gore Pass, near Kremmling. Here a bronze plaque is visible beside the highway, at an elevation of 9,000 feet. The words on the bronze give a brief version of his time here:

> HERE IN 1854 CROSSED SIR ST. GEORGE GORE. AN IRISH BARONET BENT
> ON SLAUGHTER OF GAME AND GUIDED BY JIM BRIDGER. FOR THREE YEARS
> HE SCOURED COLORADO, MONTANA AND WYOMING ACCOMPANIED USUALLY
> BY FORTY MEN, MANY CARTS, WAGONS, HOUNDS, AND UNEXAMPLED CAMP
> LUXURIES.

Lord Gore's party, we learn, dispatched "more than 2,000 buffalo, 1,600 elk and deer, and 100 bears," among others. Hunting was nothing new in a land where European trappers and fur traders had already scoured all of Colorado for beaver. But Lord Gore set a record; besides, no one matched his style. The baronet traveled with his retinue of hunters and porters from Ireland; his safari caravan eventually accumulated 112 horses, twenty-one carts, thirty wagons, and four dozen hunting dogs. He roamed the mountains for many months, shooting grizzly bear, antelope, and other animals and making elegant camp at night, complete with silver service and rare wines.

His Lordship could afford the "unexampled camp luxuries." For one thing, his income exceeded $200,000, which was quite a sum during the mid-1850s. For another, the Irish nobleman had a taste for gourmet cuisine and rare wines—and the cooks and servants to attend his needs. Lord Gore had gone to school in Oxford, and his aristocratic tastes included various mansions in Ireland and houses in East Sussex.

Lord Gore's hunt and his exploits are still studied by local children. And thanks to the Historical Society of Colorado, future visitors to the region will be reminded of the Irishman by means of the bronze plaque on Gore Pass.

The summit of Gore Pass and the plaque are 17 miles west of Kremmling and can be reached from Denver via U.S. Highway 40. There are picnic grounds on the pass. Return to I–70 by driving south on Highway 9.

Botanists have identified thousands of different flower species in the Rockies. The first sign of spring at lower elevations brings forth a rush of daisies, mountain marigolds, wild sweet peas, fairy trumpets, pink rockhill phlox, and others in a rainbow of hues. Wander up in early summer to Colorado's 8,000- or 9,000-foot levels. Here, almost overnight, you'll see leafy cinquefoils, arnicas, yellow monkey flowers, and the official state flower, the blue Rocky Mountain columbine. (The latter also grows in the foothills.) In July, you'll be welcomed by the star gentians, wood lilies, the mountain aster, and several kinds of larkspur. After the snow has melted in the alpine zone above tree line, the next wave of color arrives, brightening the rocky slopes and high valleys with lavender, crimson, azure, butter yellow, pink, and pure white.

Perhaps the most amazing aspect of these annual displays is the fact that any plant producing such delicate beauty can survive under the freezing winter

trivia

Shrine Ridge is an easy hike that can be accomplished in two to three hours. Climb through open meadows with abundant wildflowers, then up the steepest part of the trail to the 11,089-foot summit. While atop the mountain, look for "Lord Gore," a man-shaped rock to the northwest. To reach the trailhead, take I–70 to Vail Pass, exit 190. Proceed on Road #709 to Shrine Pass Summit. Turn left here and drive to Shrine Mountain Inn, where you can park.

blizzards, blazing high-altitude sun, blasting winds, and generally harsh climate that occur above timberline. Their existence up here seems miraculous.

In the tundra at high elevations, you'll notice that all the plants are small. Many have short stems or none at all. That helps; the tinier the leaves and lower to the ground, the less resistance to the wind. At the same time, roots go deep into the soil, anchoring plants so they don't get ripped away in the stiff gusts. Mountain flowers protect themselves against the elements with protective tiny umbrellas of growth, or hairs, or fine layers of woolly matter or waxy leaves that hold in moisture. And many flowers close their petals at night to hold onto the day's warmth.

Colorado is renowned for its wildflowers. Hike just about any place in the mountains from June through August and you will find flowers, often in unlikely places. Different elevations and habitats support entirely different species. The growing season is short, but the state's flora makes up for that brief window of time by putting on one of nature's loveliest of shows.

They Almost Blew It: Vail History

Vail founders never anticipated a success of such magnitude. Although thousands of mountain troopers and skiers passed through the valley during the 1940s and 1950s, none of them saw the potential of Vail Mountain, since the best slopes were out of sight high above the highway. But Peter Seibert, an ex–Tenth Mountain man and a ski racer, knew a lot about ski areas, and he spent two years hiking, climbing, and skiing all over the Rockies to look for the ideal resort location. One day in 1957, he scaled the Vail Summit with a local prospector who lived in the valley. Upon seeing the bowls and glades and open slopes, Seibert knew he'd found the ideal site. Seibert and some friends invested their savings. But more money was needed.

Unfortunately, at that time Denver's conservative bankers wouldn't gamble on a large new ski area, with Aspen already doing well. All the same, Seibert kept looking for partners. He turned to Michigan, Missouri, Wisconsin, Texas, and other states. He bought a snowcat and brought visitors to his magic mountain. He showed films of his powder bowls all over the country, and invited prospective investors to ski with him. Eventually he got lucky. A Michigan oilman-skier recognized the potential and found other wealthy backers who spread Seibert's gospel. They raised $5 million, formed Vail Associates, and successfully tapped the Small Business Administration and the no-longer-reluctant Denver bankers. And they sold real estate to precisely the people who had shaken their heads the hardest.

During the summer of 1962, the bulldozers started to dig in. An excellent Milwaukee architect had drawn up the plans and now supervised the frantic building activity. When the dust settled, there stood the first lodges, apartments, malls, homes, and lifts of Vail, Colorado.

Vail Hikes

Missouri Lakes. Hikers are sometimes discouraged by evidence of a water project at the start of this trail. However, after the first mile, the trail cuts into the plush wilderness, the likes of which experienced hikers dream about. Rustic log bridges help you cross Missouri Creek on your way to these crystal-clear lakes. Anticipate a walk of approximately five hours if you go all the way to the lakes within the Holy Cross Wilderness.

Take I–70, exit 271 to Highway 24. Drive south to Homestake Road #703. Turn right onto #704 and travel to a T in the road. The trailhead is on the left. For more information call the U.S. Forest Service Rangers Station at (970) 827-5715, or stop by the station, located ½ mile south of exit 171 in Minturn. Visit them at www.econovail .com/hiking.html.

When you're outdoors enjoying the flowers, keep in mind that the vegetation is fragile, often barely holding on under extreme growing conditions. Watch where you're walking and stay on trails. Don't pick wildflowers. They often spread their seeds through their blossoms, so picking the flowers now means there will be fewer flowers next year. Picking flowers is against the law in all national parks, forests, and monuments. And they don't last long, often wilting within an hour. Leave the flowers alive and thriving for everyone to enjoy.

There is no charge to visit the gardens, but donations are accepted. Gardens are open from dawn to dusk. For more information contact **Betty Ford Alpine Gardens,** 183 Gore Creek Dr., Vail 81657; (970) 476-0103; www.betty fordalpinegardens.org.

The **Lodge and Spa at Cordillera,** in **Edwards,** 15 miles west of Vail, offers more sports and adventure than most first-class resorts in Colorado.

While staying at this remote European castlelike lodge in winter, a guest can enjoy Alaskan dogsled rides, rent contemporary snowshoes and join a professional snowshoe guide, take lessons in cross-country skiing and skating (equipment is for rent), train for cross-country races, and get free bus service to nearby Beaver Creek for downhill skiing. In summer, the Lodge and Spa at Cordillera features guided flower hikes, mountain biking, golfing on an eighteen-hole course, swimming in an Olympic-size pool, sitting in whirlpools or in a genuine Finnish sauna, working out on Stairmasters or Lifecycles in a large gym and weight room, and being pampered with massages, body wraps, and facials at the professional spa. All this plus 360-degree mountain views, fly fishing, tennis, seclusion, and privacy on 8,000 wilderness acres. This

trivia

By the time Glenwood Canyon interstate construction was completed in 1992, more than 150,000 native trees, plants, and shrubs had been replanted in an effort to restore the area. In addition, engineers were careful to plan the route around large old trees instead of chopping them down, and the freshly made rock cuts fit right in with the natural canyon scenery—they had been stained so that they'd appear weathered.

retreat is further blessed with superb accommodations and two restaurants. It's a unique, luxurious destination for anyone wanting to be pampered. For more information contact Lodge and Spa at Cordillera; (800) 877-3529; www .cordilleralodge.com.

As you continue past Vail and Eagle on I–70 heading west, you'll soon find yourself surrounded by spectacular canyon walls. Welcome to *Glenwood Canyon.* Remarkable for its breathtaking geologic features and lovely scenery, the canyon is rendered even more extraordinary by the fact that the interstate highway running through it was constructed with a mind to retaining the canyon's wild and natural beauty. Though it's unfortunate a large interstate was constructed in this incredible setting, it is nonetheless encouraging that those in charge of building the road worked hard to make it as environmentally friendly as possible.

The interstate swoops and bends with the canyon as it drops deeper into the earth. Between the river and the canyon wall, 16-mile long *Glenwood Springs Recreation Trail* parallels the highway. You can catch occasional glimpses of it from the road. Four rest stops along I–70 allow access to the trail within the canyon. The trail starts behind the Yampah Spa and Vapor Caves in Glenwood Springs. This paved trail and the river attract not only hikers and sightseers, but also in-line skaters, cyclists, runners, rafters, and kayakers. For

Kayaking the Colorado

For an unforgettable experience, book a two-day novice kayak river trip with the *Boulder Outdoor Center.* The trips take you down the Colorado River as it winds through Glenwood Canyon. Accompanied by accredited instructors, you learn how to read the river and maneuver a kayak safely through Class II+ rapids, eddies, and through the scenery of Glenwood Canyon. They even show you how to roll yourself upright. Participants must have some previous kayaking experience and be at least twelve years old. Trips run from May through September. Write 2525 Arapahoe Ave., #E4-228, Boulder 80302 or call (303) 444-8420 or (800) 364-9376 for details; www .boc123.com.

more information call (888) 4-GLENWOOD, or contact the Eagle Ranger District at P.O. Box 720, Eagle 81631; (970) 328-6388; www.glenwoodchamber.com.

One of the hidden treats of Glenwood Canyon is *Hanging Lake.* Pull off of I–70 when you see the sign; the turnoff is well-marked but if you're not in the correct lane you will miss the exit. It's a short hike (only 1.2 miles) but in that distance it climbs 1,020 feet up the mountain. The trail follows Deadhorse Creek past box elders, cottonwoods, and lush fern gardens. Your reward at the top is a spectacular natural lake that was formed long ago when a geological fault caused the hillside to fall away. A nearby stream deposited carbonates over the fault, which hardened and formed a rim. Today the lake is 25 feet deep, crystal clear, and filled with large trout. There is no fishing so these lunkers have grown uninterrupted by anglers. A boardwalk circles part of the lake, and the mist from the waterfalls is cooling in summer. It's a fragile, pristine place, well worth the short but strenuous uphill hike.

Glenwood Springs is the gateway to some of Colorado's most dramatic and most photographed peaks, like the Maroon Bells near Snowmass or lone, spectacular Mt. Sopris, which is visible from almost everywhere in the region. The immense *White River National Forest* offers backpackers plenty of wilderness for roaming around. Anglers find world-class fishing for trout (rainbows and browns) in the surrounding rivers—the Roaring Fork, the Frying Pan, and the Colorado. Rivers attract rafters and kayakers as well; guiding services are available in Glenwood Springs. Hiking is plentiful, and hunters flock to the region for elk, deer, grouse, and waterfowl.

Despite the wealth of outdoor pursuits surrounding the town, the attraction that brings most visitors to the area is the 2-block-long *Glenwood Hot Springs* pool. No matter the season or the weather outside, the therapeutic waters are perfect for easing sore, tired muscles. With views over the conifers to the nearby peaks, the scenery and the heated pool conspire to relax even the most road-weary warrior. The Ute Indians used these springs centuries before the first explorers arrived, claiming they had miraculous healing powers. A famed architect, imported from Vienna, Austria, built the bathhouses here in 1890, and before long assorted American presidents such as Truman, Taft, Hoover and Teddy Roosevelt came to visit Glenwood's mineral spa and "Natatorium."

Today the recreational swimming—and walking—part of the pool is kept at 90° to 93°F (29° to 32°C); hotter outdoor waters at 100° to 104°F (38° to 40°C) are also available, fed by more than 3.5 million gallons. The hot springs contain a cornucopia of elements, including magnesium, calcium, sulphates, bicarbonates, phosphates, and silica. Swimmers relish the almost unlimited

trivia

Doc Holliday, the famous—or infamous—cowboy, died in Glenwood Springs in 1887; his grave marker epitaph declares only this: HE DIED IN BED.

space in the pool, while those recuperating from injuries enjoy the medical benefits.

Some guests spend much of the day in deck chairs around the pool—Colorado's version of *la dolce vita*. But no Roman bath could match Glenwood's pure air and mountain views. For additional pampering, the nearby vapor baths feature massages and natural saunas. The pool is open daily, year-round, until 10 p.m., opening at 7:30 a.m. in summer and 9 a.m. in winter. Cost is $14.75 for anyone age thirteen or older and $9.25 for children three to twelve during the summer; children two and younger are free. Contact the pool at (970) 947-2955; www.hotspringspool.com.

Glenwood Springs has plenty of lodging, but the most convenient one for soakers is the ***Hot Springs Lodge.*** It's a short walk from the pool to your room. The 107-unit Hot Springs Lodge is contemporary and ideally located. Rates are not as high as you might expect. For reservations call (800) 537-7946 or (970) 945-6571. For more information about the pool or lodgings write to the Hot Springs Lodge and Pool, P.O. Box 308, Glenwood Springs 81602; www .hotspringspool.com.

Touring Glenwood Springs

Glenwood Springs is 42 miles northwest of Aspen off Highway 82. "Glenwood," as residents call it, sits in the White River National Forest, which is a three-hour drive from Denver. Glenwood's two million acres are renowned for all manner of outdoor sports. Flat Tops Wilderness, a huge 117,000-acre plateau north of Glenwood Springs, is a popular destination for anyone seeking quiet and solitude.

Glenwood was named for its hot-spring mineral baths, which are open all year. In the 1880s, silver baron Walter Devereaux decided to convert the springs, which had been used by the Utes for centuries, into a health resort for the rich. He built the 2-block-long swimming pool, intended for the guests of the posh adjacent hotel. By the early 1900s, so many wealthy and famous people came to the spa that a rail siding was installed next to the hotel for private railroad cars. Teddy Roosevelt made Glenwood his "Summer White House" in 1901 and hunted bear in the nearby hills.

The mineral baths and vapor caves are open to visitors. Massage is also available. Locals say the water is a healthy way to ease visitors' aching muscles and stiff joints after days in the nearby wilderness, on long hikes, or on Aspen's ski slopes.

Sunlight Mountain Resort

Tired of the crowds at the big resorts? Then maybe it's time to try out *Sunlight Mountain Resort.* With more than 460 acres of terrain, plus access to plenty of Nordic trails in the adjacent White River National Forest, this resort offers a great escape. Terrific for families, almost all of the resort's ski runs come right down to the lodge. From Glenwood, head south on Highway 117. For more information contact the resort at (970) 945-7491 or (800) 445-7931; www.sunlightmtn.com. Consider staying at the cozy Sunlight Mountain Inn, located at 10252 County Rd. 117, 9 miles outside Glenwood Springs. Call (970) 945-5225 or (800) 733-4757; www.sunlightinn.com.

Glenwood Springs may be one of the state's more interesting destinations—historically, economically, scenically—yet it never gets the kind of attention accorded to trendy Aspen (41 miles to the southeast) glitzy Vail (59 miles) or cosmopolitan Denver (some 158 miles to the east). Both the town and the area are blessed with accommodations for every pocketbook. Economy travelers welcome the numerous campgrounds or inexpensive little cabins flanking the soothing rivers. Large and small motels abound. Annual festivals, yearly fishing contests, rodeos, and mountains all around the town give Glenwood Springs a true western atmosphere while preserving its small-town feel.

Glenwood can lay claim to another local attraction found nowhere else in the state. **Strawberry Days,** held in June, brings parades, carnivals, top-notch entertainment, an art and crafts market, and sporting events. Strawberry Days, now more than one hundred years old, is Glenwood Springs's oldest and most beloved annual event. The festival is Colorado's oldest civic celebration, dating back to 1898. Things have changed since the strawberry picnics of those early days, but the town's enthusiasm for this celebration is stronger than ever. The celebration goes for three days, with an estimated 30,000 people showing up to enjoy the party each year. For more information call (970) 945-6589; www .strawberrydaysfestival.com.

Today the annual Strawberry Days celebration has been extended by several days and many new activities, including sporting events, kids' events, top name entertainment, and a marketplace of handcrafted works. Attendance at the fair has risen to an estimated 30,000 people over the peak weekend.

The **Fall Art Festival,** held in September, is the largest non-juried art show in the state, attracting more than 400 entries from artists throughout Colorado and the United States. Professionals and amateurs compete in their own levels and media. And, of course, almost everything is for sale after the judging. Call (970) 945-2414 or visit www.glenwoodchamber.com for details.

While you're in Glenwood Springs, take a stroll through the stately **Hotel Colorado,** which graces the National Register of Historic Places. The 128-room hotel, one of the oldest in the state, was modeled after Italy's Villa Medici and boasts a Florentine fountain in a landscaped courtyard. The hotel's renovated beige lobby is one of the most attractive in the western United States. The sparkling chandeliers, fireplaces, oil paintings, fountains, and potted palm trees hark back to the days of royalty and the very wealthy.

The Hotel Colorado was financed by the silver mining of the nearby Aspen region and opened officially on June 10, 1893. The cost was a staggering (at the time) $850,000; some sixteen private railroad cars of the industrial barons drew up on a special Glenwood siding. Leading citizens from all over the world registered.

European millionaires arrived in droves to stay and dine here. In 1905 President Theodore Roosevelt brought his own appetite; a typical menu encouraged the presidential visitor and his entourage to consume an eight-course repast: *Caviar Canapés, Spring Lamb Consommé, Rothschild Broiled Squab, Veal, Sweetbreads, Fig's Young Turkey, and Roquefort Cheese.*

Eventually, Roosevelt—an avid bear hunter—made the hotel his Summer White House, complete with direct telegraph connections to Washington and special couriers bringing international news to the hunting head of state. Other famous guests included the "Unsinkable" Molly Brown, who managed to survive the *Titanic*'s sinking, gangster Al Capone, and President Taft. For more information and reservations contact Hotel Colorado, 526 Pine, Glenwood Springs 81601; (970) 945-6511 or (800) 544-3998; www.hotelcolorado.com.

trivia

Legend has it that the Teddy Bear was born at the Hotel Colorado. One time when frequent visitor President Teddy Roosevelt had a fruitless day of bear hunting, the hotel's maids sewed a stuffed bear in an effort to cheer him up. When he did succeed in hunting down a real bear, his daughter named the bear "Teddy," a name that stuck.

For more information about the Glenwood Springs area, contact the Glenwood Springs Chamber Resort Association at (888) 4-GLENWOOD or (970) 945-6589; www.glenscape.com. Glenwood Springs is easily reached from Denver by rental car, bus, or train. Motorists use I–70. The distance from Denver is 158 miles.

Even by Colorado standards, the trip to **Redstone** is long, but it is worth it. The scenery along the way is classic Rockies landscape and the distance only enhances the charms of the little hamlet of Redstone and its historic inn and castle. The imposing **Redstone Inn** and Tudor clock tower are an unexpected sight in this remote mountain landscape.

The thirty-five rooms are cozy and unpretentious, although many furnishings are in need of replacement. It's a quirky, one of a kind place, and if you don't need 4-star accommodations, this historic hotel in a beautiful setting is a nice escape from the city. The lobby and the restaurant are filled with antiques and have a Victorian atmosphere. The Crystal River is quiet and lovely, with fishing and horseback riding available in the warm months. In winter, the inn serves as headquarters for sleigh rides, cross-country skiing, ice climbing, and snowshoeing.

Contact Redstone Inn at 82 Redstone Blvd., Redstone 81623; (970) 963-2526 or (800) 748-2524; www.redstoneinn.com. Get to Redstone via I–70 west to Glenwood Springs, then Highway 82 south out of Glenwood toward Aspen; turn right at Carbondale on Highway 133—it's 18 miles to Redstone. For more information about the community and surrounding area, visit www .redstonecolorado.com.

If you continue along Highway 82 south out of Glenwood, it won't be long until you reach the famous town of ***Aspen.*** This pretty town is famous around the world as a mountain retreat for movie stars, music moguls, and the wealthy. The gated communities in the hills above town are where the rich and famous stay and party during ski vacations or summer getaways. It's the best celebrity-spotting place in Colorado.

But Aspen is much more than glitz and glamour, and as you approach the edge of town you will see why it's become a haven for celebrities. Aspen sits at the upper end of Roaring Fork Valley, surrounded by abundant aspen groves. The Roaring Fork River, a tributary of the Colorado River, runs through town. Mountains and wilderness rise above Aspen on three sides. Nearby Maroon Bells and Maroon Lake are among the most photographed and easily recognizable of Colorado's many natural landmarks. Mention Colorado to someone who's never been here, and the scenery around Aspen is likely the sort of place they have in mind.

Aspen called itself Ute City at first because it was in Ute territory. Silver gave the town its big start back in the early 1880s. The first news made the prospectors head up the passes and rush to Aspen—a hard, punishing journey, even from nearby Leadville. Some men dropped dead before they could stake their first claim. Western historians still mention the stampede of that winter in 1879. They came on burro, on foot, or on horseback.

Sometimes a man would keel over and die on the Aspen street. Other

trivia

One nugget from the Molly Gibson Mine in Aspen weighed 1,840 pounds. It was 93 percent pure silver.

prospectors just stuck the body into a snow bank and kept up the frantic search for silver riches. The best years were from 1885 to 1889, when mines galore—with names like the Smuggler or Montezuma—operated above the mountain town. The smelter was booked for weeks, and silver rock would pile up everywhere.

Some miners got rich fast. "The men filled their pockets and fled," wrote one observer of the era. The silver barons built the luxurious Victorian **Hotel Jerome** (330 East Main St., 970-920-1000; www.hoteljerome.com) and an opera house. Singers and musicians came from Europe to perform.

The crash came in 1893 and brought lean times. Aspen shriveled from a population of 13,000 to a mere 500. The 1930 census shows a total population of 705 residents. Many Aspen dwellings stood empty. But several investors saw potential. In the 1940s the rebirth begin, and by the early 1950s skiing was well established. Aspen was on its way to a second chance, this time as a world-class ski resort.

Today the town is an eclectic mix of architectural styles: original log cabins, Victorian homes, "mineshaft" condos, and mansions in the hills. Yet despite its flaws, Aspen retains a simplicity that keeps visitors coming back. Aspen summers are a delight, with classical music, lectures, trails for hikers and bikers, rivers for anglers, and an expanded airport for private planes. The ski facilities, with four different ski areas and countless lifts, are all extraordinary,

Versatile Aspen

Most Colorado ski centers consist of dozens of condos, a resort, and a ski hill. By contrast, Aspen has many ski areas, and it was a full-fledged town long before skiing arrived. A pedestrian mall and flower boxes and benches invite lingering. Aspen's red, Old West-style brick buildings and Victorian gingerbread homes are periodically restored. The antique cherry-wood bars shine, as do the contemporary Tiffany lamps and the stained-glass windows. Aspen outranks most North American ski resorts when it comes to the sheer number and variety of restaurants and nightlife possibilities.

There are close to a hundred eating establishments in Aspen ready to satisfy just about any craving. From American to ethnic, gourmet to down home, Aspen has enough bistros, grills, bars, saloons, pubs, subterranean dives, cafeterias, cafes, pastry shops, coffeehouses, and high-end eateries to keep even the most dedicated foodie happy for a long time. It's a cosmopolitan, polyglot, diverse town. Aspen is everything to every level of skier and, happily, to every non-skier as well; the town is ideal for couples or families where one member doesn't ski. Several hundred shops invite browsers; amusements and sports of every kind beckon.

Aspen Highlands

Few people know that at one point in mining history—circa 1879 to 1882—Aspen had a nearby competitor named Ashcroft. Located in an adjacent valley, Ashcroft actually boasted several hotels, numerous bars, a jail, and even a newspaper. (The Ashcroft silver riches attracted silver millionaire H. A. W. Tabor and his pretty young bride, Baby Doe.) By 1883, Aspen was famous for its silver wealth, and fortune hunters arrived by the thousands; the inhabitants of Ashcroft, meanwhile, dwindled to about 100 (from 2,600 in its heyday).

And today? Aspen is a successful ski resort and Ashcroft is a ghost town. A half-dozen rickety buildings stand silently below Castle Peak, bleached by sun and wind, pummeled by snow and rain, slowly returning to the earth.

More than one hundred years after the silver boom and bust, Ashcroft still holds value. **Ashcroft Ski Touring Center** offers 35 kilometers of cross country trails, along with rentals, instruction, and advice on where to ski. You reach this quiet area by driving west for a ½ mile on Highway 82, and then turning on Castle Creek Road. After 12 miles, you see the cross country trails. Call (970) 925-1971 for more information; www.pinecreekcookhouse.com.

rivaling anything in the Swiss Alps. Restaurants and hotels cater to every budget. And on Red Mountain, where the movie stars live, the parties still go on most every night.

The scene is an early Saturday morning in ***Ashcroft,*** a remote Colorado ghost town near Aspen. The sun's first rays work their way down nearby Castle Peak and begin spilling across the snowy valley. Nothing stirs in this silent, wintry landscape. Then comes full daylight, bright, golden, and topped by a china-blue Colorado sky.

A few people assemble down the road from Ashcroft's weathered, abandoned buildings. Several more join them, all carrying snowshoes. By 9 a.m. forty snowshoers stand ready, almost twice as many as the Colorado Mountain Club leader had expected.

After a long decline in popularity, ***snowshoeing*** is back in fashion, and for several good reasons. Over the last couple of decades the equipment has evolved into lightweight, high-tech gear that makes walking in the snow easy. You don't need lessons; within minutes you will be ready to take off up the trail. And it's excellent exercise. Snowshoeing is really nothing more than winter hiking. You get to enjoy great views,

trivia

When the silver boom went bust in the 1890s, Aspen's population plummeted and Aspen almost became a ghost town.

trivia

A 130-pound woman burns about 340 calories per hour of snowshoeing.

stop whenever you like, and have a solid outdoor workout at a time when others are indoors hiding from Old Man Winter.

On snowshoes you can go just about anywhere, on trail or off, wherever you can find at least a few inches of snow. From the steep winter meadows of the Continental Divide, across the gentle mounds of eastern Colorado, over frozen Lake Dillon, and into the dramatic deep-snow regions above Silverton and Ouray, snowshoers find many hundreds of places to explore. There are no lift lines or tickets to buy. There's no expensive outfit to buy, just standard outdoor winter clothing. Many outdoor shops in Colorado rent snowshoes; cost is around $15 per day for the first day, less for each additional day. In Denver try REI; their flagship store is at 1416 Platte St.; (303) 756-3100; www.rei.com/stores/18.

Summertime in the Colorado mountains is a delight to the ears. Tumbling streams, trilling birdsong, wind whistling down the canyons; it's a daily free concert. But the Colorado Rockies also happen to be home to a world-famous music festival in a mountain setting unlike any other. Far from any urban center, the music at this altitude seems even more pure and lifting.

The Aspen Music Festival was founded in 1949 with the belief that combining art and nature encourages the growth of the human spirit. This internationally renowned festival presents some of the world's most accomplished classical musicians in a magnificent alpine setting. Over a nine-week period attendees can choose from more than 200 events, including chamber and contemporary music, orchestral concerts, classes, lectures, and kid's programs. Events are held in concert halls, churches, and a permanent tent structure

Aspen Flights

If you're ready to try something totally different, how about taking to the skies on a paraglider?

With no prior experience necessary, you can soar with an experienced certified pilot from near the summit of Aspen Mountain. Scheduled on a daily basis, these summer flights are absolutely unforgettable.

The *Aspen Paragliding School* offers an instruction course, including flights, technique, and equipment. For information, call (970) 925-7625 or visit www .aspenparagliding.com.

Aspen Dog Sledding

And you thought dog sledding only happens in Alaska! Snuggle down into a sled and be prepared for a thrilling ride though a pristine Aspen landscape. Each sled is pulled by ten Alaskan sled dogs and guided by an experienced musher. The dogs are born and bred to run, and they are as excited as the riders to move quickly down the trail. Rides last 1.5–2 hours and are available from mid-December through mid-April depending on snow conditions. They are located at 4250 Divide Rd. in Snowmass Village, 10 miles from Aspen. For more information call (970) 923-3953 or visit www .krabloonikrestaurant.com.

with excellent acoustics. Many events are free, and there's always free seating on the lawn outside the tent. Contact the organization at 2 Music School Rd., 81611; (970) 925-3254/9042; www.aspenmusicfestival.com.

Nature and the outdoors are among the main reasons people visit Colorado. The first step for many is experiencing the region through road trips, camping, hiking, skiing, rafting, and biking. But many visitors seduced by the grandeur and beauty of the state are curious about the geography, flora, and fauna, and want to learn more about the ecology and the environment that makes the area unique.

The *Aspen Center for Environmental Studies* (ACES) was formed in 1968 to provide a way for an increasingly urbanized world to rediscover nature. Along with establishing a wildlife preserve in Aspen, the initial focus was to educate school children about nature and teach environmental responsibility.

Today ACES is an important part of the Aspen community. Thousands of adults and children visit every year to participate in the Naturalist Field School. Instructors from around the country come each summer to teach close to 50 different workshops and courses on the diverse Rocky Mountain ecosystem. Daily courses include hawk, eagle, and owl demonstrations; naturalist-guided walks, a variety of programs for kids, sunset beaver walks, and campground programs. Course topics include birds, plants, backcountry navigation, families in nature, geology, mushrooms, field journaling, astronomy, and farming.

In the winter, ACES leads snowshoe tours to Castle Creek Valley and Ashcroft ghost town, and ski tours at Snowmass. Each Wednesday at 7:30 during Potbelly Nights, weekly photo presentations by adventurers and biologists transport audiences to faraway lands. For more information and a complete list of courses contact ACES at 100 Puppy Smith St., 81611; (970) 925-5756; aces@ aspennature.org; or www.aspennature.org.

Naturalist Nights

Interesting and educational, Naturalist Nights take place every Thursday evening at Aspen Center for Environmental Studies (ACES) from 7:30 to 8:30 p.m., January through March. Naturalist Nights cover a variety of topics, such as "Survival in the Avalanche Zone," "Wolves in the West," and "Birds of the Winter Forest." Admission is $3, free for members.

Snowmass Village just ten miles from Aspen, may not have the instant name recognition enjoyed by its nearby neighbor, but it compensates by offering a wide variety of activities and events throughout the year. You're still deep in the Rockies, so expect to find miles of hiking and mountain biking, fly fishing, rafting, golf, jeep tours, and horseback riding.

But just like Aspen, Snowmass is also a cultural destination. Winter means skiing and other winter sports, but the summer and fall months bring a non-stop selection of unique festivals, concerts, and events. Summer begins with the Chili Pepper and Brew Fest, featuring a chili cook-off, microbrew tasting, and live music. Snowmass Rodeo begins in mid-June and stretches through mid-August. Snowmass Village puts on free music concerts featuring major acts through the summer at the Village Mall on the mountain. The Jazz Aspen Snowmass June Festival is ten days of some of the best jazz on the planet.

Taking It Slow in Aspen

The Aspen/Snowmass Nordic Trail System offers cross-country skiers numerous opportunities around the valley. This systems is unique because it links two towns (Aspen and Snowmass Village), meandering through meadows, wooded areas, and across three valleys. Choose from 60 kilometers of groomed trails or set off on your own across fresh powder. Two Nordic centers, Aspen Cross-Country Center, (970) 925-2145, and Snowmass Cross-Country Center, (970) 923-5700, are on the trail network, providing instruction, rentals, snacks, waxing advice, and information on choosing the right trail for your skill level. Directions and information for both centers can be found at www.aspennordic.com or www.utemountaineer.com/aspenxc.html.

A third Nordic center, Ashcroft Ski Touring, (970) 925-1971, is located up the Castle Creek Valley on the Ashcroft Trail System. They offer rentals, instruction, and trail advice, and with 35 kilometers of trail, the center has some of the prettiest routes in the valley. You can also ski or snowshoe into and out of the Pine Creek Cookhouse for a memorable gourmet meal. Visit online at www.skiashcroft.com, www.pinecreek cookhouse.com.

Snowmass Balloon Festival in September fills the sky for three colorful days with one of the highest-altitude balloon events in the country. Jazz Aspen Snowmass Labor Day Festival brings a wide variety of music to the mountain for three days.

In case this partial list isn't enough to entice you to visit Snowmass, there's more. From late spring through fall, Snowmass hosts bike races, theater, a film festival, Octoberfest, food and wine festivals, volleyball competition, and a great July 4th party. But not all visitors come for the festivals and outdoor activities. Some visitors are drawn to Snowmass to follow their muse. Artists come here from around the country and abroad to study at **_Anderson Ranch Arts Center,_** where more than 140 workshops are offered each summer. Classes are available for all age groups, and include subjects such as ceramics, painting and drawing, photography, printmaking, furniture design, woodworking, and sculpture. Courses on the five-acre ranch run from two days to two weeks, giving artists of all levels a place to be inspired, learn new skills, and immerse themselves in the creative process. For more information contact the ranch in Snowmass at 5263 Owl Creek Rd., 81615 or P.O. Box 5598, 81615; (970) 923-3181; www.andersonranch.org. For general information on activities and events at Snowmass call (888) 649-5982; www.stayaspensnowmass.com or www.snowmassvillage.com.

Aspen, Snowmass, and Aspen Highlands have some of the best skiing in the country, including many advanced intermediate and expert runs. The fourth local ski area, little **_Buttermilk Ski Resort,_** would at first glance seem to be up against some tough competition. But Buttermilk has carved out a name for itself in two areas. First, it focuses on beginners and skiers who don't need the

Snowmass Summers

Snowmass summers are mellow. The rocks are warm and meadows fill with wildflowers: anemones, bluebells, gentian, and Indian paintbrush. Hikers move into the high country. Classes begin at the arts center. Aspen's music festival is only twenty minutes away.

In summer, Snowmass is a center for picnickers, hikers, kayakers, four-wheel enthusiasts, and mountain bikers. Climbers set out for the Maroon Bells. Fishermen arm themselves with flies, rods, and nets, and set out for the many area trout streams. Horseback riders climb into saddles and disappear into the woods.

Miles of trails, ranging from gentle forest paths to muscle-aching switchbacks, will transport you into an alpine world of mountain flowers, snowmelt streams, and shady aspen groves.

heart-racing intensity of black diamond slopes. Although Buttermilk has expert runs, it's known as an excellent place for beginners with an outstanding ski school. The hills are gentle and friendly to those just starting out, or for those who want to take it easy and enjoy the slopes at a mellower pace.

Buttermilk's other specialty is snowboarding. The resort has five separate terrain parks, more than 30 rails, a super pipe and a beginner's pipe, all within the world's longest (two miles) terrain park. From beginner to Winter X Games pro, snowboarders of every skill level will find plenty to keep them happy. For more information on Buttermilk skiing, contact Aspen Skiing Company, P.O. Box 1248, Aspen 81612; (970) 925-1220 or toll-free (800) 525-6200; www .aspensnowmass.com.

Vail. Aspen. Telluride. Copper, Winter Park. Crested Butte. Snowmass. In the world of skiing, these are household names, spoken in almost reverential tones. Colorado is justifiably famous for its skiing. The snow is light, fluffy, and easy to ski. With so much of the state at high elevations, the region has the terrain, the altitude, and the weather for world-class skiing. And the western landscapes, especially when viewed from the upper slopes, are grandiose.

The state's ski meccas are deserving of their fame. None of Colorado's ski resorts look alike; each has its special character made up of a dozen variables. Century-old mining towns like Breckenridge and Crested Butte have been revived. Aspen is immense and complex. Vail is a giant in every way, an American St. Moritz. Winter Park serves vacationers during the week and Denverites on weekends. Loveland Basin and Keystone yield consistent snow. Uncrowded Telluride with its fast, epic runs nestles in a beautiful box canyon.

If you come to this state anytime between late November and April, you should try to ski, even if you've never done it before. Each resort area offers excellent instruction and beginner slopes. And there are numerous other

Skier's Locomotion up Aspen Mountain

When the Aspen Skiing Corp. (now the Aspen Skiing Company) opened its first lifts on Aspen Mountain in 1947, it eliminated one of skiing's biggest drawbacks: climbing the hill.

Skiing sixty years ago was for the truly committed, because if you wanted to enjoy the slopes in winter, you had to hoof it. If skiers were lucky, they could catch a ride with miners up the back side of Aspen Mountain.

A year later, you could ascend Aspen Mountain in a single chair. The trip took more than an hour and you could get a free ticket by helping to "pack" the slopes in the morning. As many as 100 volunteers worked the slopes at the same time.

Rifle Falls State Park

Before you head too much farther west, consider making a side trip to **Rifle Falls State Park.** Though small, this unique gem of a state park offers visitors the unlikely opportunity to get downright tropical—or close to it! The triple waterfall plummets down 80 feet past limestone cliffs, keeping the lush vegetation moist. Dark, cool caves beckon to curious explorers, and interpretive signs help explain the phenomena. With its $6 per car entry fee, the park makes for a worthwhile side trip and a terrific place to have a family picnic.

From Aspen, take Highway 82 north about 41 miles. In Glenwood Springs turn left onto Sixth Street then left onto North River Drive, following signs to I–70 west. Take I–70 west about 25.5 miles to the Rifle exit. Go north on Highway 13 for 4 miles. Turn right on Highway 325 and drive 9.8 miles. Call (970) 625-1607 or write Rifle Falls State Park, 5775 Highway 325, Rifle 81650; http://parks.state.co.us/parks/riflefalls.

winter activities, such as cross-country skiing, snowshoeing, sledding and tubing, and sleigh rides. For more information contact Colorado Ski Country USA, 1507 Blake St., Denver 80202; (303) 837-0793; www.coloradoski.com.

Grand Junction is at the west end of Colorado, close to the Utah border. This is expansive, wide open country. To the south lies Grand Mesa, the largest mesa in the world. To the north are the towering Bookcliffs, stretching for nearly 200 miles. It's the largest town on the Western Slope, and this region has an entirely different feel than the mountains or eastern plains. Instead of thick forests and jagged peaks, the area around Grand Junction is all about geology. Drier than points east, this region is a land of mesas, arroyos, plateaus and pinnacles, a striking landscape sculpted by annual cycles of heat and cold, of rain, wind, sun and snow. With little vegetation to hide the formations, this part of Colorado has a stark beauty that for many feels like the true West.

The town was named in 1881 for the nearby confluence of the Grand River and the Gunnison River. When the Grand was renamed Colorado River in 1921, nobody bothered to change the name of the city. Today the downtown historic area retains some of that much of the old west charm with its Victorian-era architecture. Coffeehouses, restaurants, and shops invite lingering. And the streets of downtown Grand Junction are home to one of the country's largest sidewalk sculpture galleries with close to 100 sculptures.

The *Museum of Western Colorado* covers the history of the area, beginning with the earliest residents and displays of prehistoric pottery, Navajo paintings, and rock art. The old west comes alive with a uranium mine, a stagecoach, a one-room schoolhouse, firearms exhibit, and the Pastime Saloon. Contact the museum at 462 Ute Ave., (970) 242-0971; www.wcmuseum.org.

Also at the museum, the ***Cross Orchards Living History Farm*** recreates life as it was lived by Grand Valley pioneers in the early 1900s. A country store, blacksmith shop, bunkhouse for workers, and an extensive collection of equipment from the era are part of this 24-acre site. Costumed interpreters add authenticity and explain what life was like for early settlers. The museum is located at 3073 F Rd.; (970) 434-9814.

At Dino Digs, spend the day with a paleontologist working in a real dinosaur quarry, digging for dinosaurs, turtles, lizards, and mammals in the 150 million year-old badlands of the Morrison Formation. The digs fill fast and the number of participants is limited, so call ahead for reservations. Contact the Museum of Western Colorado at (888) 488-3466, ext. 212; www.wcmuseum.com.

Grand Junction and the surrounding areas are known for producing some of the best fruit and vegetables in the state. And one of the best places to sample them while enjoying one of the town's signature events is at the weekly Farmers' Market Festival. Every Thursday during the summer Main Street is closed to car traffic, and farmers, artisans, vendors, musicians, and merchants gather for an evening of socializing, eating, music, and fun. It's a great place to experience a community party, and everyone is welcome. The market runs from mid-June until mid-September, Thursday from 5p.m. to 8:30 p.m. For more information, visit www.visitdowntowngj.org.

The region around Grand Junction doesn't seem like vineyard country. But the Grand Valley, stretching from Palisade to Fruita, has grown into a productive winery region. The climate here is milder than along the Front Range, with almost 300 days of sun a year. The warm, dry days and cool nights result in a microclimate that is ideal for wine grapes. The area is worth a day trip from Grand Junction to drive through the vineyards and peach orchards, stopping for lunch in Palisade. Many wineries offer tours demonstrating how the wine gets from grape to glass. The Colorado Mountain Winefest takes place in mid-September, (800) 704-3667; www.coloradowinefest.com. For more information and directions to the wineries, contact Grand Valley Winery Association at P.O. Box 99, Palisade, 81526-0099; (970) 464-5867 or (303) 399-7586; www.grand valleywine.com.

Each summer Grande River Vineyards hosts the Grapevine Summer Concert Series, musical events featuring jazz, soul, classical, rock, and blues. Guests bring picnics, and of course wine, to enjoy in the beautiful outdoor setting. For more information, 787 Elberta Ave.; (970) 464-5867; www.granderiverwines.com.

Each summer Colorado residents look forward to the Western Slope peach harvest. First come the Elbertas and Red Havens, followed a few weeks later by Suncrest, Sullivan, and Blake. Toward the end of summer the Redskin and Hale arrive. As each variety ripens, peach lovers search fruit markets for the peach of the week. Peach jams, cobblers, and pies show up in restaurants and kitchens. Palisade celebrates this esteemed fruit with the Palisade Peach Festival for four days in mid-August, (970) 464-7458; www.palisadepeachfest.com.

Many people drive to the orchards to buy peaches, as well as apricots and cherries. Numerous fruit stands also sell local jams, preserves, salsas, and other condiments. For more information on fruit season around Palisade, contact the Palisade Chamber of Commerce at 319 Main St., 81526; (970) 464-7458; e-mail info@palisadecoc.com; or visit www.palisadecoc.com.

Travelers in search of deep canyons, red rock walls, and sandstone spires often head to the parks of Utah. But Colorado has its own park, **Colorado National Monument,** where a world of steep plateaus, sheer drop-offs, and craggy rock spires awaits. This 31-square mile park is easily explored via a 23-mile loop road that offers numerous overlooks across the high-desert scenery. If you're a cyclist, it's a great way to absorb the scenery. Thirteen backcountry trails lead into the far reaches of the park.

To reach Colorado National Monument, follow Monument Road out of downtown Grand Junction, which will take you to the entry gate. Fees are $4 per person or $7 per vehicle. For more information call (970) 858-3617 or write Colorado National Monument, Fruita 81521; www.nps.gov/colm.

To reach the Colorado National Monument, follow Monument Road out of downtown Grand Junction, which will take you to the entry gate. Pick up a map there. Fees are $4 per person or $7 per vehicle. For more information call (970) 858-3617 or write Colorado National Monument, Fruita 81521; www.nps.gov/colm.

trivia

In Colorado, state law considers bicycles to be vehicles and they must obey the same traffic laws as automobiles. Ride single file on the right in the same direction as traffic. Always signal when stopping or turning. When you need to catch your breath, move off the road. It's also good advice to wear a helmet and protective glasses.

trivia

Despite receiving only 11 inches of rainfall annually, the area encompassed by the Colorado National Monument was continuously inhabited for thousands of years until 1881. That year, the area's most recent inhabitants, the Utes, were moved by the U.S. military to a Utah reservation. Past inhabitants left evidence of their existence through rock art and other artifacts.

Places to Stay in the Central Mountains

The rating scale for hotels is based on double occupancy and is as follows:
Inexpensive:
Less than $75 per night
Moderate:
$75 to $100 per night
Expensive:
$101 to $150 per night
Deluxe:
More than $150 per night

ASPEN

Aspen Mountain Lodge,
311 West Main St.;
(970) 925-7650 or
(800) 362-7736
www.aspenmountainlodge
.com
Expensive to Deluxe

Hotel Aspen,
110 W. Main St.;
(970) 925-3441 or
(800) 527-7369
www.hotelaspen.com
Moderate to Expensive

Hotel Jerome,
330 E. Main St.;
(970) 920-1000 or
(800) 331-7213
www.hoteljerome.
rockresorts.com
Deluxe

Limelight Lodge,
335 Monarch St.;
(970) 925-3025 or
(800) 433-0832
www.limelightlodge.com
Expensive

Little Nell,
675 E. Durant Ave.;
(970) 920-4600 or
(888) 843-6355
www.thelittlenell.com
Deluxe

St. Regis Resort,
315 Dean St.;
(970) 920-3300 or
(888) 454-9005
www.stregisaspen.com
Deluxe

BRECKENRIDGE

Allaire Timbers Inn,
9511 S. Main St.;
(970) 453-7530 or
(800) 624-4904
www.allairetimbers.com
Moderate–expensive

Barn on the River Bed & Breakfast,
303 North Main St.;
(970) 453-2975 or
(800) 795-2975
www.breckenridge-inn.com
Expensive to Deluxe

Lodge & Spa at Breckenridge,
112 Overlook Dr.;
(970) 453-9300 or
(800) 736-1607
www.thelodgeatbreck.com
Moderate to Expensive

River Mountain Lodge,
100 South Park Ave.;
(970) 453-4711 or
(800) 627-3766
www.resortquest.com
Expensive to Deluxe

Skiway Lodge,
275 Ski Hill Rd.;
(970) 453-7573 or
(800) 472-1430
www.skiwaylodge.com
Expensive to Deluxe

DILLON

Best Western Ptarmigan Lodge,
652 Lake Dillon Dr.;
(970) 468-2341 or
(800) 842-5939
www.ptarmiganlodge.com
Moderate to Expensive

La Quinta Inn (Summit County),
560 Silverthorne Lane;
(970) 468-6200
www.lq.com
Moderate to Deluxe

GEORGETOWN

All Aboard Inn,
(located in historic district)
605 Brownell St.;
(303) 569-2525
www.allaboardinn.com
Expensive

Mad Creek Bed & Breakfast,
167 West Park Ave.,
Empire;
(303) 569-2003 or
(888) 266-1498
www.madcreekbnb.com
Expensive

Rose Street Bed & Breakfast,
200 Rose St.;
(303) 569-2222 or
(866) 569-2221
www.rosestreetbed
breakfast.com
Moderate to Expensive

SELECTED CENTRAL MOUNTAINS GENERAL INFORMATION RESOURCES

ASPEN

Aspen Chamber Resort Association,
425 Rio Grande Place;
(970) 925-1940 or (800) 670-0792
www.aspenchamber.org

BRECKENRIDGE

Breckenridge Resort Chamber,
P.O. Box 1909, 80424;
(888) 251-2417
www.gobreck.com

GEORGETOWN

Downtown Georgetown Community Center,
P.O. Box 834, 80444;
(303) 569-2888 or (800) 472-8230
www.georgetowncolorado.com

GLENWOOD SPRINGS

Glenwood Springs Chamber Resort Association,
1102 Grand Ave.;
(970) 945-6589 or (888) 4-GLENWOOD
www.glenwoodchamber.com

IDAHO SPRINGS

Idaho Springs Chamber of Commerce,
P.O. Box 97, 80452;
(303) 567-4382
www.historicidahosprings.com

PALISADE

Palisade Chamber of Commerce,
319 Main St.;
(970) 464-7458
www.palisadecoc.com

VAIL

Vail Valley Chamber and Tourism Bureau,
100 East Meadow Dr.;
(970) 476-1000 or (800) 653-4523
www.visitvailvalley.com

GLENWOOD SPRINGS

Hot Springs Lodge,
(across from Glenwood pool)
415 Sixth St.;
(970) 945-6571 or
(800) 537-7946
www.hotspringspool.com
Expensive to Deluxe

Hotel Colorado,
(historic hotel; well-restored)
526 Pine St.;
(970) 945-6511 or
(800) 544-3998
www.hotelcolorado.com
Expensive to Deluxe

Redstone Inn,
82 Redstone Blvd,
Redstone;
(970) 963-2526 or
(800) 748-2524
www.redstoneinn.com
Inexpensive to Deluxe

GRAND JUNCTION

The Chateau at Two Rivers,
2087 Broadway;
(866) 312-9463 or
(970) 255-1471
www.tworiverswinery.com/
Expensive

Grand Vista Hotel,
2790 Crossroads Blvd.;
(800) 800-7796 or
(970) 241-8411
www.grandvistahotel.com
Moderate to Expensive

Hampton Inn Grand Junction,
205 Main St.;
(970) 243-3222
www.hamptoninn.com
Moderate to Expensive

Los Altos B&B,
375 Hill View Dr.;
(970) 256-0964 or
(888) 774-0982
www.losaltosgrandjunction.com
Expensive

GRANT

The Tumbling River Ranch,
(large swimming pool; outstanding stables; a stay here guarantees a quality experience)
P.O. Box 30;
(303) 838-5981 or
(800) 654-8770
www.tumblingriver.com
Deluxe

IDAHO SPRINGS

H & H Motor Lodge,
(simple, clean motel)
2445 Colorado Blvd., Idaho Springs;
(303) 567-2838
Inexpensive to Moderate

Heritage Inn,
(quiet motel; within walking distance of cafes)
2622 Colorado Blvd.;
(303) 567-4473
www.theheritageinn.com
Inexpensive to Expensive

KEYSTONE

Ski Tip Lodge,
(one of Colorado's first lodges; great atmosphere; a little cramped; make reservations far in advance)
764 Montezuma Rd., Keystone;
(970) 496-4950
Moderate to Deluxe

Places to Eat in the Central Mountains

The rating scale for restaurants is as follows:
Inexpensive:
Most entrees less than $10
Moderate:
Most entrees $10 to $15
Expensive:
Most entrees $16 to $20
Deluxe:
Most entrees more than $20

ASPEN

Boogie's Diner,
534 E. Cooper Ave.;
(970) 925-6610
Moderate

Cantina,
(Mexican, American)
411 East Main St.;
(970) 925-3663
www.cantina-aspen.com
Moderate to Expensive

Hickory House Ribs,
730 W. Main St.;
(970) 925-2313
www.hickoryhouseribs.com
Moderate to Expensive

Little Annie's,
517 East Hyman Ave.;
(970) 925-1098
www.littleannies.com
Moderate to Expensive

Main St. Bakery & Cafe,
201 E. Main St.;
(970) 925-6446
Inexpensive to Moderate

Paradise Bakery & Cafe,
(delicious muffins, homemade ice cream)
320 South Galena St.;
(970) 925-7585
www.paradisebakery.com
Inexpensive

Takah Sushi,
320 South Mill St.;
(970) 925-8588 or
(877) 925-8588
www.takahsushi.com
Deluxe

Toppers,
300 Puppy Smith St.;
(970) 920-0069
www.toppersaspen.com
Moderate to Expensive

Wienerstube,
(Austrian; continental)
633 East Hyman Ave.;
(970) 925-3357
www.wienerstube.com
Moderate to Expensive

Wild Fig,
315 E. Hyman Ave.;
(970) 925-5160
www.thewildfig.com
Expensive

BRECKENRIDGE

Blue Moose,
(breakfast)
540 South Main St.;
(970) 453-4859
Inexpensive to Moderate

OTHER ATTRACTIONS WORTH SEEING IN THE CENTRAL MOUNTAINS

ASPEN

Aspen Historical Society Wheeler/ Stallard Museum,
(970) 925-3721
www.aspenhistory.org/wsh.html

Independence Pass,
(Highway 82, closed in winter)
www.independencepass.org

DILLON

Copper Mountain Resort Ski Area,
(866) 841-2481
www.coppercolorado.com

GEORGETOWN

Loveland Ski Area,
(800) 736-3754
www.skiloveland.com

GLENWOOD

White River National Forest,
(970) 945-2521
www.fs.fed.us/r2/whiteriver

IDAHO SPRINGS

Idaho Springs National Historic District,
(303) 567-4660 or (866) 674-9237
www.historicidahosprings.com

Breckenridge Brewery,
(ribs, fish & chips, fajitas)
600 South Main St.;
(970) 453-1550
www.breckbrew.com
Moderate

Cafe Alpine,
(continental)
106 East Adams Ave.;
(970) 453-8218
www.cafealpine.com
Deluxe

Clint's Bakery and Coffee House,
131 S. Main St.;
(970) 453-2990
Inexpensive to Moderate

Giampietro Pasta and Pizzeria,
100 N. Main St.;
(970) 453-3838
Inexpensive to Moderate

DILLON

Marcellos,
135 Main St.;
(970) 468-0551
www.marcellosattown
center.com
Moderate to expensive

Silverheels at the Ore House,
(Spanish tapas and southwestern specialties)
603 Main St., Frisco;
(970) 668-0345
www.silverheelsrestaurant
.com
Moderate to Expensive

GEORGETOWN

The Happy Cooker,
(homestyle American; breakfast and lunch only)
412 Sixth St.;
(303) 569-3166
Inexpensive to Moderate

Red Ram,
606 Sixth St.;
(303) 569-2300
Moderate

GLENWOOD SPRINGS

Daily Bread Cafe,
(sandwiches, salads, soups)
729 Grand Ave.;
(970) 945-6253
Inexpensive to Moderate

Dos Hombres,
(Mexican)
52783 Hwy. 6;
(970) 928-0490
www.doshombres
glenwood.com
Inexpensive

Florindo's,
(Italian)
721 Grand Ave.;
(970) 945-1245
Moderate to Expensive

Juicy Lucy's Steakhouse,
308 Seventh St.;
(970) 945-4619
www.juicylucyssteakhouse
.com
Moderate to Expensive

River's,
(seafood, wild game)
2525 South Grand Ave.;
(970) 928-8813
www.theriversrestaurant
.com
Moderate to Expensive

GRAND JUNCTION

**Crystal Cafe & Bake
Shop,**
314 Main St.;
(970) 242-8843
Inexpensive to Moderate

il Bistro Italiano,
400 Main St.;
(970) 243-8622
www.ilbistroitaliano.com
Expensive

Main Street Bagels,
559 Main St.;
(970) 241-2740
www.mainstreetbagels.net
Inexpensive to Moderate

Pablo's Pizza,
319 Main St.;
(970) 255-8879
www.pablospizza.com
Moderate

636 on Rood,
626 Rood Ave.;
(970) 257-7663
www.626onrood.com
Expensive to Deluxe

IDAHO SPRINGS

BeauJo's,
(famous homemade pizza)
1517 Minor St.;
(303) 567-4376
www.beaujos.com
Moderate

Two Brothers Deli,
1424 Miner St.;
(303) 567-2439
www.twobrothersdeli.com
Inexpensive to Moderate

VAIL

Bart & Yeti's,
(burgers, chili, ribs)
551 East Lionsheads
Circle;
(970) 476-2754
Moderate

Larkspur,
Golden Peak Lodge,
458 Vail Valley Dr.;
(970) 479-8050
Expensive

Left Bank,
(French)
183 Gore Creek Dr. #4;
(970) 476-3696
www.leftbankvail.com
Expensive to Deluxe

Pazzo's Pizzeria,
(calzone, pizza)
122 East Meadow Dr.;
(970) 476-9026
www.pazzosvail.com
Moderate

Sweet Basil,
(award-winning American
cuisine)
193 East Gore Creek Dr.;
(970) 476-0125
www.sweetbasil-vail.com
Expensive to Deluxe

SOUTHERN COLORADO

Colorado Springs and Beyond

Southern Colorado is far from the Front Range, and in many ways it's another world. Too far from Denver for a day trip or short weekend getaway, the area escapes the crowds that can congregate at destinations further north. No interstates cross the region, which somehow translates to a slower pace of life in this corner of the state. This is all good news for anyone wanting to explore this varied landscape, because many of the state's highlights lie in this area. Mountain ranges such as the Sangre de Cristo, San Juan, La Plata and San Miguel are home to Colorado's most rugged peaks and largest wilderness tracts. The San Luis Valley and Great Sand Dunes are unexpected and imposing in their vastness. Mining ghost towns, plunging canyons, and alpine meadows jam-packed with wildflowers wait to be explored. Friendly western towns offer a mix of mountain biking, ranching culture, and brewpubs that bring together eclectic communities. The region contains well-preserved evidence of the ancient Puebloans who lived in the area for centuries before the first Europeans rode up on horseback.

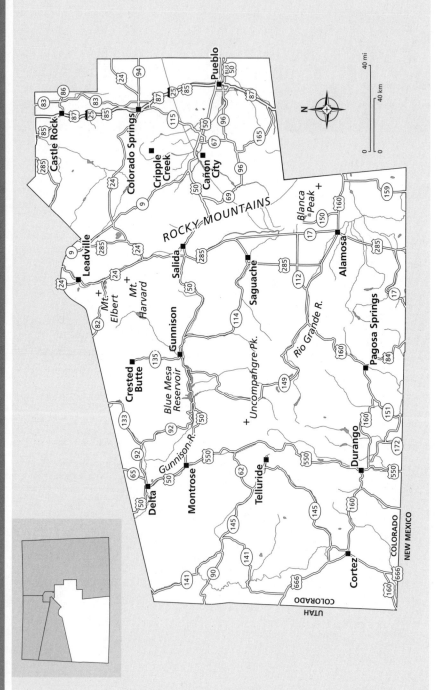

Dozens of different vacations await visitors to Southern Colorado. Take your pick of Victorian mountain towns, red rock canyons, local festivals, challenging mountain biking, counter-culture communities, ancestral cliff dwellings, rodeo, and some of the best scenery, hiking, camping, fishing, and other outdoor pursuits to be found on the planet.

The *Devil's Head Lookout Trail,* in the Rampart Range west of the little community of Sedalia (south of Denver) offers a 360 degree view of surrounding Pike National Forest. On clear days you can see mountain peaks over 100 miles away. It got its name from the red rock formations that stick out like two horns. The trail winds through deep pine forests interspersed with aspen, past giant red cliffs. The trail's length—just 1⅜ miles—doesn't sound like much; it climbs steeply, though, and includes a 950-foot vertical elevation gain, beginning at 8,800 feet.

Along the way, you get views of Pikes Peak, a number of "fourteeners" (peaks over 14,000 feet high), some of the peaks in Rocky Mountain National Park, and the Great Plains. Benches for the tired line the uphill paths. Bring water since there is none along the trail.

AUTHOR'S FAVORITES IN SOUTHERN COLORADO

Garden of the Gods,
(719) 634-6666
www.gardenofgods.com

Great Sand Dunes National Monument,
(719) 378-6300
www.nps.gov/grsa

Manitou and Pikes Peak Railway,
(719) 685-5401
www.cograilway.com

Mesa Verde National Park,
(970) 529-4465
www.nps.gov/meve

Town of Salida Downtown and Riverfront,
(877) 772-5432 or (719) 539-2068
www.salidachamber.org

Durango & Silverton Narrow Gauge Railroad,
(970) 247-2733 or (877) 872-460
www.durangotrain.com

Royal Gorge Bridge and Park,
(719) 275-7507 or (888) 333-5597
www.royalgorgebridge.com

Shelf Road,
(719) 269-8500
www.co.blm.gov/recweb/rectouring.htm

Town of Telluride,
(888) 605-2578
www.visittelluride.com

To reach the trailhead, from Denver take Santa Fe (U.S. Highway 85) south to Sedalia (13 miles); turn west toward Deckers (Highway 67) for 10 miles and make another left turn onto the Rampart Range Road (Highway 5); go another 8.5 miles until you see the Devil's Head sign. For more information contact South Platte Ranger District, 19316 Goddard Ranch Court, Morrison 80465; (303) 275-5610; www.coloradolookouts.com/dhead.html.

trivia

The Devil's Head Lookout Tower at the end of the Devil's Head Lookout Trail sits atop the highest point in the Rampart Range. It is the last operational lookout on the Front Range.

En route from Denver to Colorado Springs via the interstate, you may see a modest sign that says **Larkspur.** Few travelers have ever heard of it. Even many Denver residents are unfamiliar with this hamlet.

Yet on weekends from mid-June through July, tiny Larkspur comes alive with a bang. Cannon shots can be heard from afar. When your car draws closer to the hillside, the cannons are followed by medieval trumpets played in unison.

For more than twenty years, the zany, lively **Colorado Renaissance Festival** has entertained summer visitors on a wooded Colorado hillside above Larkspur, part theater, part learning experience, part petting zoo for children, part commerce. The Renaissance theme begins when you enter the walled compound and you're greeted as "My Lord" or "My Lady." Artisans galore demonstrate their craft: blacksmiths hammer away, glassblowers regale onlookers with their art, potters shape at their wheels, leather workers show their stuff. Bands of costumed musicians wander up the mountainside. Harpists, flutists, bagpipers, and minstrel singers materialize and harmonize.

Several times a day, "King Henry" and his "Court" introduce you to knights jousting on horseback at a gallop, doing tricks with their lances. The stages are busy with storytellers and merrymakers; the pubs dispense barrels of beer and huge turkey legs. Processions of celebrities—Shakespeare, Anne Boleyn—promenade among the visitors, while a few yards away, you can be a medieval archer or knife thrower or dart artist. Encounter the unexpected: Youngsters ride real camels and elephants; jugglers and puppet masters dazzle onlookers. A good time is had by everyone.

No charge for parking weekends June through July. To reach Larkspur, take exit 172 from Interstate 25 and follow the signs. Open 10 a.m. to 6:30 p.m. Saturday and Sunday. Admission costs $17.95 for adults and teenagers thirteen and older and $8 for children five to twelve; children four and younger free. Discount tickets can be purchased at any King Soopers (a local grocery store

TOP ANNUAL EVENTS IN SOUTHERN COLORADO

Pagosa Springs Winter Fest,
Second weekend in Feb;
(800) 252-2204
www.pagosa-springs.com

Music and Blossom Festival,
Cañon City; spring;
(719) 275-7234
www.ccblossomfestival.com

Royal Gorge Rodeo,
Cañon City; May;
(719) 275-0118
www.horsestop.net/royalgorgerodeo
.htm

Pikes Peak or Bust Rodeo,
Colorado Springs; summer;
(719) 635-3547
www.coloradospringsrodeo.com

Donkey Derby,
Cripple Creek; late June;
(877) 858-4653
www.cripple-creek.co.us

Telluride Bluegrass Festival
Late June;
(303) 823-0848 or (800) 624-2422;
www.bluegrass.com/telluride

Colorado Renaissance Festival,
Larkspur; June and July;
(303) 688-6010 or (877) 259-3328
www.coloradorenaissance.com

Crested Butte Wildflower Festival,
July
(970) 349-2571
www.crestedbuttewildflowerfestival.com

Cattlemen's Days Rodeo and County Fair,
Gunnison; mid-July;
(970) 641-1501
www.gunnison-co.com

Boom Days and Burro Race,
Leadville; first full weekend of Aug;
(719) 486-1900
www.leadville.boomdays.com

Colorado State Fair,
Pueblo Fairgrounds; late Aug–early Sept;
(719) 561-8484 or (800) 876-4567
www.coloradostatefair.com

Colorado Springs Balloon Classic,
Labor Day weekend;
(719) 471-4833
www.balloonclassic.com

Telluride Film Festival,
Sept
(510) 665-9494
www.telluridefilmfestival.com

Durango Cowboy Gathering,
Durango; first week of Oct;
(970) 247-0312 or (888) 414-0835
www.durangocowboygathering.org

chain). For more information contact the festival at 409F South Wilcox St., Castle Rock 80104; (303) 688-6010; www.coloradorenaissance.com.

A ten-minute drive south of Larkspur, on the same little Country Road 105, and you will reach quiet, photogenic **Palmer Lake.** Almost no travel guide mentions it, and most people bypass it via I–25. Palmer Lake was once a refueling stop for steam railroad engines; now it's almost forgotten. Its colorful history includes gold mines, Indian raids, the occasional scalping, posses hunting murderers, and saloon shootings. Several trailheads in town lead into the hills, and there are good restaurants, shops, and a historical museum. People come here to get away from the city, walk around the lake, or take their young children to the small playground. Traffic is minimal, and it's a fine place to relax. For more information contact the Town Offices at 42 Valley Crescent, Palmer Lake 80133; (719) 481-2953; www.ci.palmer-lake.co.us.

For those who like to hike or bike, the 15-mile *Santa Fe Regional Trail,* one of the largest continuous trails in El Paso County, begins at *Palmer Lake Recreation Area.* It goes through the town of Monument to the south, ending at the southern boundary of the *United States Air Force Academy.* For more information call (719) 520-6375; http://adm.elpasoco.com/Parks/Facilities.htm.

The Air Force Academy north of Colorado Springs is one of eastern Colorado's most recognized landmarks. Whether you hike, bike, or drive, consider a stop at the academy's visitor center, located at exit 150B off I–25. A nature trail and the *Cadet Chapel* are open for visitors. The chapel is stunning with its seventeen silver-hued spires that sweep to heights of more than 150 feet. Completed in 1963, the chapel, considered to be the architectural centerpiece of the academy's campus, holds Protestant, Catholic, Jewish, Buddhist, and Muslim services. It is open Monday through Saturday, 9 a.m. to 5 p.m.; Sunday from 1 p.m. to 5 p.m. Sunday services are open to all; call (719) 333-2636 for times.

When visiting the academy, ask for a map at the gate. The visitor center is open from 9 a.m. to 5 p.m. daily. For more information call (719) 333-2025; www.usafa.af.mil.

Not far from the U.S. Air Force Academy, you'll discover your next stop— the *ProRodeo Hall of Fame and Museum of the American Cowboy,* which presents the West's unique cowboy heritage in a facility that is both entertaining and educational. The cowboy played a vital role in opening the West to the expansion of the nineteenth century, and his reputation for courage and individualism has become part of our national folklore and culture.

Families with children will enjoy the outdoor corral with its live animals. Inside, dioramas and exhibits display saddles, boots, buckles, spurs, ropes, chaps, branding equipment, and other paraphernalia, all telling the story of rodeo's history in this country. Rodeo as a sport comes alive through the mementos of America's major rodeo champions.

Visitors can learn about such colorful rodeo champs as bull rider Warren G. "Freckles" Brown, reputed to be the oldest man in ProRodeo history to win a riding event. His long career was interrupted by a broken neck, as well as by World War II. With typical spirit during wartime parachute jumps into China, Brown put on a rodeo using army mules and native cattle and declared himself the Orient's all-around champion of 1942.

Over the years, rules and equipment were standardized, judging was streamlined, prize money increased, and the freewheeling entertainment of the 1800s evolved into the modern sport of professional rodeo.

Here the visitor can learn the fine points of saddle bronc riding and how to judge a rider's performance, and can get the jolting sensation, through film with stereo sound, of what it's like to ride a bucking Brahma bull. Other films trace the historical development of rodeo.

The ProRodeo Hall of Fame is located just north of Colorado Springs on I–25 at exit 147. Hours are 9 a.m. to 5 p.m. daily except for major holidays. A small fee is charged to help defray expenses of the nonprofit museum. Call (719) 528-4764 or write 101 ProRodeo Dr., Colorado Springs 80919; www.pro rodeohalloffame.com.

The wonders of nature blend together at the *Garden of the Gods* in Colorado Springs to create one of the most varied natural settings in Colorado. Established as a free city park in 1909, the almost 1,370 acres are filled with silent and spectacular red sandstone rock formations, including Gateway Rocks, Cathedral Spires, and the Balanced Rock. Grasslands meet mountain forests to provide contrasts of scenic beauty. A common resident of the park is the great horned owl, whose keen, light-gathering eyes and superior hearing make it an effective nighttime hunter. Hike, picnic, and horseback ride to fully appreciate the park's natural beauty. But most of all, bring your camera and photograph these wonders (especially at sunset or sunrise when the low sun accents the naturally colorful red stone).

trivia

The Air Force Academy's Cadet Chapel received a 1996 American Institute of Architects' award. The chapel conducts services for Protestant, Catholic, Buddhist, Muslim, and Jewish worshippers.

The park itself is open daily from November 1 through April 30 from 5 a.m. to 9 p.m. and May 1 through October 31 from 5 a.m. to 11 p.m. The Garden of the Gods Visitor and Nature Center is open from 9 a.m. to 5 p.m. in the winter months and 8 a.m. to 8 p.m. Memorial Day weekend through Labor Day weekend. The center offers free color maps of the park and free entrance to the *Museum of Natural and Cultural History.* Arrive via exit 146 off I–25. Go west on Garden of the Gods Road, and then south on North Thirtieth Street. The visitor center will be on your left at Gateway Road. For more information: Garden of the Gods Visitor and Nature Center, 1805 North Thirtieth St., Colorado Springs 80904; (719) 634-6666; www.gardenofgods.com.

If you want to vacation in the lap of luxury, consider the five-star *Broadmoor,* which has 14,110-foot Pikes Peak for a backdrop. The Broadmoor actually began in the 1850s with a Silesian count. He hoped to create another Monte Carlo against the backdrop of Colorado's mountainscape. Eventually, two Philadelphians, Charles Tutt and Spencer Penrose, took over. They'd gotten rich in Cripple Creek mining and real estate, and as world travelers, they knew what they wanted—a regal, Renaissance-style hotel.

trivia

The Garden of the Gods was once sacred ground to Native Americans.

The Broadmoor's doors opened on June 29, 1918; among several notables, the first to register was John D. Rockefeller Jr. Since that day, there has been a stream of industrialists, diplomats, movie moguls, film stars, and titled ladies and gentlemen. They mingle nicely nowadays with anyone who can afford this pricey, year-round retreat. It is the largest, plushest, and most elegant in Colorado, offering every conceivable amenity. For more information call (866) 837-9520 or (719) 634-7711; www.broadmoor.com.

Seven Falls is ten driving minutes west of the Broadmoor resort. "The Grandest Mile of Scenery in Colorado" lives up to its slogan: A 1,000-foot-high granite canyon leads to seven waterfalls flanked by healthy forests of juniper, blue spruce, Douglas fir, and ponderosa pine. Not far from the dramatic, perpendicular "pillars of Hercules," you can climb several hundred steep steps to platforms from which you view these scenic wonders.

You get to Seven Falls via Cheyenne Boulevard and Mesa (exit 140B off I–25). Hours vary from 8:30 a.m. to 10:30 p.m. in midsummer to 9 a.m. to 4:15 p.m. in winter; call for details. Daytime admission ranges from $5.50 to $10.50, with a slightly higher nighttime admission with special lighting. Seniors and military receive a $1 discount. For more information write to Seven Falls Company, P.O. Box 118, Colorado Springs 80901 or call (719) 632-0765; www.sevenfalls.com.

The year was 1806; the discoverer of Colorado Springs's "Great Mountain" was Lieutenant Zebulon Montgomery Pike. Neither he nor any of his party got even close to the summit, due to bad weather and perhaps a lack of planning. At that time, it certainly wasn't conceivable that one of America's most unusual railroads ever constructed would carry thousands of persons to its summit.

Located on Cheyenne Mountain just above the Broadmoor resort is the *Cheyenne Mountain Zoo.* With 146 acres and 172 species, the zoo mirrors the natural habitats of animals from Africa, Australia, Asia, and North America. A petting zoo and oversized garden are a delight for kids. To reach the zoo, from I–25 go south on Nevada Avenue. Turn right on Lake Avenue. Turn onto Mirada Road and follow signs. Admission is $14.25 for adults, $12.25 for seniors sixty-five and older and $7.25 for children three to eleven; children two and younger free. For more information call (719) 633-9925 or visit www .cmzoo.org. Today you can journey on the country's highest railroad to the summit of famous Pikes Peak. The *Manitou and Pikes Peak Cog Railway,* which is 46,158 feet long, climbs from an elevation of 6,571 feet at the Manitou Springs station to one of 14,110 feet at the summit. This is a vertical gain of 7,539 feet, or an average of 846 feet per mile. Actually, the distance is longer than any covered by the famous cogwheel rails in Switzerland.

Along the entire route you'll be treated to a continuous panorama. At the 11,578-foot level, the train emerges from a sea of quaking aspen into the windswept stretches of timberline and climbs into the Saddle, where you get an unparalleled view of Manitou Springs and of the Garden of the Gods in the valley below. You also see the vast expanses of the Great Plains stretch toward the horizon.

On clear days, you can spot Denver 75 miles to the north of Colorado Springs and the dramatic Sangre de Cristo Mountains in southern Colorado. The view of the west is astounding; mile upon mile of snowcapped giants rise into the blue Colorado sky.

The Steamer Stop Shop (clothing and curios) is a good place to pick up gifts at the Manitou Springs Station. You can purchase a box lunch at the cafe to eat on the patio or take on the train ($9 per lunch). The Cog Railway runs from April through December. Depending on the season, tickets run about $30 to $34 for adults and $17 to $19 for children three to eleven, and children younger than two ride free if held on a lap throughout the ride. Reservations are highly recommended. The round-trip takes three hours and ten minutes; call for departure times. Take exit 141 (U.S. Highway 24) off I–25. Head west on US 24 for 4 miles to the Manitou Springs exit. Go west on Manitou Avenue for 1½ miles. Turn left on Ruxton Avenue. The station is ¾ mile up the road. For more information call (719) 685-5401, or visit www.cograilway.com.

Florissant Fossil Beds

One of the richest and most diverse fossil deposits in the world lies in this grassy mountain valley. Once a primeval rain forest, the area was covered by volcanic ash 30–40 million years ago, perfectly preserving insects, plants, and redwood stumps up to 14 feet wide. The visitor center with exhibits and a brief film is a good first stop before exploring the monument. There are 14 miles of trail, and hourly ranger talks at the amphitheater during the summer. The monument is two miles south of the town of Florissant. For directions and more information, (719) 748-3164; www.nps.gov/flfo.

trivia

Some of the bristlecone pine trees along the Manitou and Pikes Peak Cog Railway are estimated to be almost 2,000 years old, making them among the oldest living things on earth.

Back in 1891, the ***Cripple Creek*** gold strike proved to be the last major gold rush in North America. Within a few years, those mines in the mountains west of Colorado Springs yielded almost a billion dollars' worth of the valuable mineral. By 1900 Cripple Creek grew to some 50,000 inhabitants. The miners could patronize seventy-five saloons, forty grocery stores, seventeen churches, and eight newspapers. Every day a dozen passenger trains steamed into the depot. Eventually, 500 gold mines operated in the area. Some 8,000 men brought on a gambling, carousing, and whoring boom.

Ironically, the man who discovered the first gold vein sold his claim for $500 and proceeded to drink it all away. Colorado Springs owes part of its existence to the prospectors. In time, celebrities came and went. Adventurer Lowell Thomas was born in nearby Victor, now nearly a ghost town. Groucho Marx once drove a grocery wagon in Cripple Creek. Jack Dempsey, for a brief bout a miner, trained and boxed in the region. Financier Bernard Baruch worked as a telegrapher here. Teddy Roosevelt, after a Cripple Creek visit, told the world that "the scenery bankrupts the English language." The politicians arrived in droves to see for themselves.

Over the years, gold prices dropped. Production began to slip and the miners scattered. By 1920 fewer than 5,000 people lived here.

And today? Cripple Creek attracts hordes of summer tourists. They come for the narrow-gauge train rides. They pan for gold on Main Street. They play at the slot machines. They attend one of the summer theater performances put on at the renovated ***Historic Butte Opera House.*** This building, originally constructed in 1896, has had many uses throughout its history. Before its

Some Little-Known Facts about Manitou Springs

It was actually from Manitou Springs's mineral springs that Colorado Springs got its name.

"Manitou" is a Native American word for "Great Spirit."

Native Americans attributed supernatural powers to Manitou Springs's waters and temporarily reserved the surrounding area as a sanctuary.

Some Little-Known Facts about Cripple Creek

In its heyday, the Cripple Creek area produced $25 million in gold in one year.

Famous Cripple Creek workers included Jack Johnson and Jack Dempsey. Dempsey once fought a bloody, drawn-out battle here in Cripple Creek . . . for fifty dollars.

Speakeasy hostess "Texas" Guinan started in Cripple Creek. Perhaps this is one of the reasons why the city is now best known for its Las Vegas–style gambling.

renovation in the late 1990s, the building served as home to the Cripple Creek Fire Department.

Extensive renovations by the city of Cripple Creek restored the theater's splendor. The Historic Butte Opera House now seats 174 people and has a 1,350-square-foot stage, state-of-the-art sound equipment and movie projectors, and snack bar. For more information and performance dates, contact the Opera House at (719) 689-6402; www.butteoperahouse.com.

The old railroad depot has become the ***Cripple Creek District Museum,*** along with an old assay office and the Colorado Trading and Transfer Company building, constructed in 1893. These three buildings are crammed with mementos of the mining age. Superbly kept up, the museum is well worth a visit. Hours are 10 a.m. to 5 p.m. daily Memorial Day through September; Friday through Sunday 10 a.m. to 4 p.m. for the rest of the year. Call (719) 689-2634 or (719) 689-9540; www.cripple-creek.org. The museum is on Bennett Avenue in Cripple Creek.

Cripple Creek is a popular destination, especially in summer. Visitors come to browse the antique and souvenir shops housed in historic buildings. They play blackjack, poker, and the slots in more than a dozen casinos. The Cripple Creek District Museum, Jail Museum, and Old Homestead (former bordello) Museum offer a glimpse back in time to life during an untamed era. Small cafes serve home-cooked food.

trivia

Mining experts considered Cripple Creek worthless despite frequent reports of gold; still, novice prospectors, mining with pitchforks, eventually developed the "300-million-dollar cow pasture."

Not many visitors venture beyond the town and into the surrounding hills. This leaves plenty of room on the miles of hiking and biking trails leading through stunning scenery in Pikes National Forest. Several local outfitters offer horseback riding trips ranging from one hour to all day. The mountains are studded with old abandoned mines that can be reached by hiking up old mining roads past rusting machinery and old wooden trestles. View the mines from outside only; they are dangerous and unstable inside, and should not be entered.

trivia

The Cripple Creek Mining District, made up of roughly 25 towns in the Cripple Creek area, was once known as "The World's Greatest Gold Camp."

The story of the *Mollie Kathleen Gold Mine* is a Cripple Creek legend. Back in 1891, Mollie Kathleen Gortner moved to the area with her family, including her attorney husband, Henry. On an excursion by herself to see a herd of elk (she'd never seen them before), Mollie Kathleen came upon an outcropping of quartz that was veined with gold. Upon attempting to file her claim in town, she was informed that as a woman, she had no right to do so. Not to be deterred, Mollie Kathleen seized the papers and signed them anyway, declaring that the issue could be taken up with her husband if there was a problem. Thus Mollie Kathleen Gortner became the first woman in the area to stake a gold claim. Her mine continued to produce gold uninterrupted for the next seventy years, with the exception of a period of time during World War II when all gold production ceased due to a nationwide ban. Today the gold that came out of the mine would be worth more than $100 million.

The Mollie Kathleen Gold Mine stopped producing long ago, but now visitors can descend 1,000 feet below ground on the country's only historic gold mine tour. Learn about the life and working conditions of the hard rock gold miner. The tour begins with a ride on a skip (elevator) down to the lower levels of the mine. There you can see equipment used to mine at these

Take a Ride on the Railroad

For an unusual perspective, explore the area from a car on the *Cripple Creek and Victor Narrow-Gauge Railroad.* It takes about forty-five minutes to complete the winding 4-mile ride behind a coal-burning steam locomotive. The train travels through the historic gold mining district, passing abandoned mines, and stopping at several points of interest and photo opportunities. The railroad is open daily from mid-May through the second week of October. Call (719) 689-2640 for departure times. The fare is $12.25 for adults and teenagers thirteen and older, $11.25 for senior citizens sixty-five and older, and $7.75 for children three to twelve; children two and younger ride free; www.cripplecreekrailroad.com.

depths and ride on the last air-powered Tram-Air Locomotive Appropriate for all ages (there are no steps or ladders to climb), the forty-minute tours of the Mollie Kathleen Gold Mine depart at frequent intervals during the peak season. The mine is open for tours daily from early April through October. During the off-season, tours take place, weather permitting, Friday, Saturday, and Sunday. Call ahead. Rates are $15 for adults and $10 for children three to twelve; children under three tour free. For more information call (719) 689-2466 or (888) 291-5689-9101. When using the toll-free phone number, you must enter a PIN number (9101); www .goldminetours.com.

trivia

Cripple Creek's Mollie Kathleen Gold Mine, the longest continually operating gold mine tour in the world, boasts the only vertical-shaft gold mine tour in the United States.

Many people come to Cripple Creek just for gaming at the dozen or more casinos. But regardless of whether you enjoy gambling, the wealth of historical sites and the plentiful outdoor activities are well worth a visit. Cripple Creek is 45 miles west of Colorado Springs. From there it can be reached via US 24 west, then Highway 67. For more information write the Cripple Creek Welcome Center, P.O. Box 430, Cripple Creek 80813; call (877) 858-4653; or visit www.cripple-creek.co.us.

Pueblo, located some 40 miles south of Colorado Springs, hosts the yearly ***Colorado State Fair & Exposition,*** the largest single event in the state. Every summer, the fair delivers an action-packed seventeen-day experience for all who visit.

The Colorado State Fair is unique. Come to see the PRCA Championship Rodeo, and stroll the largest carnival and midway in the state. In the agricultural section, view prize lambs, hogs, steers, horses, and other animals. Young animals are available to pet in the children's barnyard. Competition for the best baked goods, jams and preserves, quilting, and scores of exhibits and creative arts displays give visitors literally hundreds of things to see. At night there are performances by some of the nation's top entertainers.

General admission to the state fair is $8 Friday through Sunday and $5 Monday through Thursday; children six and younger get in free. Hours run 10 a.m. to midnight throughout the course of the fair. From I–25, take exit 97A west (Central Avenue). This will take you to Northern Avenue. Follow Northern west; the state fairgrounds will be on your right. Call (719) 561-8484 or (800) 876-4567 for details, or visit www.coloradostatefair.com.

In a nearby residential district, there awaits one of Colorado's most stately bed-and-breakfasts, the ***Abriendo Inn.*** This distinguished hostelry, not far

Pueblo's El Pueblo History Museum

Designed to be the gateway to *Historic Arkansas Riverwalk of Pueblo (HARP)*, the new *El Pueblo History Museum* includes a permanent gallery covering the history of Pueblo along with an atrium gallery and a children's gallery. The museum also serves as a central location for tourist information. Contact the museum at (719) 583-0453 for details or visit www.coloradohistory.org/hist_sites/pueblo/pueblo.htm. The museum is located at 301 North Union St. in Pueblo. Hours are Tuesday through Saturday 10 a.m. to 4 p.m.

from the community college and the historic Union Avenue, couldn't have a better location. The inn has only ten rooms, each unique, but all with period furniture, old-fashioned lace curtains, canopied or brass beds, fresh flowers, oak antiques, and original art. The staff serves free evening snacks and gourmet breakfast creations. Some rooms have a whirlpool tub for two; all rooms have free Wi-Fi. All this cozy comfort comes at a very reasonable price. For more information call (719) 544-2703, or visit www.abriendoinn.com.

trivia

Pueblo is known to many as the home of the Federal Citizen Information Center, where Americans can write to "Pueblo, Colorado 81009" for information on hundreds of subjects.

For more information on visiting the Pueblo area, contact the Greater Pueblo Chamber of Commerce, 302 N. Santa Fe Ave., Pueblo 81003; (800) 233-3446 or (719) 542-1704; www.pueblo chamber.org.

From Pueblo, head west on U.S. Highway 50 to Cañon City, known as Colorado's Prison Capitol for the abundance of prisons in the area. One of the nearby attractions is *Shelf Road.* Shelf Road makes up part of the *Gold Belt Tour.* a designated Colorado Scenic Byway. From stunning limestone cliffs that attract rock climbers from all over the world to the sheer drop-offs on the side of the road (hence the name) into lush green valleys, the views and the isolation encountered along Shelf Road are idyllic. Abundant wildlife viewing potential rounds out the area's special charm—past sightings include mule deer, foxes, hawks, American black bears, and owls.

Some of the driving is on rough roads (it's not for the faint of heart) and should be avoided in wet or icy weather; furthermore, four-wheel-drive is recommended for portions of Upper Shelf Road. However, any two-wheel-drive vehicle can navigate the scenic portion of Shelf Road that leads out of

Cañon City. The road becomes narrow once it turns to dirt, so drive carefully and slowly, watching for oncoming traffic. Plan ahead where you are going to turn around; a good place is at mile marker 14. The entire Gold Belt Tour encompasses 131 miles of driving and takes roughly five hours.

To get there from Cañon City, drive north on Raynolds, and then head north again on Fields after Raynolds swings west. Nine miles along Fields takes you directly to Shelf Road. For more information call (719) 269-8500; www.co.blm .gov/ccdo/canon.htm.

trivia

Originally, Pueblo was a crossroads for travelers, including Spaniards, fur traders, and Native Americans.

After a jaunt along Shelf Road, another scenic wonder awaits you at the **Royal Gorge Bridge and Park.** The gorge, at 1,200 feet deep, has been compared to the Grand Canyon. With its striking reds, mauves, browns, and yellows, the deep and narrow gauge stopped Lieutenant Zebulon Pike (of Pikes Peak fame) in his tracks back in 1806. He couldn't forge the gorge (and he didn't climb Pikes Peak, either).

In 1929 the Royal Gorge Bridge opened up to traffic after seven months of construction. The bridge is able to support more than two million pounds, so don't worry about your car's weight! Today people flock from all over to drive across this mighty suspension bridge, allegedly the highest of its kind in the world.

The 2,200-foot-long **Aerial Tram** offers another viewing option as it takes visitors for a ride across the fabulous canyon. Painted a fiery red, the thirty-five-passenger tram cabin comes with a guide-conductor who assures timid passengers that the tram will not plunge into the Arkansas River, which rages and roars below. Three braking systems and an extra motor guarantee your safety. In the terminals, a total of about one hundred tons of concrete and steel anchor the conveyance's enormous cables, providing reassurance with their heftiness. In fact, a helicopter had to string the tram's pilot cable, and more than $350,000 was needed to rig up this tourist attraction.

After looking at it from above, hop aboard for a five-and-a-half-minute ride on the **Incline Railway** to the bottom

trivia

In December 1999, the city of Pueblo was astonished to find seventeen trees on its *Historic Arkansas Riverwalk of Pueblo (HARP)* destroyed within a matter of days. The culprit? A Colorado beaver whom officials affectionately deemed "Bandit" before they relocated the creature to a place a little farther out of town.

Bureau of Land Management and U.S. Forest Service

The Bureau of Land Management (BLM) administers millions of acres of public lands around the country, including 8.4 million acres in Colorado, while the U.S. Forest Service (USFS) manages 14.3 million acres in the state. State offices for both organizations can direct you to specific regional and local offices, many of which are listed throughout this book as well. For more information, look on the USFS Web site—www.fs.fed.us/r2—or contact the USFS Rocky Mountain Regional Office at (303) 275-5350. For information about BLM lands in Colorado, visit www.co.blm.gov/index.htm or contact the BLM Colorado state office at (303) 239-3600.

of the gorge. The world's steepest conveyance of its kind, the Incline Railway gives you a view from below as you look back up at the gorge and bridge above you. Built by the same crew who built the bridge, the railway opened in 1931 and has been operating ever since.

These days there is much more to the gorge than the aerial tram and the railway. Horse and donkey rides, a rollercoaster, carousel, petting zoo, wildlife pavilion, cliff walk, scale-model railway, and mule team wagon rides are just a few of the many activities that keep families busy. Park admission is $24 for adults and teenagers and $19 for children four to eleven; children three and younger are admitted free. Park hours vary throughout the year. Admission offers unlimited access to all park attractions, although some attractions are seasonal. Call for details. The Royal Gorge Bridge and Park is 12 miles west of Cañon City on US 50. Call (719) 275-7507 or (888) 333-5597; www.royalgorgebridge.com. The Cañon City Chamber of Commerce is located at 403 Royal Gorge Blvd.; (719) 275-2331 or (800) 876-7922; www.canoncitychamber.com.

trivia

The Royal Gorge Bridge cost more than $10 million to construct.

US 50 west from Cañon City takes you to **Salida.** There are few more outdoorsy places in Colorado. With the Arkansas River running along the edge of town, and an excellent whitewater course created by the city, Salida is famous for white-water rafting, kayaking, and fishing. Locals bring their kids to the river to laze on the warm boulders and splash in the shallows. Mountain bikes and road bikes are popular modes of transportation. And the historic district, several blocks of century-old red-brick buildings, is filled with casual cafes and coffeehouses, fine dining, art galleries, a bookstore, and unique boutiques.

Stop by Bongo Billy's just a block from downtown, grab a coffee or a bite to eat, and sit out on the deck overlooking the Arkansas River. The town often shows up on those "Best Places to Live in America" lists. Spend a few hours walking the streets and strolling along the river, and you'll see why.

At the relaxed, western-style *Tudor Rose Bed & Breakfast,* located 1.5 miles from downtown, you're welcome to bring your own horse (stables available; humans can stay in one of the six guest rooms, most of which have spectacular views). The innkeeper will point out the Sangre de Cristos and the

trivia

The Royal Gorge Bridge and Park averages about 500,000 visitors annually.

Sawach Range. As you wake up and prepare for your day, the Tudor Rose gets ready to serve a hearty western breakfast. For more information on Salida contact the Heart of the Rockies Chamber of Commerce, 406 West Highway 50, Salida 81201; (719) 539-2068 or (877) 772-5432; www.salidachamber.org.

The *Tenth Mountain Division Hut Association* manages a system of twenty-nine backcountry huts connecting 350 miles of suggested routes. Named in memory of the U.S. Army men who trained during World War II at Camp Hale in central Colorado, each far-flung Colorado cabin can accommodate from six to twenty hikers, mountain bikers, or cross-country skiers.

The shelters are rugged; bring your own food, water, and sleeping bag. The huts are reachable from such major highways as Interstate 70 or from Tennessee Pass and Highway 24, among others. Distances vary. Some are short, such as the three-mile hike from Vail Pass to Shrine Mountain hut. All the same, you need to be fit and adequately equipped. One option is to hire and pay a guide. Weekends are busiest, but to ensure a space, make reservations beforehand. Rates are about half of what you'd pay for a cheap ski area motel per night. This is a true Colorado backcountry experience. Contact the Tenth Mountain Division Hut Association, 1280 Ute Ave., Suite 21, Aspen 81611; (970) 925-5775; www.huts.org.

trivia

Cañon City is the county seat of Fremont County, which has nine state prison facilities and a federal prison complex with four facilities. The state and federal prisons are the largest employers in the area, together accounting for more than 3,000 workers.

Now for a story of love and power, of wealth and poverty, of joys and tragedy, of a Colorado mining town whose fortunes flourished and vanished. A story so extraordinary that it became the subject of an opera, a play, and many biographies, some of them bad ones.

The characters were bigger than life. Begin with Horace Austin Warner Tabor, a onetime Vermont stonecutter, and his straitlaced hardworking wife, Augusta. The couple gave up a Kansas homestead to try their luck first in Denver, then under Pikes Peak, then at Oro City. They arrived in **Leadville** with a rickety wagon and an old ox during the 1860s, some years after the first gold had been discovered in California Gulch.

The Tabors established themselves as best as they could—Augusta with a tiny rooming house and a small bakery, Horace with a store and later a part-time job as mayor. The Tabors' first break came on April 20, 1878. Two destitute miners, new in town, dropped into Horace's shop. Could he help out with some tools and a basket of groceries? The accommodating mayor agreed to help for a third of whatever minerals they might find. A few days later, some hard digging produced a rich silver vein.

The Tabors were launched. By summer that first mine—the Little Pittsburgh—lavished $8,000 a week on its owners. Before long there was $100,000 worth of silver per month; this was followed by other Tabor ventures, all successful. In time, Tabor invested in many mines, controlled a good chunk of the local bank, built the Leadville Opera House, and erected mansions in the mining town and in Denver. He owned a lot of real estate and a hotel. By 1879 Leadville had seventeen independent smelters; it took 2,000 lumberjacks to provide enough wood to fire the machinery that processed the silver riches. Thanks to Tabor's new wealth and almost daily discoveries of more ore, the immigrants flooded to Leadville in droves. Celebrities like the "Unsinkable" Molly Brown showed up, as did various Dows, Guggenheims, and Boettchers.

Tabor soon bought an additional mine—the Matchless. He prospered while Leadville grew to a city of 30,000. Oscar Wilde appeared in the famous **Tabor Opera House.** The Chicago Symphony Orchestra and the Metropolitan Opera came there, to faraway Colorado. Well-known singers, ballet dancers, actresses, and entertainers arrived to perform.

trivia

Leadville, at 10,152 feet above sea level, is North America's highest incorporated city.

H. A. W. Tabor became a millionaire many times over. He was a tall man, mustached, kindly, and, as a local historian writes, "outgoing, gregarious, and honest as the falling rain." By contrast, Horace was married to a woman who, although she worked hard, brought Tabor no happiness. She allegedly nagged; she was described as prim and humorless. Colorado's richest man thought he deserved better.

Horace Tabor's luck changed one day in 1882. That evening the fifty-year old silver magnate saw Elisabeth Doe-McCourt in the restaurant of Leadville's Clarendon Hotel.

"Baby" Doe was twenty-two—a beauty with shining blue eyes and curly, dark blonde hair. Round-faced and charming, she'd been born into an Irish immigrant family of fourteen children. Baby Doe had just emerged from a brief, unhappy marriage with an unsupportive miner in Central City. Recently divorced, she had the good sense to look for a better partner in booming Leadville. She was a respectable young woman. And her search was crowned by success.

What began as a simple flirtation deepened into an abiding love that scandalized people in the Rockies and became the celebrated story of Colorado's opera *The Ballad of Baby Doe,* by Broadway veterans John Latouche and Douglas Moore.

Horace and Baby Doe were snubbed by Denver High Society when Tabor divorced his wife, Augusta, who allegedly received a $500,000 settlement. Tabor soon married his new love. The wedding took place in Washington, D.C., in the presence of President Chester Arthur and other dignitaries. Baby Doe received a $90,000 diamond necklace, and she wore a $7,500 gown.

Although young, she actually had greater substance than most of her biographers gave her credit for. She was honest and loyal, helpful to others, and interested in a variety of things. Best of all, she was in love with her much older Colorado husband. Her love was returned.

The Tabors lived the lavish life of luxury to the hilt. Most historians estimate that the Tabors spent some $100 million. Horace Tabor made few new worthwhile investments. For a brief time he was elected to the U.S. Senate.

Some Little-Known Facts about Leadville

As the highest incorporated city in the United States, Leadville is just below the timberline.

Legend says that in the old days, the worth of a barrel of Leadville whiskey was as high at $1,500.

Tents were once pitched on Main Street, and it was boasted that each was "the best hotel in town."

"Unsinkable" Molly Brown made her fortune here; also David May, Charles Boettcher, Charles Dow, and Meyer Guggenheim.

In 1893 disaster struck Leadville. Silver was replaced by paper money. The nation experienced a financial panic. The Tabors were ruined. The mines began to fail. Real estate was sold to satisfy creditors.

The couple moved to Denver, still in love. Thanks to some contacts, Horace got a postmaster's job for a short time. But the financial plunge must have been too much for him. Soon he was ailing. His final hours came on April 10, 1899, at Denver's Windsor Hotel. His wife, Baby Doe, was by his side, holding his hand.

Before Horace Tabor died, he once more spoke about his Matchless Mine in Leadville. It had long played out after yielding some $1 million during its fourteen years of operation. "Hold on to the Matchless," Tabor whispered. "It'll make millions again." His wife nodded.

Baby Doe kept her promise. She moved back to Leadville. Penniless, she lived in a shack beside the mine pit for thirty-six years. She remained faithful to Tabor.

During the winter of 1935, while in her seventies, she shopped at a local grocery for some food. The grocer gave her a ride home in his truck. Baby Doe was dressed in tatters. Her feet were sheathed in sackcloth instead of shoes. The cabin next to the Matchless Mine was squalid, but she kept a rifle in it, protecting her mine.

Leadville's altitude is more than 10,000 feet. It gets cold there on winter nights. Baby Doe Tabor was found in her shack on March 7, 1935. She had frozen to death. No one knows how long the body had been there. Ironically, there were some unopened boxes with new blankets sent by some Leadville sympathizers, which the dying woman had refused to use.

The Tabors are buried side by side in Denver. *The Ballad of Baby Doe* was added to the New York City Opera's repertoire shortly after its 1956 debut in Central City. The role of Baby Doe was among the first that Beverly Sills sang for a company she was to head many years later.

And how about the current Leadville? Thanks to the town's solid mining history, there is a 70,000-square-foot ***National Mining Hall of Fame & Museum.*** This museum should be essential for ore seekers, mining school students, and history buffs. Located in a restored Victorian schoolhouse, the facility retraces the entire Leadville history; you can also view old equipment, assorted rocks and crystals, various artifacts, and dioramas.

The Last Chance is a realistic replica of a hard-rock mine tunnel. Stretching more than 120 feet, the "rock" walls have exposed ore veins. Mine-gauge rail tracks are underfoot on the rock-strewn floor. Dripping water adds to the illusion of being underground in a real mine. Admission costs $7 for adults and teenagers twelve and older, $6 for seniors sixty-two and older, and $4

Leadville Visit

While in Leadville, well-conditioned adventurers won't want to miss a chance to hike Colorado's highest mountain, *Mt. Elbert* (14,433 feet).

Depending on time and ability, hikers can choose one of the Mountain's two main trails:

North Mt. Elbert Trail is a 5-mile hike to the summit. From Sixth Street in Leadville, head south on US 24 for about 4 miles. Go west on Highway 300 for ¾ mile, and then south (left) on Lake County Road 11 for 1¼ miles. Head west (right) on Forest Road 110 for 5 miles, which will take you to the parking area at Halfmoon Campground.

South Mt. Elbert Trail can be serene; it is seldom crowded. It is 5½ miles to the summit with a trailhead near Lakeview Campground. Go south on US 24, and then head west on Highway 82 for about 3½ miles. Go north on Lake County 24 for just over a mile to reach the parking area, just north of the campground.

With a 4,500-foot elevation gain, both trails should be attempted only by hikers who are in good shape and are knowledgeable about safety in hiking.

For more information contact the San Isabel National Forest, Leadville Ranger District, 810 Front St., Leadville 80461; (719) 486-0749; www.fs.fed.us/r2/psicc/leadville/.

---

for children six to eleven; children five and younger are admitted free. Hours are 11 a.m. to 4 p.m. daily. For more information call (719) 486-1229; www.leadville.com/miningmuseum.

More than 70 square blocks of Leadville have been designated as a National Historic Landmark District, making it one of the largest such districts in Colorado.

You can enjoy this town's history at any time of year by going on a short historic walking tour through this district. Start your free, self-guided tour at **Ice Palace Park** in the 100 block of West Tenth. Plenty of parking can be found here. The park commemorates the ill-fated Ice Palace, built nearby in 1896. The palace, constructed of 5,000 tons of ice and 307,000 board feet of lumber, lasted only a few months before going under. From the park, you walk southeast to Harrison Avenue, where most of the tour's attractions await your exploration, including the Heritage Museum, the Hyman Block (where the infamous Doc Holliday shot—but failed to kill—his last victim), and the Tabor Opera House.

For a map of the tour, visit the Web site www.leadville.com/walktour/ or call the Leadville/Lake County Chamber of Commerce at (800) 933-3901. To

St. Elmo

Far up a dirt road, deep in the mountains of Chaffee County, lies the ghost of St. Elmo. This weathered ghost town, where creaking wooden sidewalks meander past splintered wooden buildings with false fronts, is among Colorado's best-preserved.

Once a rollicking mining town, St. Elmo sits quietly in a wooded valley, home to hummingbirds and chipmunks. From Buena Vista take US 24 south for 8 miles to Nathrop, then County Road 162 west for 16 miles. For more information see www .coloradoghosttowns.com/st-elmo-area.htm.

reach Leadville from Denver, take I–70 west, turning off at Highway 91 (exit 195, Copper Mountain).

South and west of Leadville is *Crested Butte,* a laid-back mountain town with a scenic ski center. Thirty minutes up the road from Gunnison, Crested Butte is too far from Front Range cities to attract crowds. (Denver is 199 miles to the northeast.) The town is surrounded by almost two million acres of pristine wilderness, giving everyone plenty of elbow room to find his or her own private Eden. Crested Butte has become a major mountain-biking destination with hundreds of miles of trails outside of town. The sport is celebrated during Fat Tire Bike Week each June. An entire week is devoted to racing, guided tours, and fun competitions like the Chainless Race, where spectators have as much fun as riders. A beer garden and live music liven things up. For more information call the Chamber of Commerce at (800) 545-4505 or (970) 349-6438; www.ftbw.com.

In a state filled with beautiful mountains, the scenic peaks around Crested Butte rank among the best. The town sits at the end of a long valley, up the road from Gunnison. As the crow flies, it's not far from Aspen, just over the Elk Mountains. And like Aspen, the town retains some of its mining-town past with restored Victorian houses.

But the similarities end there. Crested Butte never became a playground for the wealthy and famous. The town is mountain-hip without being pretentious. There may be more bikes than cars here. And some of the locals would probably have fit in just fine back in the old mining days. A marketing campaign for the ski area some years back said it best: "Aspen like it used to be, and Vail like it never was."

The skiing here is as good as it gets in Colorado. But summer is a magical time in Crested Butte. One of the state's major festivals is the *Crested Butte Wildflower Festival.* The wildflower displays here are among the best in the state. In fact, Crested Butte is recognized by the Colorado Legislature as the Official Wildflower Capital of Colorado. All mountain towns have wildflowers, but the climate in this sheltered valley seems to produce more floral quantity and variety than other places around the state. And the festival is scheduled right around the peak wildflower season each summer.

Guided hikes and bike rides, 4x4 tours into the back country, photo and art classes, garden tours of historic homes, medicinal plant classes, wildflower gardening, and birds and butterflies are some of the ways to enjoy the festival. Call (970) 349-2571 for more information; www.crestedbuttewildflowerfestival.com.

Crested Butte was the site of the first mountain biking in Colorado. In the mid-1970s, after a motorcycle group rode their Harley Davidsons from Aspen over the rough Pearl Pass Jeep road, some "Butte" locals decided to one-up the bikers by doing the same route on bicycles. They hopped on their basic clunkers and rode the 40 miles back over the mountain. With that, a sport was born.

Since then these bikes have evolved from one-speed clunkers into sophisticated machines of lightweight carbon alloy with up to 27 gears. Crested Butte has a wealth of trails available to mountain bikers. Keep in mind that most of these trails are open for public use. Cyclists are required to yield to hikers and horses. If this means you have to get off your bike and move off the trail, then do it. Around the United States, failure of cyclists to yield has caused some popular trails to be closed to them.

Crested Butte celebrates the sport with the ***Mountain Bike Hall of Fame and Museum,*** which documents the people and events that helped shape the sport of mountain biking. You can see vintage bikes and components, classic photos, memorabilia, and press clippings and highlights from historic races and events. The hall of fame is at 331 Elk Ave., open daily 10 a.m. to 8 p.m. in summer, noon to 6 p.m. in winter; (970) 349-1880; www.mtnbikehalloffame.com.

Another museum well worth a visit is the ***Crested Butte Mountain Heritage Museum.*** Housed in an 1883 building formerly used as a gas station and hardware store, the collection and displays depict early mining, ranching, skiing, and settler life around Crested Butte. Open daily 12 p.m. to 7 p.m.; 331 Elk Ave.; (970) 349-1880.

Highway of the Fourteeners

From Buena Vista, this 19-mile stretch of US 24 along the Collegiate Peaks Scenic Byway offers dramatic, close-up views of ten of Colorado's 14,000-foot mountains. Nowhere else in the United States will you see so many high peaks in one place. Allow about thirty minutes for the drive, more if you stop for photos. In Buena Vista, drop by ***Bongo Billy's*** (713 US 24) for coffee, sandwiches, and pastries.

Artistic types have been drawn to the area for decades, and as a result, Crested Butte offers a diverse and rich calendar of cultural activities throughout the year. The *Crested Butte Center for the Arts* at 606 Sixth St. hosts concerts, art displays, classes, films, events and more. Call (970) 349-7487 or www.crestedbuttearts.org.

The *Crested Butte Mountain Theatre* is located at 403 Second St. in the 1880s-era Old Town Hall. Since 1972 this venue has entertained locals and visitors with live theatrical performances ranging from drama and musicals to comedy and beyond. It's a delightful way to spend an evening. For more information, (970) 349-0366; www.cbmountaintheatre.org.

Three miles up the road from town is *Crested Butte Mountain,* another of Colorado's premier ski destinations. The majority of the mountain (57 percent) is for the intermediate skier, with the remaining 43 percent almost equally divided between beginning and advanced runs. There are numerous long, intermediate runs, as well as gentle, rolling meadows with plenty of places to go at your own pace. The trail network is well-planned, and an excellent children's ski school and childcare facility make this an attractive family ski resort.

For many, though, the big draw at Crested Butte is extreme skiing and snowboarding. That can be found at the Extreme Limits, more than 580 acres of ungroomed, double-black diamond terrain. It's no coincidence that the U.S. Extreme Skiing Championships are held here. Steep bowls, narrow chutes, cliff drops, and through-the-trees skiing await adrenaline junkies who are ready for some of the steepest lift-served runs in North America. Tours are available for expert skiers who want a taste of the mountain's wild side.

Crested Butte's ski season runs from mid-December through mid-April. The ski slopes are open from 9 a.m. to 4 p.m. daily. Prices vary throughout the season. For more information call (800) 810-7669; www.skicb.com.

Located at the edge of town, the Crested Butte Nordic Center is unique. No other cross-country center in Colorado offers in-track skiing so close to a town. An extensive, 50-kilometer network of trails spreads out from three nearby trailheads, making it easy to ski a few morning hours, ski into town for lunch, then take off into the woods again in the afternoon. Choose trails ranging from novice to advanced. The Nordic Center offers lessons, rentals, backcountry tours, ice skating, sledding, and snowshoeing. For information contact (970) 349-1707; www.cbnordic.com.

Crested Butte is 28 miles north of Gunnison on Highway 135. Contact the Crested Butte–Mt. Crested Butte Chamber of Commerce at P.O. Box 1288, Crested Butte 81224; (970) 349-6438 or (800) 545-4505; www.cbchamber.com.

Between Crested Butte and Gunnison, where the East and Taylor Rivers meet to form the Gunnison River, lies the small community of *Almont.* Winter visitors on their way to the resort rarely stop here, but in warm-weather months the area is a good base for nearby camping, canoeing and kayaking, 4x4 driving, hiking, rock climbing, horseback riding, fishing, rafting, and exploring nearby Taylor Canyon. Ranch resorts and riverside cabins offer a quieter, simpler vacation where you can slow down and enjoy the western landscape. For information call (800) 814-7988; www.gunnisoncrestedbutte .com/area-tour/almont.

Don't overlook *Gunnison* on your way to Crested Butte. With its legacy of ranching and farming, the town and surrounding area are as authentically Western as it gets in Colorado. Cowboy boots and wide-brimmed hats are worn as work clothes. Western State College adds a subtle college-town feel to the community. And nature lovers use Gunnison as a base for excellent nearby fishing and hunting.

If you want to learn about early life in the area, visit the *Gunnison Pioneer Museum* at 803E. Tomichi Ave. These six acres contain an antique car collection, a narrow gauge train, two rural schoolhouses, a log cabin chapel, carpenter shop, blacksmith shop, print shop, and displays of pioneer life. Open Memorial Day weekend–mid-September 9 a.m.–5 p.m., Monday–Saturday, and 1–5 p.m., Sunday, (970) 641-4530.

The *Gunnison Valley Observatory* houses the largest public telescope in Colorado. Located off Gold Basin Road at the base of "W" Mountain, just southwest of town on U.S. Highway 50, the observatory houses a 30-inch reflector telescope, taking advantage of the unpolluted atmosphere here to scan the skies. The observatory is open to visitors every Friday evening at 7:30 from early April until late September. For more information call (970) 642-1111; www.gunnisonobservatory.org.

For those who enjoy whitewater sports and for those who enjoy watching them, *Gunnison Whitewater Park* is a pleasant place to spend a few hours. A series of rock structures along a several-hundred-foot section of the Gunnison River created a paddling playground for kayaking, canoeing, and rafting. A walking path and picnic area offer good vantage points to watch the action. For more information, call (800) 814-7988; www.gunnisoncrestedbutte .com/whitewater-park.

Hartman Rocks Recreational Area, located just five minutes from downtown Gunnison, has more than 20 trails on 8,000 acres of public land. This network of trails welcomes hiking, single track and double track mountain biking, rock climbing, and horseback riding. In winter the area is popular for cross country skiing and snowshoeing. The routes pass through rolling hills of sagebrush with granite rock outcrops and occasional cottonwood groves. To get there, drive west on Highway 50 from downtown, and turn left/south on Gold Basin Road (City Road 38 just before the twin bridges). Turn right and go for about 2.5 miles where you will find an entrance through a wooden fence into the parking area.

Nine miles west of Gunnison along Highway 50 is ***Curecanti National Recreation Area,*** a series of three reservoirs set in a starkly beautiful volcanic landscape. One of them, Blue Mesa Reservoir, is the largest body of water in the state, and from its depths have come several state record lake trout. Swimming, camping, boat rentals, sailboarding, and other activities are available.

Continuing along US 50, an hour out of Gunnison you will come to the dramatic ***Black Canyon of the Gunnison National Park,*** which became a national park in 1999. In the sunlight, the massive black granite towers, pillars, and stone blocks turns mauve. In all, the Black Canyon of the Gunnison National Park comprises some 30,385 acres. Carved by the river, the canyon measures 53 miles long and 2,722 feet from rim to bottom at its deepest point.

There are three roads in the park: East Portal, North Rim, and South Rim. Each offers spectacular views, but only East Portal allows access to the bottom by car. The South Rim Visitor Center offers exhibits detailing the geology and history of the canyon. This is a good place to learn about the scenic overlooks along each drive, and to find out about the hiking trails, from easy to moderate, leading to different vistas. The area can be hot in summer, so come prepared with water and a hat. Two campgrounds offer tent and RV camping, but vehicles more than 35 feet long are discouraged. The closest lodging outside the park is in Montose, 15 miles southwest.

Rock climbing in the canyon is considered one of Colorado's best bigwall destinations, and is only for experienced climbers. Some routes can take several days to complete, requiring climbers to overnight on narrow ledges or in hammocks slung from the rock wall.

The national park is open in winter and summer. The entrance fee is $15 per vehicle or $7 per pedestrian, bicyclist, and motorcyclist (no charge for visitors age sixteen or younger). The North and South Rim stations are open daily, but access is limited in winter. To get to the South Rim take US 50 from Montrose for 15 miles to Highway 347. The visitor center is at the South Rim. The North Rim is 11 miles south of Crawford via U.S. Highway 92 and North

Rim Road, which is closed during winter. Contact Park Headquarters, 102 Elk Creek, Gunnison 81230; (970) 641-2337; www.nps.gov/blca.

Accommodations are available nearby in Montrose at a variety of motels. Try the **Best Western Red Arrow,** 1702 East Main (US 50 East); (970) 249-9641 or (800) 468-9323; www.bestwesterncolorado.com/hotels/best-western-red-arrow.

Southwestern Colorado

As you approach the southwestern corner of Colorado from the northeast, you have the chance to visit one of the most geologically unique areas on the continent. **Great Sand Dunes National Park** is on the short list of "don't miss" places that both residents and visitors return to year after year, and for good reason. These dunes, the tallest in North American at 750 feet high, run eight miles in length at their longest point, covering 30 square miles in the main dune field.

The 150,000-acre park offers hiking, overnight camping, and bird watching here and in nearby wetlands such as in the San Luis State Wildlife Area. But most visitors come to climb the dunes. There are few experiences that can compare with being on them. Climb to the top of a ridge and take in the view of golden sandy waves stretching for miles to the distant Sangre de Cristo Mountains, then drop into a trough until you are in a valley surrounded by towering hills of sand. Stop and listen to the silence broken only by the wind as it pushes thousand of tiny grains of sand. Climb back several ridges into the dunes and you will be alone.

Most visitors come during the hot months of July and August. Make sure you wear shoes to climb the dunes during this season—the sand can reach temperatures of 140°F. Save the bare feet for wading across the soft, water-cooled sand of Medano Creek. Flowing at the base of the dunes during the spring snow melt, Medano Creek is one of the few places in the world to experience "surge flow" where creek water comes in rhythmic waves. The best times to experience surge flow depend on annual snow levels. The creek often begins flowing in March and may last until July or longer after a heavy snowfall winter. After dry winters the creek may not even reach the main parking area.

trivia

For amateur geologists, most sand at Colorado's Great Sand Dunes is between 0.2 and 0.3 mm in diameter, composed of 51.7 percent volcanic rock fragments, 29.1 percent quartz, 8.9 percent feldspar, 2.5 percent sandstone, 0.7 percent magnetite, 3.4 percent other minerals, and 3.7 percent other rocks.

Southwest Colorado Overview

In the San Juan Range of southwest Colorado, piñons and junipers yield to spruce and aspen as you go up in elevations. The weather in towns like Durango and Cortez is remarkably mild year-round, despite copious snowfall at high elevations. The mountains are always cooler than the lower, drier elevations, but usually comfortably so, especially in summer when days are short-sleeves warm, and a light blanket is de rigeur for sleeping at night.

As is common throughout Colorado, summer is the main tourist season in southwest Colorado, followed by the ski months of winter. Caution: Skiing through waist-deep, soft powder in the high, dry air on a typical sunny winter day may be addictive. The sun always comes out after a storm, so skiers sans jackets by noon are another common sight.

Colorado's legendary outdoor world has much to do with its geography. The state has 1,143 mountains rising to an altitude of at least 10,000 feet above sea level—and 1,000 are 2 miles high or more. Fifty-four often snow-crowned peaks towering above 14,000 feet give the state more than six times the mountain area of Switzerland. For more information on hiking and climbing the mountains, contact the Colorado Fourteeners Initiative at (303) 278-7650; www.coloradofourteeners.org.

Great Sand Dunes National Park is located on Highway 150 in the south-central part of the state, just 16 miles off US 160, the main cast-west highway through southern Colorado. Individuals age seventeen or older pay a $3 entry fee. The site is open daily. The visitor center also is open daily except for federal holidays. Visitor center hours are 9 a.m. to 6 p.m. in summer, and 9 a.m. to 4:30 p.m. or 5 p.m., as staffing permits, the rest of the year. The 88-site campground is available on a first-come, first-served basis, and fills up fast on summer weekends. Campers should come prepared to face gnats and hungry mosquitoes in late spring and early summer. For more information contact Great Sand Dunes National Park, 11500 Hwy. 150, Mosca 81146; (719) 378-6300; www.nps.gov/grsa.

Farther west, and just south of Wolf Creek Pass on US 160 is *Pagosa Springs.* Named for the Ute word Pahgosa, meaning "boiling water," Pagosa Springs has a ready supply of natural geothermal energy. Many a weary traveler has stopped for a day or more to soak in these healing waters, and to enjoy nearby San Juan National Forest and Weminuche Wilderness. Nearby stables rent horses and lead trips. Fishing, mountain biking, and hiking are all options.

Another water wonder near Pagosa is *Treasure Falls.* This is the longest waterfall in the entire San Juan National Forest. The short hike is a perfect place to break up a long drive and stretch the legs. To get there, follow US 160 east for 15 miles toward scenic Wolf Creek summit. The parking lot and trailhead are on the right (east) side of the road. A short ¼-mile well-worn trail climbs 300 feet up the canyon through dense pine and oak forest to Colorado's mini-version of Niagara. For more information write to Pagosa Ranger District, 180 Pagosa St., P.O. Box 310, Second Springs 81147; (970) 264-2268; www.fs .fed.us/r2/sanjuan.

trivia

Although Pagosa Springs water is used primarily for bathing, some of the hotter springs, at 153°F, are used for energy to heat houses and buildings.

To the west of Pagosa Springs stands a man-made wonder built a thousand years ago. The stone ruins of **Chimney Rock** were home to the ancestors of the modern Pueblo Indians and are of great spiritual significance to these tribes. More than 200 homes and ceremonial buildings were built around the area, and archeologists have found hundreds of individual sites. Named for the towering twin spires of natural stone that dominate the landscape, Chimney Rock provides expansive views to the far distance.

The Chimney Rock Interpretive Program leads tours four times daily and operates the visitor center during the open season (May 15 through September 30). Tour costs are $10 for adults and teenagers twelve and older and $5 for children five to eleven; children four and younger get in free. Fees are paid at the visitor center, which is open from 9 a.m. to 4:30 p.m. daily during the season. Chimney Rock is located 17 miles west of Pagosa Springs via US 160, and then southwest on Highway 151.

For more information write to Chimney Rock Interpretive Program, P.O. Box 1662, Pagosa Springs 81147; (970) 883-5359 (May 15 through September 30) or (970) 264-2287 (off-season, October 1 through May 14); www.chimney rockco.org. For more information about the Pagosa Springs area write to Pagosa Springs Area Chamber of Commerce, 402 San Juan St., Pagosa Springs 81147; (970) 264-2360 or (800) 252-2204; www.pagosa-springs.com.

Hot Springs

Set along the banks of the San Juan River, Pagosa Springs offers numerous therapeutic, mineral-rich pools for soaking weary muscles after a long day of skiing, backpacking, golfing, or driving. Two spas in the middle of town offer day rates and overnight accommodations. For more information, (970) 264-5236; www.pagosa .com; www.pagosahotsprings.com.

Another 17 miles south past Chimney Rock on Highway 151, **Navajo State Park** is Colorado's version of Lake Powell. Sprawling Navajo Reservoir is surrounded by piñon and juniper hillsides that look more like New Mexico than Colorado. That's no surprise, since the reservoir extends 35 miles across the state line. Boating, fishing, hiking, biking, and camping keep visitors busy during the day, while quiet nights under starry skies promise a good night's sleep. For more information call (970) 883-2208; www.parks.state.co.us/parks/navajo.

The chute opens and the cowboy holds on to the horse's riggings with one hand. The horse rears wildly, resenting the man on his back, hooves flailing in all directions, a bucking, pitching, twisting, snorting, wild-eyed animal. The cowboy's hat flies off and lands in the dust. He has been on the horse for five seconds now, and he still hangs on. Leaning back until his shoulder blades graze the animals back, the man's outstretched arm hits the horse's flank. Six seconds now. Seven. Eight.

The buzzer sounds and the cowboy jumps safely to the ground. Eight seconds of bareback riding can seem like eight hours. In the early days of rodeo, the rider stayed in the saddle "until the horse was rode or the cowboy throwed." Today, the saddle bronc rider must stay aboard eight seconds, while at the same time not disqualifying himself in any number of ways. It takes a tough person to ride at the rodeo.

These western riding competitions are an important income source for some Colorado cowboys. Rodeo began in the 1700s with the vaqueros, Spanish cattlemen in the American west. In the 1800s, American cowboys would hold informal riding, roping, and cattle driving competitions. The sport caught on and became commercialized with the early efforts of entrepreneurs such as Buffalo Bill Cody and Will Rogers. By the 1970s rodeo turned professional, and today it is a big business, earning the top performers a comfortable living.

Every summer Colorado towns such as Leadville, Brush, Walden, Steamboat Springs, La Junta, Las Animas, Kiowa, Kremmling, Salida, and others are part of the rodeo circuit for a few days. Each offers a standard mix of bull riding, steer wrestling, bareback, team roping, and other events that comprise this slice of true Americana. As you drive around the state, ask locally; there's bound to be a rodeo not too far away. For more information contact the Colorado Pro Rodeo Association at (719) 647-2828; www.coloradoprorodeo.com.

Durango lies in the Animas River Valley against a backdrop of the San Juan Mountains. It's the largest town in southern Colorado, but with only 15,000 you'll quickly fall under its small-town charm. The lovingly-preserved historic downtown area is filled with restaurants, art galleries, coffeehouses, and shops. Wander south from the intersection of Thirteenth Avenue and Main past elegant buildings from the 1800s, then head east to Third Avenue, where an eclectic mix of period homes and mansions line the street. With more restaurants per capita than San Francisco, the town takes pride in cuisines ranging from French and American Southwestern to sushi and Himalayan. Four brewpubs keep the town supplied with hand-crafted, award-winning beers. The Rocky Mountain Chocolate Factory is based here, sending premium chocolate candies across the United States and Canada.

But as inviting as the culinary scene may be, there's much more to do and see in the area. Start with a walk along the five-mile long Animas River Trail that goes through town and watch rafters, kayakers, and canoeists navigate the rapids. A two-mile stretch of the Animas south of down town is designated Gold-Medal water for fishing. Outside of town, more than 350 miles of trails await hikers, horseback riders, mountain bikers, wildflower enthusiasts, and anyone who enjoys stunning outdoor scenery.

Durango is the departure point for the ***Durango & Silverton Narrow Gauge Railroad,*** a heritage railway that takes passengers on a 45-mile, seven-hour round trip from Durango to the historic mining town of Silverton. These steam-powered trains date back to the 1920s and before, and the nicely-restored coaches and open air cars allow you to enjoy the changing scenery. It's easily one of the classic Colorado sightseeing journeys. The train has both a summer and winter schedule with a range of prices depending on the class,

Colorful Locals

In the early days in Durango, there was a rowdy local gang that went by the name of the Stockton–Eskridge gang. These boys and a group of local vigilantes once fought an hourlong gun battle on the main street through town.

In 1885, locals set out on an expedition to New Mexico. Their goal? To "dig up Aztecs." Included in the supplies for the expeditions were five cases of tobacco, three cases of beer, ten gallons of "heavy liquids," four burro-loads of "the stuff that busted Parliament," seven reels of fuse, soap, cigars, one fish line, rubber boots, bread, lard, and a pound of bacon.

Newspaperman "Dave" Day, the witty, often profane editor of the *Durango Herald-Democrat* in the 1890s, once had forty-two pending libel suits against him.

In 1922, after the paper had split into two papers, William Wood, city editor for the *Durango Herald,* was shot dead in front of the barber shop by Rod Day (son of former editor "Dave" Day), editor of the *Durango Democrat,* after a long squabble that started over Prohibition and reached a peak over the printing of a scandal. Ah, the good old days.

and several departures a day in summer. For more information contact the railroad at 479 Main Ave., 81301; (970) 247-2733, (877) 872-4607; www.durangotrain.com.

Anyone interested in experiencing an authentic western rodeo should head to the La Plata County Fairgrounds in Durango. Each summer the fairgrounds hosts a series of rodeos where spectators enjoy a variety of events, including bare back riding, saddle bronc riding, barrel racing, and the most dangerous sport in the world, bull riding. For information on summertime rodeos, contact Durango Tourism at (800) 525-8855, www.durango.org.

Located 18 miles north of Durango on U.S. Highway 550, the year-round **Durango Mountain Resort** remains a secret to many Coloradans. This remote oasis has everything—nature, atmosphere, and amenities. Guided horseback expeditions depart each day from the stables, bringing you into the one-million-acre San Juan National Forest. Fishing, river rafting, jeep tours into the high country, mountain biking, golfing, an alpine slide, and a day camp for kids are just a few of the activities. In winter the resort is the lodging base for Purgatory, one of the state's classic ski mountains. For more information contact Durango Mountain Resort, 1 Skier Place, Durango 81301; (970) 247-9000 or (800) 982-6103; www.durangomountainresort.com.

For more information about Durango and surrounding areas contact the Durango Area Tourism Office, 111 South Camino del Rio, P.O. Box 2587, Durango 81302; (888) 414-0835 or (970) 247-3500; www.durango.org.

Just 35 miles west of Durango is **Mesa Verde National Park.** With more than 4,700 archeological sites in the park, this is an extraordinary place, made even better by the restraint with which the national park service has limited development. Aside from the narrow road, the museum and visitor center, a small restaurant and shop, and trails leading to the cliff dwellings, almost nothing here hints at the twenty-first century. Ravens and vultures drift across the ridges. Coyotes yip and howl on moonless nights. The fragrance of pinon and juniper sweetens the dry mesa air after a summer squall. The only thing missing are the hundreds of people who called this place home some 800 years ago.

Mesa Verde is best known for its Ancestral Puebloan Cliff Dwellings. A UNESCO World Heritage Site, these structures represent an astonishing culture that thrived for 700 years in this harsh land. A good place to begin your visit is at the **Chapin Mesa Archeological Museum,** where you can see baskets, pottery, agricultural tools, and exhibits describing these first residents. At Far View Visitor Center you can purchase tickets for ranger-guided tours of the three main cliff dwelling areas. Self-guided tours to two of the cliff dwellings as well as several hiking trails are available for further exploration. Drive across

Wetherill Mesa through the ponderosa, spruce, and juniper, stopping to explore the mesa top sites and admire the views from various overlooks. Dawn and dusk offer quiet moments when the cliffs are bathed in warm, golden light.

Devote at least a full day to the park, two if possible. It is an eight-hour drive southwest of Denver and is about an hour and a half west of Durango on US 160, midway between Mancos and Cortez. About 500,000 visitors come here each year, with most of them visiting during the summer months. The park is open all year, with some activities closed during winter.

Mesa Verde National Park is open daily year-round. Park entry fee is $10 per vehicle. The Chapin Mesa Archeological Museum is open daily at 8 a.m., closing at 6:30 p.m. in summer and fall and at 5 p.m. in winter and spring. The Far View Visitor Center is open from mid-April through mid-October from 8 a.m. to 5 p.m. For park information call (970) 529-4465; www.nps.gov/meve. Camping is available at Morefield Campground, four miles inside the park, on a first-come, first-served basis. The campground is never full. Lodging is available at Far View Lodge. For more information on both options call (888) 896-3831; www.visitmesaverde.com.

When visiting Mesa Verde you're not too far from the Four Corners area of Colorado, Utah, New Mexico, and Arizona. The sky seems even bluer here against the red rock buttes, mesas, and canyons. Mesa Verde was the major population center for the Ancestral Pueblo people, but there were many communities scattered for hundreds of miles across the four-state area of Colorado, Utah, New Mexico, and Arizona. The remains of many are hidden in remote areas and can only be reached on foot. But others are vehicle accessible, and exploring them will increase your fascination for the culture that flourished here long ago.

A quieter, less known site west of Cortez is ***Hovenweep National Monument.*** Six Puebloan-era villages lie in a landscape of arroyos, mesas, and sage, straddling the Colorado-Utah border. With artistic skill that would rival a stonemason's today, ancient Pueblo Indians built these towers in several configurations. Round, square, and oval structures dot the canyon edge. Each rock was trimmed to fit exactly with its neighbor, and the lines of the buildings are straight and almost smooth. Small peepholes and keyhole entrances could have provided views of a possible enemy approaching or just been a way to keep an eye on the rest of the community. Hiking and interpretive trails link most structures. These towers and buildings were constructed around the same time as Mesa Verde, but the monument's solitude and fewer visitors make for a very different experience from the better-known park to the east. Allow at least a half-day to explore the monument.

The ranger station is open year-round and operates a bookstore and a small museum. Bring your own food; there is none available. A small campground with picnic tables and water offers overnight stays. A $3 entry fee per person or $6 per vehicle is charged. Call for directions; the only paved entrance is from Utah. Hovenweep is open year-round. The visitor center is open from 8 a.m. to 6 p.m. daily April through September, and 8 a.m. to 5 p.m. the rest of the year (closed Thanksgiving, Christmas, and New Year's Day). For more information call (970) 562-4282; www.nps.gov/hove.

For those with an interest in Native American culture, the city of Cortez is the gateway to both the **Southern Ute** and **Ute Mountain Ute Indian Reservations.** The **Ute Mountain Utes** are one of seven original Ute bands that once inhabited the entire state of Colorado. The Ute Mountain Tribal Park, set in a classic southwestern landscape of mesas and canyons, contains an impressive collection of Ancestral Puebloan cliff dwellings, ruins, petroglyphs, and pictographs. Access is restricted to tours with Ute guides, who provide interpretation of the culture and history of these homelands.

The half-day tour visits petroglyphs, pictographs, scenic landmarks, and some surface archeological sites. All sites on this tour are within easy walking distance of the gravel road. The full-day tour is more strenuous, including climbs up rock faces via a series of ladders and a three mile walk on unpaved trails. The reward is a visit to four well-preserved cliff dwellings.

Tours begin at the Visitor Center/Museum, 20 miles south of Cortez at Highway Junction 160/491. For more information contact the Ute Mountain Tribal Park, P.O. Box 109, Towaoc, 81334; (970) 565-3751 ext. 330 or (800) 847-5485, or the Visitor Center at (970) 749-1452; www.utemountainute.com/tribalpark.htm.

Whenever the Rio Grande Southern rolled into the **Telluride** station back in the boomtown days of the early 1900s, legend has it the conductor would yell, "To hell you ride!" reminding passengers of the jarring, dusty journey they'd just completed. These days most people arriving at this former gold-mining town think they've pulled into paradise. Nestled in a box canyon where waterfalls roar down from surrounding peaks, Telluride sparkles as one of Colorado's crown jewels.

The town has two personas. In winter, heavy snowfall makes it a deep-powder ski destination. But when the snows melt each spring, wildflowers bloom, hummingbirds return, and Telluride becomes a sun-drenched alpine village where festivals, fun, and a funky mountain atmosphere drive away winter's chill.

At less than a mile long, the place is made for walking. Victorian buildings line Main Street. While the brothels and gambling dens are gone and the saloons have lost their rough edges, the town offers delights and distractions those miners never imagined. Throughout the summer, festivals celebrate everything from jazz, blues, and bluegrass to wine, film, and mushrooms.

Colorful shops, cafe bakeries, galleries, and bookstores provide plenty of low-volume entertainment. But sometimes paradise means nothing more than a morning latte and a comfortable bench along Main Street to watch the local color and wonder whether it's true that there are more dogs than residents in Telluride.

With rugged mountains on all sides, there are plenty of reasons to leave the pavement. The San Miguel River Trail follows the river for 2⁷/₁₀ easy miles.

Bridal Veil Falls, the tallest free-falling waterfall in Colorado, can be reached via a steeper hike of 1⅕ miles. For an easier route and a panoramic view, ride the free, twelve-minute gondola from town up to Mountain Village, Telluride's upscale sister hamlet. Once there, ogle the sky-high real estate, or take off on one of many hiking and biking trails that start here.

Telluride's gold-rush era left numerous high country roads, and today those tracks lead to weathered mining ruins. Local companies offer jeep tours to Tomboy and Alta ghost towns, Imogene and Ophir Passes, and points beyond.

Experienced 4x4 enthusiasts can buy a detailed map and take off on their own past flower-filled meadows to panoramic vistas. For more information call (888) 605-2578; www.visittelluride.com.

The name says bluegrass, but don't let that fool you. The famous ***Telluride Bluegrass Festival*** may be one of the country's most progressive bluegrass gatherings, but expect to hear folk, rock, blues, country, pop, Celtic, world beat, and just about everything in between. Set in the box canyon amid soaring mountains, the four-day event takes place at one of the most spectacular locations in America. When it's time for a break from the music, Telluride is a short stroll away, where eclectic eateries, galleries, coffeehouses, quirky shops, and bars await in the Victorian-era historic district. As a true Colorado tradition with stunning scenery, superb music, and plenty of friendly folks, this festival is a national treasure. Call (303) 823-0848 or (800) 624-2422; www.bluegrass.com/telluride.

Telluride

Telluride is renowned for its breathtaking alpine beauty, but many people don't realize that Telluride lies in the center of the greatest diversity of geology and archaeology in the nation. This area, known as the Grand Circle, encompasses four states, numerous state and national parks, and a variety of topography from the Rocky Mountains to the Painted Desert.

Places to Stay in Southern Colorado

The rating scale for hotels is based on double occupancy and is as follows:
Inexpensive:
Less than $75 per night
Moderate:
$75 to $100 per night
Expensive:
$101 to $150 per night
Deluxe:
More than $150 per night

ALMONT

Almont Resort,
(lodge, cabins, fishing outfitter)
10209 Hwy. 135;
(970) 641-4009
www.almontresort.com
Moderate to Deluxe

Best Western Royal Gorge Inn,
1925 Fremont Dr.;
(719) 275-3377 or
(800) 231-7317
www.book.bestwestern
.com
Inexpensive to Moderate

Harmel's Ranch Resort,
County Road 742;
(970) 641-1740 or
(800) 235-3402
www.harmels.com
Moderate to Deluxe

Lost Canyon Resort
(cabins),
8264 Hwy. 135;
(970) 641-0181
Moderate to Expensive

Quality Inn and Suites,
3075 East US 50;
(719) 275-8676
www.qualityinn.com
Inexpensive to Moderate

Royal Gorge Inn,
217 North Reynolds Ave.;
(719) 269-1100 or
(866) 495-8403
www.royalgorgeinn.com
Inexpensive

Three Rivers Resort,
(cabins, fishing/rafting/
kayaking outfitter)
130 County Rd. 742;
(970) 641-1303 or
(888) 761-3473
www.3riversresort.com
Inexpensive to Deluxe

COLORADO SPRINGS

Antlers Hilton Colorado Springs,
4 South Cascade Ave. at
Pikes Peak Avenue and
Cascade Avenue;
(719) 955-5600
www.antlers.com
Expensive to Deluxe

The Broadmoor,
1 Lake Ave.;
(719) 577-5775 or
(866) 837-8520
www.broadmoor.com
Deluxe

Garden of the Gods Motel,
2922 West Colorado Ave.;
(719) 636-5271 or
(800) 637-0703
www
.gardenofthegodsmotel/
pikes-peak.com
Inexpensive to Moderate

Holden House,
1902 Bed & Breakfast Inn
1102 West Pikes Peak;
(719) 471-3980
www.holdenhouse.com
Expensive

Old Town Guesthouse Bed & Breakfast,
115 South Twenty-Sixth
St.;
(719) 632-9194 or
(888) 375-4210
www.bbonline.com/co/
oldtown
Moderate to Deluxe

Rodeway Inn & Suites Garden of the Gods,
1623 South Nevada Ave.;
(719) 623-2300 or
(877) 424-6423
www.rodewayinn.com
Inexpensive to Moderate

CORTEZ

Best Western Turquoise Inn and Suites,
535 E. Main St.;
(970) 565-3778 or
(800) 547-3376
www
.bestwesternmesaverde
.com
Moderate to Expensive

Lebanon School House B&B,
24925 Road T, Dolores;
www.lebanonschoolhouse
.com
(970) 882-4461

CRESTED BUTTE

Crested Butte International Lodge & Hostel,
615 Teocalli;
(970) 349-0588 or
(888) 389-0588
www.crestedbuttehostel
.com
Inexpensive to Deluxe

Cristiana Guesthaus,
621 Maroon Ave.;
(800) 824-7899
www.cristianaguesthaus
.com
Moderate to Expensive

Elizabeth Anne Bed & Breakfast,
703 Maroon Ave.;
(970) 349-0147 or
(888) 745-4620
www.crested-butte-inn
.com
Expensive to Deluxe

Elk Mountain Lodge,
129 Gothic Ave.;
(970) 349-7533 or
(800) 374-6521
www.elkmountainlodge
.com
Moderate to Deluxe

Inn at Crested Butte,
510 Whiterock Ave.;
(970) 349-2111 or
(877) 343-2111
www.innatcrestedbutte.net
Deluxe

Nordic Inn,
14 Treasury Rd.;
(970) 349-5542 or
(800) 542-7669
www.nordicinn.com
Moderate to Expensive

Old Town Inn,
210 North Sixth Ave.;
(970) 349-6184 or
(888) 349-6184
www.oldtowninn.net
Moderate to Expensive

The Ruby of Crested Butte,
624 Gothic Ave.;
(970) 349-1338 or
(800) 390-1338
www.therubyofcrestedbutte
.com
Deluxe

CRIPPLE CREEK

Carr Manor,
(luxury historic inn)
350 East Carr Ave.;
(719) 689-3709
www.carrmanor.com
Moderate to Expensive

Gold King Mountain Inn,
601 East Galena Ave.;
(719) 689-2600 or
(800) 445-3607
www.gkmi.com
Moderate to Expensive

Imperial Casino Hotel,
(historic Victorian inn; authentic Old West atmosphere)
123 North Third St.;
(719) 689-7777 or
(800) 235-2922
www.imperialscasinohotel
.com
Inexpensive to Moderate

J.P. McGill's Hotel and Casino,
232 Bennett Ave.;
(719) 689-2446 or
(888) 461-7529
www.triplecrowncasinos
.com
Inexpensive to Moderate

DELTA COUNTY

Best Western Sundance,
903 Main St., Delta;
(970) 874-9781
www.bestwesternsundance
.com
Moderate to Expensive

The Bross Hotel B&B,
312 Onarga Ave., Paonia;
(970) 527-6776
www.paonia-inn.com
Moderate to Expensive

Fresh and Wyld Farmhouse and Garden,
1978 Harding Rd, Paonia;
(970) 527-4374
www.freshandwyld.com
Moderate to Expensive

Leroux Creek Inn & Vineyard,
12388, 3100 Road, Hotchkiss;
(970) 872-4746
www.lerouxcreekinn.com
Deluxe

DURANGO

Bear Paw Lodge at Vallecito Lake,
18011County Rd. 501, Bayfield;
(970) 884-2508
www.bearpawlodge.com
Expensive

Durango Mountain Resort,
1 Skier Place;
(970) 247-9000 or
(800) 982-6103
www.durangomountain
resort.com
Deluxe

SELECTED SOUTHERN COLORADO GENERAL INFORMATION RESOURCES

CAÑON CITY

Cañon City Chamber of Commerce,
403 Royal Gorge Blvd., 81212;
(719) 275-2331 or (800) 876-7922
www.canoncitychamber.com

COLORADO SPRINGS

Colorado Springs Convention and
Visitors Bureau,
515 South Cascade Ave., 80903;
(719) 635-7506 or (800) 368-4148
www.experiencecoloradosprings.com

CRESTED BUTTE

Crested Butte–Mt. Crested Butte
Chamber of Commerce,
601 Elk Ave.; P.O. Box 1288, 81224;
(970) 349-6438 or (800) 545-4505 or
(800) 323-2453
www.crestedbuttechamber.com,
www.gunnisoncrestedbutte.com

CRIPPLE CREEK

Cripple Creek Heritage Center,
Fifth and Bennett Ave.;
P.O. Box 430, 80813;
(719) 689-3315 or (877) 858-4653
www.visitcripplecreek.com

DURANGO

Durango Area Chamber Resort
Association,
111 South Camino del Rio;
P.O. Box 2587, 81302;
(970) 247-3500 or (888) 414-0835
www.durango.org

GUNNISON

Gunnison Country Chamber of
Commerce,
500 East Tomichi Ave., 81230;
(970) 641-1501 or (800) 323-2453
www.gunnison-co.com, www
.gunnisoncrestedbutte.com

LEADVILLE

Leadville/Lake County Chamber of
Commerce,
809 Harrison Ave.;
P.O. Box 861, 80461;
(719) 486-3900 or (888) 532-3845
www.leadvilleusa.com

MANITOU SPRINGS

Manitou Springs Chamber of
Commerce & Visitors Bureau,
354 Manitou Ave., 80829;
(800) 642-2567 or (719) 685-5089
www.manitousprings.org

General Palmer Hotel,
(historic bed-and-breakfast)
567 Main Ave.;
(970) 247-4747 or
(800) 523-3358
www.generalpalmerhotel
.com
Moderate to Deluxe

The Historic Strater
Hotel,
699 Main Ave.;
(970) 247-4431 or
(800) 247-4431
www.strater.com
Expensive to Deluxe

Iron Horse Inn,
5800 North Main St.;
(970) 259-1010 or
(800) 748-2990
www.ironhorseinndurango
.com
Moderate to Expensive

MESA VERDE

Mesa Verde Country Visitor
Information Bureau,
(800) 530-2998
www.swcolo.org

Cortez Chamber of Commerce,
928 East Main St., 81321;
(970) 565-3414
www.cortezchamber.org

MONTROSE

Montrose Chamber of Commerce,
1519 East Main St., 81401;
(970) 249-5000 or (800) 923-5515
www.montrosechamber.com

MOSCA

Great Sand Dunes National Park,
11999 Hwy. 150, 81146;
(719) 378-6300 (main) or (719) 378-6399 (visitor center)
www.nps.gov/grsa

PAGOSA SPRINGS

Pagosa Springs Area Chamber of
Commerce,
P.O. Box 787, 81147;
(970) 264-2360 or (800) 252-2204
www.visitpagosasprings.com

PUEBLO

Greater Pueblo Chamber of
Commerce,
P.O. Box 697, 81002;
302 N. Santa Fe Ave. 81003;
(800) 233-3446 or (719) 542-1704
www.pueblochamber.org

SALIDA

Salida Chamber of Commerce,
406 West Highway 50, 81201;
(877) 772-5432, (719) 539-2068
www.salidachamber.org/visitor

TELLURIDE

Telluride Tourism Board,
P.O. Box 1009, Telluride, 81435;
(888) 605-2578
www.visittelluride.com

Lightner Creek Inn,
999 County Rd. 207;
(970) 259-1226 or
(800) 268-9804
www.lightnercreekinn.com
Expensive to Deluxe

**Rochester Hotel/Leland
House Bed & Breakfast,**
721 East Second Ave.;
(970) 385-1920 or
(800) 664-1920
www.rochesterhotel.com
Expensive to Deluxe

Wilderness Trails Ranch,
23486 County Rd. 501,
Bayfield;
(970) 247-0722 or
(800) 527-2624
www.wlidernesstrail.com
Deluxe

GREAT SAND DUNES/ ALAMOSA

Great Sand Dunes Lodge,
(next to park entrance)
7900 Hwy. 150 North
(Mosca);
(719) 378-2900
www.gsdlodge.com
Moderate to Expensive

GUNNISON

Gunnison Inn,
412 E. Tomichi Ave.;
(866) 641-0700
www.gunnisoninn.com
Moderate

Holiday Inn Express Hotel & Suites,
910 E. Tomichi Ave.;
(970) 641-1228 or
(877) 863-4780
www.hiexpress.com
Moderate to Expensive

Island Acres Resort,
38339 W. Hwy. 50;
(970) 641-1442
www.islandacresresort.com
Inexpensive

Quality Inn,
400 E. Tomichi Ave.;
(970) 641-1237
www.qualityinn.com
Inexpensive to Moderate

Super 8,
411 East Tomichi Ave.;
(970) 641-3068
www.super8.com
Inexpensive

Water Wheel Inn,
37478 West Highway 50;
(970) 641-1650 or
(800) 642-1650
www.waterwheelinnat
gunnison.com
Inexpensive to Expensive

Wildwood Resort and Cabins,
1312 West Tomichi;
(970) 641-1663
www.wildwoodmotel.net
Inexpensive to Deluxe

LEADVILLE

Ice Palace Inn Bed-and-Breakfast,
(historic bed-and-breakfast)
813 Spruce St.;
(719) 486-8272 or
(800) 754-2840
www.icepalaceinn.com
Expensive to Deluxe

Timberline Motel,
216 Harrison Ave.;
(719) 486-1876 or
(800) 352-1876
www.timberlinemotel.net
Moderate and Expensive

MT. CRESTED BUTTE

Crested Butte Lodging,
Various Properties;
(970) 349-2400 or
(888) 412-7310
www.crestedbuttelodging
.com
Inexpensive to Deluxe

Crested Butte Retreat,
39 Whetstone Dr.;
(970) 349-1701
www.crestedbutteretreat
.com
Deluxe

Elevation Hotel & Spa,
500 Gothic Rd.;
(800) 334-9236
www.elevationhotelandspa
.com
Deluxe

Grand Lodge Crested Butte,
6 Emmons Loop;
(888) 823-4446
www.grandlodgecrested
butte.com
Deluxe

Lodge at Mountaineer Square,
500 Gothic Rd.;
(800) 334-9236
www.mountaineersquare
.com
Deluxe

Nordic Inn,
14 Treasury Rd.;
(970) 349-5542 or
(800) 542-7669
www.nordicinn.com
Moderate to Deluxe

WestWall Lodge,
14 Hunter Hill Rd.;
(970) 349-1349 or
(888) 349-1280
www.westwalllodge.com
Deluxe

MANITOU SPRINGS

Black Bear Inn,
5250 Pikes Peak Highway,
Cascade;
(719) 684-0151 or
(877) 732-5232
www.inntravels.com
Moderate to Expensive

El Colorado Lodge,
(historic cottage)
23 Manitou Ave.;
(719) 685-5485 or
(800) 782-2246
http://Elcolorado.pikes-
peak.com
Moderate to Expensive

Red Crags Bed-and-Breakfast Inn,
302 El Paso Blvd.;
(719) 685-1920 or
(800) 721-2248
www.redcrags.com
Expensive to Deluxe

Town-N-Country Cottages,
(quiet accommodations)
123 Crystal Park Rd.;
(719) 685-5427 or
(800) 366-3509
www.townncountryc.com
Moderate to Expensive

MESA VERDE

Far View Lodge,
(motel; busy in summer,
reserve far in advance)
At Navajo Hill; in the park
15 miles from entrance;
(602) 331-5210 or
(800) 449-2288
www.visitmesaverde.com
Expensive to Deluxe

MONTROSE

Best Western Red Arrow,
(comfortable)
1702 East Main;
(970) 249-9641
www.bestwesterncolorado
.com/hotels/best-western-
red-arrow
Inexpensive to Moderate

Black Canyon Motel,
160 East Main;
(970) 249-3495 or
(800) 348-3495
www.blackcanyonmotel
.com
Inexpensive to Moderate

Country Lodge,
1624 East Main St.;
(970) 249-4567
www.countrylodgecolorado
.com
Inexpensive to Moderate

Uncompahgre Bed-and-Breakfast,
21049 Uncompahgre Rd.;
(970) 240-4000 or
(800) 318-8127
www.uncbb.com
Moderate to Expensive

Western Motel,
1200 East Main St.;
(970) 249-3481 or
(800) 445-7301
www.westernmotel.com
Inexpensive to Moderate

PAGOSA SPRINGS

Fairfield Resorts Pagosa,
(tennis, golf, restaurant on
premises)
538 Village Dr.;
(970) 731-8000
www.fairfieldpagosa.net
Deluxe

High Country Lodge,
(motel),
3821 East Highway 160;
(970) 264-4181 or
(800) 862-3707
www.highcountrylodge
.com
Inexpensive to Expensive

The Pagosa Lodge,
(newly remodeled)
3505 West Hwy. 160;
(970) 731-4141 or
(800) 523-7704
www.pagosalodge.com
Moderate to Expensive

The Springs Resort,
(hot springs)
165 Hot Springs Blvd.;
(970) 264-4168 or
(800) 225-0934
www.pagosahotsprings
.com
Moderate to Expensive

PUEBLO

Abriendo Inn,
(bed-and-breakfast)
300 West Abriendo Ave.;
(719) 544-2703
www.abriendoinn.com
Inexpensive to Expensive

Days Inn,
(good value)
4201 North Elizabeth;
(719) 543-8031
www.daysinn.com
Inexpensive to Moderate

Guest House Inn,
730 North Santa Fe Ave.;
(719) 543-6530
www.guesthousepueblo
.com
Inexpensive

SALIDA

Days Inn,
402 East Hwy. 50;
(719) 539-6651
www.daysinnsalida.com
Inexpensive to Moderate

Tudor Rose Bed-and-Breakfast,
6720 County Rd. 104;
(719) 539-2002 or
(800) 379-0889
www.thetudorrose.com
Moderate to Expensive

OTHER ATTRACTIONS WORTH SEEING IN SOUTHERN COLORADO

COLORADO SPRINGS

Flying W Ranch,
(719) 598-4000 or (800) 232-3599
www.flyingw.com

Old Colorado City,
(719) 577-4112
www.shopoldcoloradocity.com

U.S. Olympic Visitor Center,
(888) 659-8687
www.olympic-usa.org/content/
index/1374

DURANGO

Durango Mountain Resort,
(970) 247-9000 or (800) 982-6103
www.durangomountainresort.com

LEADVILLE

**Leadville, Colorado & Southern
Railroad Train Tour,**
(719) 486-3936 or (866) 386-3936
www.leadville-train.com

MANITOU SPRINGS

Cave of the Winds,
(719) 685-5444
www.caveofthewinds.com

MONTROSE

Owl Creek Pass,
(970) 249-5000 or (800) 923-5515
(Chamber of Commerce)
www.montrosechamber.com

OURAY

Million Dollar Highway,
(970) 325-4746
(Chamber of Commerce)
www.ouraycolorado.com

PAGOSA SPRINGS

Navajo State Park,
(970) 883-2208
http://parks.state.co.us/parks/navajo

Wolf Creek Pass,
(800) 252-2204
(Chamber of Commerce)
http://sangres.com/features/
wolfcreekpass.htm

PUEBLO

**The Greenway and Nature & Raptor
Center of Pueblo,**
(719) 549-2414
www.gncp.org

SILVERTON

Silverton Historic District,
(800) 752-4494 or (970) 387-5654
(Chamber of Commerce)
www.silvertoncolorado.com

Woodland Motel,
903 West First St.;
(719) 539-4980 or
(800) 488-0456
www.woodlandmotel.com
Inexpensive to Expensive

TELLURIDE

Lumiere Telluride,
118 Lost Creek Lane;
(970) 728-4224 or
(866) 530-9466
www.lumieretelluride.com
Deluxe

Mountain Lodge,
457 Mountain Village Blvd.;
(970) 369-5000
www.mountainlodge
telluride.com
Expensive to Deluxe

New Sheridan,
231 W. Colorado Ave.;
(970) 728-4351 or
(800) 200-1891
www.newsheridan.com
Expensive to Moderate

San Sophia Inn,
300 West Pacific Ave.;
(970) 728-3001 or
(800) 537-4781
www.sansophia.com
Expensive to Deluxe

Places to Eat in Southern Colorado

The rating scale for restaurants is as follows:
Inexpensive:
Most entrees less than $10
Moderate:
Most entrees $10 to $15
Expensive:
Most entrees $16 to $20
Deluxe:
Most entrees more than $20

ALMONT

Almont Resort,
10209 Hwy. 135;
(970) 641-4009
www.almontresort.com
Inexpensive to Expensive

Harmel's Ranch Resort,
(seasonal)
County Road 742;
(970) 641-1740
www.harmels.com
Deluxe (all-inclusive)

Three Rivers Resort Smokehouse,
(seasonal)
130 County Rd. 742;
(970) 641-1303 or
(888) 761-3474
www.3riversresort.com
Deluxe (all-inclusive)

BUENA VISTA

Bongo Billy's Buena Vista Cafe,
414 E. Main St.;
(719) 395-4991
www.buenavistaroastery.com
Inexpensive

CANON CITY/ROYAL GORGE

Merlino's Belvedere,
(Italian, American)
1330 Elm Ave.;
(719) 275-5558
www.belvedererestaurant.com
Moderate

Pizza Madness,
509 Main St.;
(719) 276-3088
Inexpensive

COLORADO SPRINGS

Charles Court at Broadmoor,
(true elegance; large menu)
1 Lake Ave.;
(719) 577-5733
www.broadmoor.com
Deluxe

Edelweiss,
(German; authentic European)
34 East Ramona Ave.;
(719) 633-2220
www.edelweissrest.com
Moderate to Expensive

Flying W Ranch,
(Western atmosphere; chuck wagon suppers)
3330 Chuckwagon Rd.;
(719) 598-4000 or
(800) 232-FLYW (3599)
www.flyingw.com
Expensive

Giuseppe's Old Depot,
(Italian, American)
10 South Sierra Madre;
(719) 635-3111
www.giuseppes-depot.com
Inexpensive to Moderate

La Casita Patio Cafe,
(Mexican)
3725 E. Woodmen Rd.;
(719) 536-0375
Inexpensive to Moderate

La Petite Maison,
(French)
1015 West Colorado Ave.;
(719) 632-4887
www.lapetitemaisoncs.com
Deluxe

CORTEZ

Metate Room,
(Mesa Verde National Park);
(602) 331-5210 or
(800) 449-2288
www.visitmesaverde.com/lodging-dining/index.cfm
Expensive to Deluxe

Nero's Restaurant,
3303 W. Main St.;
(970) 565-7366
www.subee.com
Inexpensive to Deluxe

Silver Bean Coffee Shop,
410 W. Main St.;
(970) 946-4404
Inexpensive

CRESTED BUTTE

Donita's Cantina,
(Tex-Mex, Mexican)
332 Elk Ave.;
(970) 349-6674
www.donitascantina.com
Inexpensive to Expensive

Izzy's,
(breakfast & lunch)
218 Maroon Ave.;
(970) 349-5026
Inexpensive

Le Bosquet,
(French)
Sixth & Belleview, Majestic
Plaza;
(970) 349-5808
Expensive

Lil's Sushi Bar & Grill,
(seafood & meat)
321 Elk Ave.;
(970) 349-6233
Moderate to Expensive

Paradise Cafe,
(breakfast & lunch)
303 Elk Ave.;
(970) 349-6233
Inexpensive

Secret Stash,
(gourmet pizzeria)
21 Elk Ave.;
(970) 349-6245
www.thesecretstash.com
Moderate

Slogar Bar & Restaurant,
(chicken & steak, family
style)
517 Second St.;
(970) 349-5765
Expensive to Deluxe

Soupcon,
(French)
127 A. Elk Ave.;
(970) 349-5448
www.soupconcrestedbutte
.com
Moderate to Deluxe

Timberline Restaurant,
(American bistro)
210 Elk Ave.;
(970) 349-9831
www.timberlinerestaurant
.com
Moderate to Deluxe

CRIPPLE CREEK

**The Stratton's Grill at
Imperial Casino Hotel,**
(historic; American)
123 North Third St.;
(719) 689-7777
www.imperialcasinohotel
.com
Moderate to Expensive

DURANGO

**Arianos Italian
Restaurant,**
150 East College Dr.;
(970) 247-8146
Moderate

**Brickhouse Cafe &
Coffee,**
(breakfast and lunch)
Nineteenth & Main Avenue;
(970) 247-3760
www.brickhouse.com
Inexpensive to Moderate

**Carver's Bakery & Brew
Pub,**
1022 Main Ave.;
(970) 259-2545
Moderate to Expensive

Common Sense Cafe,
1480 East Second Ave.;
(970) 259-9106
www.commonsensecafe
.com
Inexpensive

Cyprus Cafe,
(Mediterranean cuisine)
725 East Second Ave.;
(970) 385-6884
www.cypruscafe.com
Inexpensive to Expensive

Ken & Sue's,
636 Main Ave.;
(970) 385-1810
www.kenandsues.com
Inexpensive to Moderate

**Mahogany Grille at the
Strater,**
699 Main Ave.;
(970) 247-4433
www.mahoganygrille.com
Deluxe

Ore House,
147 East College Dr.;
(970) 247-5705
www.orehouserestaurant
.com
Deluxe

Serious Texas Bar-B-Q,
3535 North Main Ave.;
(970) 247-2240
www.serioustexasbbq.com
Inexpensive to Moderate

Steamworks Brewery,
801 East Second Ave.;
(970) 259-9200
www.steamworksbrewing
.com
Moderate

GUNNISON

The Bean Coffeehouse & Eatery,
(breakfast & lunch)
120 N. Main St.;
(970) 641-2408
Inexpensive

Garlic Mike's,
(Italian)
2674 North Hwy. 135;
(970) 641-2493
www.garlicmikes.com
Inexpensive to Expensive

Gunnysack Cowboy Bistro,
(southwestern)
142 N. Main St.;
(970) 641-5445
Moderate

Gunnison Brewery,
138 N. Main St.;
(970) 641-2739
Moderate to Expensive

Ol' Miner Steakhouse,
139 N. Main St.;
(970) 641-5153
Moderate to Expensive

Quarter Circle Restaurant,
(American)
323 East Tomichi Ave.;
(970) 641-0542
Moderate

The Trough,
(steak, seafood, game)
37550 U.S. Highway 50;
(970) 641-3724
Inexpensive to Moderate

LEADVILLE

Columbine Cafe,
(American)
612 Harrison Ave.;
(719) 486-3599
Moderate

La Cantina,
(Mexican)
1942 US Hwy. 24;
(719) 486-9021
Inexpensive to Moderate

MT. CRESTED BUTTE

Avalanche Bar & Grill,
15 Emmons Rd.;
(970) 349-7195
www.avalanchebarandgrill.com
Inexpensive to Moderate

Butte 66 Roadhouse BBQ,
Slopeside at Ski Base;
(970) 349-2999
Inexpensive to Expensive

Camp 4 Coffee,
Mountaineer Square Courtyard & Top of Painter Boy Lift
(also locations in Crested Butte and Crested Butte South)
www.camp4coffee.com
Inexpensive

django's,
620 Gothic Rd.;
(970) 349-7574
www.djangos.us
Inexpensive to Expensive

Prime 9380,
Elevation Hotel & Spa;
(970) 251-3030
www.skicb.com
Inexpensive to Expensive

Woodstone Bar & Grille,
Grand Lodge Crested Butte;
(970) 349-8030
www.grandlodgecrestedbutte.com
Inexpensive to Expensive

MANITOU SPRINGS

Adam's Mountain Cafe,
(vegetarian)
934 Manitou Ave.;
(719) 685-1430
www.adamsmountain.com
Inexpensive to Moderate

The Briarhurst Manor,
(continental)
404 Manitou Ave.;
(719) 685-1864 or
(877) 685-9000
www.briarhurst.com
Expensive to Deluxe

Craftwood Inn,
(Colorado cuisine; seafood, game)
404 El Paso Blvd.;
(719) 685-9000
www.craftwood.com
Expensive to Deluxe

Mission Bell Inn,
(Mexican)
178 Crystal Park Rd.;
(719) 685-9089
www.missionbellinn.com
Moderate to Expensive

Stagecoach Inn,
(buffalo, prime rib)
702 Manitou Ave.;
(719) 685-9400
www.stagecoachinn.com
Moderate to Expensive

MONTROSE

Cafe 110,
110 North Townsend;
(970) 249-0777
www.cafe110montrose.com
Moderate

Garlic Mike's Italian Cuisine,
103 Rose Lane;
(970) 249-4381
www.garlicmikes.com
Moderate

Sakura,
(sushi, Japanese)
411 North Townsend;
(970) 249-8230
Modérate to Expensive

PAGOSA SPRINGS

Branding Iron Bar-B-Que,
(western)
3961 East Hwy. 160;
(970) 264-4268
Inexpensive to Moderate

Elkhorn Cafe,
(Mexican, American)
438 Pagosa Blvd.;
(970) 264-2146
Moderate to Expensive

Ole Minor's Steakhouse,
3821 Hwy. 160;
(970) 264-5981
www.highcountrylodge
.com
Moderate to Expensive

PUEBLO

Cactus Flower,
(Southwestern)
4610 North Elizabeth St.;
(719) 545-8218
Moderate

Cafe Del Rio,
(continental)
5200 Nature Center Rd.;
(719) 549-2009
Moderate

Gaetano's,
(Italian, large portions)
910 W. US Hwy. 50;
(719) 546-0949
Moderate to Expensive

La Renaissance,
(continental)
217 East Routt Ave.;
(719) 543-6367
www.larenaissance
restaurant.com
Expensive to Deluxe

SALIDA

Bongo Billy's Salida Cafe,
300 West Sackett Ave.;
(719) 539-4261
www.salidacafe.com
Inexpensive

SEDALIA

Gabriel's,
(historic; fine dining)
5450 Manhart Ave.
(Highway 67);
(303) 688-2323
www.gabrielsdenver.com
Deluxe

TELLURIDE

Allreds,
Top of San Sophia
Gondola;
(970) 728-7474
www.allredsrestaurant.com
Deluxe

Baked in Telluride,
127 S. Fir St.;
(970) 728-4775
Inexpensive

Fat Alley Barbecue,
122 S. Oak St.;
(970) 728-3985
Inexpensive to Moderate

Honga's Lotus Petal,
135 E. Colorado Ave.;
(970) 728-5134
www.hongaslotuspetal.com
Expensive to Deluxe

La Marmotte,
150 W. San Juan Ave.;
(970) 728-6232
www.lamarmotte.com
Moderate to Deluxe

La Piazza Del Villagio,
117 Lost Creek Lane,
Mountain Village;
(970) 728-8283
www.lapiazzadelvilla
ggioristorante.com
Moderate to Deluxe

Steaming Bean Coffee,
221 W. Colorado Ave.;
(970) 369-5575 or
(800) 230-2326 (bean)
www.thebean.com
Inexpensive

DENVER AND THE PLAINS

Denver Metropolitan Area

For years Denver has wrestled with an identity crisis. Should it proudly accept the folksy label of "cow town" bestowed on it long ago? Or should it point to the long list of metropolitan achievements and traits that has earned it acclaim over the last 30 years as a cultured metropolis?

Although the presence of the Western Stock Show every January fills the streets with Stetson hats and cowboy boots, few would deny that Denver has become an exciting cultural center. With the nation's second-largest theatrical venue, a sizzling culinary scene, diverse music and nightlife choices, world-class museums, excellent library system, numerous brewpubs, five major-league sports teams, and one of the largest bike trail systems in the country, the historical moniker of cow town is fading fast.

Long before the cows and the city culture arrived, there were Native American tribes living here at the junction of Cherry Creek and the South Platte River. Ute, Cheyenne, Arapahoe, and Cherokee hunted the plains and traveled into the mountains each summer in search of game. Trappers and

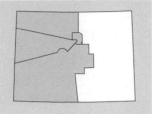

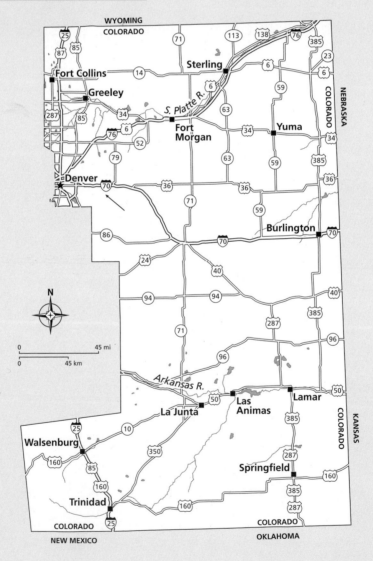

WYOMING
COLORADO

Fort Collins
Greeley
S. Platte R.
Sterling

Fort
Morgan
Yuma

Denver

Burlington

N

0   45 mi
0   45 km

Arkansas R.

La Junta
Las
Animas
Lamar

Walsenburg

Springfield

Trinidad

COLORADO
NEW MEXICO

COLORADO
OKLAHOMA

NEBRASKA

COLORADO
KANSAS

explorers wandered through in the 1800s but overall this prairie wilderness was a quiet place. In July of 1858 an event took place near the mouth of Little Dry Creek that would change the landscape and its Native people forever. Gold was discovered.

From 1859 to 1861, around 100,000 gold seekers streamed into the region, lured by exaggerated tales back east of riches waiting to be found. Within 18 years Denver was the capital of the nation's 38th state, and 35,000 people lived here. Not much gold was discovered in the local streams, but in the nearby mountain towns of Central City and Blackhawk, large deposits were uncovered. Denver became a supply center and much of the money earned in the mining camps made its way back to town. Gold brought more fortune hunters from all over North America, but most of them did not strike it rich. Still, they flocked to the area.

AUTHOR'S FAVORITES IN DENVER AND THE PLAINS

Bent's Old Fort,
(719) 383-5010
www.nps.gov/beol/

Brown Palace Hotel,
(800) 321-2599 or (303) 297-3111
www.brownpalace.com

Confluence Park and Denver Bike Paths,
South Platte River at downtown REI store

Denver Art Museum,
(720) 865-5000
www.denverartmuseum.org

Denver Botanic Gardens,
(720) 865-3500
www.botanicgardens.org

Denver Performing Arts Complex,
(303) 893-4000
www.denvercenter.org

Denver Museum of Nature & Science,
(800) 925-2250 or (303) 323-7009
www.dmns.org

El Chapultapec Jazz Club,
(303) 295-9126

Larimer Square,
(303) 534-2367
www.larimersquare.com

Rockmount Ranch Wear,
(303) 629-7777
www.rockmount.com

South Platte River Trail,
Thirty mile biking/walking path along South Platte River
www.denver.org/metro/features/bike-trails

Tattered Cover Bookstore,
(800) 833-9327
www.tatteredcover.com

Washington Park,
(303) 698-4930
www.denvergov.org

Residents endured some rough times during these years. Early in 1863, a great fire destroyed much of the business district. The following summer the lush plains were scorched by a drought. The winter was cold beyond all previous experience. Then, in the spring of 1864, a flash flood churned along the Cherry Creek sand bed through the city, washing over houses and bridges and killing twenty people. Nearly $1 million worth of property was destroyed. In the wake of these natural disasters, there were skirmishes with Indians. Stage stations were sacked, and communication and supply lines to the East severed.

But the city and its people bounced back. By 1890 over 100,000 called Denver home. Silver had been discovered in the previous decade and a new era of opulence arrived. Corruption was common as city officials and police partnered with underworld figures such as Soapy Smith and Lou Blonger to profit from gambling, con games, and other illegal enterprises. Miners returning from the fields found bawdy houses along Market Street catering to every budget. Hustlers were waiting at gambling tables to separate the miners from their hard-earned gold. Denver's vice district during these early days was second only to those in San Francisco's Barbary Coast and New Orleans' Storyville.

trivia

In the 1850s, as Denver competed with other mining towns for the status of being Colorado's premier city, Denver was made up of nothing but crude cabins and one saloon—Colorado's first.

According to local historian Richard Grant, "The silver barons built elaborate mansions on Capitol Hill. Gamblers, drifters and gunmen flooded the saloons and gaming halls on Larimer and Market streets. Bat Masterson tended bar here, Soapy Smith ran the West's largest gang of thieves, crooks and con artists, and anyone who was anyone in the 'Old West' paid at least a visit to Denver's mud-filled, honky-tonk streets."

Colorado moved forward into the twentieth century, and as the gold and silver petered out, ranching, farming, and manufacturing replaced mining. By 1910 the city had become the commercial and industrial center of the Rocky Mountain region, with a large cattle market and the largest sheep market in the world. By 1940, 322,000 people lived here. Denver was on its way to becoming the city it is today. Thanks to a proliferation of government offices, Denver was in the process of becoming the nation's second capital. This is still the case; with 26 government agencies based at the Federal Center in the suburb of Lakewood, the area has the largest concentration of Federal agencies outside of Washington, D.C.

AUTHOR'S FAVORITE EVENTS IN DENVER AND THE PLAINS

First Friday Art Walks,
Santa Fe Drive Art District, First Fri of
each month;
www.artdistrictonsantafe.com

**National Western Stock Show, Horse
Show, and Rodeo,**
National Western Complex in Denver;
early to mid-Jan;
(303) 295-6124
www.nationalwestern.com

Denver March Pow Wow,
Denver Coliseum, Mar;
(303) 934-8045
www.denvermarchpowwow.org

Cinco de Mayo Festival,
Civic Center Park; May 5;
(303) 534-8342
http://cincodemayodenver.com

La Piazza dell'Arte,
LoDo; early June;
(303) 685-8143
www.larimerarts.org/la_piazza_dell_arte
.html

Cherry Blossom Festival,
Sakura Square; June or July;
(303) 295-1844
www.tsdbt.org/cherryblossom

Greeley Stampede and Rodeo,
Greeley; late June through early July;
(800) 982-2855
www.greeleystampede.org

Cherry Creek Arts Festival,
Cherry Creek; July 4th weekend;
(303) 355-2787
www.cherryarts.org

Colorado Dragon Boat Festival,
Lakewood; late July;
(303) 722-6852
www.coloradodragonboat.org

Larimer County Fair and Rodeo,
Loveland; early August;
(970) 619-4009
www.larimercountyfair.org

Great American Beer Festival,
Colorado Convention Center; late Sept
to early Oct;
(303) 447-0816 or (888) 822-6273
www.beertown.org/events/gabf

Zoo Lights,
Denver Zoo; nightly in Dec;
(303) 376-4800
www.denverzoo.org

As Denver modernized, old edifices were torn down and replaced with new structures. Unfortunately, many of the classic architectural gems, the Tabor Grand Opera House and the Windsor Hotel among them, were razed to make way for modern glass-and-steel skyscrapers. Parts of Denver died each time another historic building was demolished.

Quite a few of the Victorian buildings still exist. The historic **Brown Palace Hotel** (321 Seventeenth St.; 303-297-3111 or 800-321-2599; www.brown-palace.com) and The **Oxford Hotel** (1600 Seventeenth St.; 303-628-5400 or 800-228-3858; www.theoxfordhotel.com) are alive and well. The Brown Palace is well worth stopping in for afternoon tea or a drink in the Ship Tavern. One of the city's pleasures is to relax in the expansive, beautifully detailed atrium while sipping tea and listening to piano music.

Anyone interested in history will enjoy the **Molly Brown House Museum,** where Colorado's past is well-preserved. After she became wealthy, the "Unsinkable" Molly Brown lived her flamboyant life in this 1889 mansion of native Colorado lava stone. Following Molly's death in 1932, the building served as a rooming house. At the whim of each successive owner, it was remodeled or divided. Rescued in 1971 by Historic Denver Inc., the mansion was decorated as Molly herself had done, using old photographs Molly had taken of her home's interior. The Molly Brown House has been restored to its exaggerated, extreme opulence. It is located at 1340 Pennsylvania St.; (303) 832-4092; www.mollybrown.com. Admission costs $8 for adults and teenagers thirteen and older, $6 for senior citizens sixty-five and older, and $4 for children six to twelve; children five or younger free. Open year-round Tuesday through Saturday from 10 a.m. to 3:30 p.m. and Sunday from noon to 4 p.m.; closed Monday and major holidays.

Colorado's **Governor's Mansion** (also known as the **Cheesman-Boettcher Mansion** and the Executive Residence), a redbrick colonial building with white stone trim, was built by one of the state's distinguished pioneer families, the Cheesmans. (Cheesman Park is named for them.) After serving as the home of John Evans, Colorado's second territorial governor, the property passed into the Boettcher family. Then it became part of their Boettcher Foundation, a philanthropic organization that presented it as a gift to the state of Colorado in 1960. The mansion has been the executive residence of the state's governors ever since.

trivia

Denver has 300 days of sunshine annually—more hours of sun each year than Miami Beach!

Furnished with luxurious art, antiques, and furniture, the house is available for limited tours. It is located at 400 East Eighth St. in Denver. For information about tours, contact the Colorado Historical Society's Office of Archaeology and Historic Preservation, 1300 Broadway, Denver 80203; (303) 866-3681; www.colorado.gov/dpa/doit/archives/govs/mansion/front1.htm.

If you enjoy visiting stately old Denver mansions, consider the **Pearce McAllister Cottage,** located at 1880 Gaylord St. This 1899 structure also contains the **Denver Museum of Miniatures, Dolls and Toys.** Open Tuesday through Saturday from 10 a.m. to 4 p.m. and Sunday from 1 to 4 p.m. Admission costs $5 for anyone age seventeen through sixty-one and $4 for ages five

Black American West Museum & Heritage Center

Did you know that nearly one-third of America's working cowboys in the Old West were African American? The *Black American West Museum* offers a unique and much-needed look at the history of these and other African Americans and the roles they played in our nation's past. The museum is housed in the former home of Denver's first African-American doctor, Dr. Justina Ford, who delivered more than 7,000 babies during her illustrious career. Admission prices are $8 for adults, $7 for seniors sixty-five and older, and $6 for children under twelve. Call for hours. For more information: 3091 California, Denver 80205, (303) 482-2242; www.blackamericanwest museum.com.

to sixteen and senior citizens sixty-two and older. Call (303) 322-1053 or log on to www.dmmdt.com.

The *Grant-Humphreys Mansion* was built in 1902 and named after former Colorado governor James B. Grant. It has more than forty rooms. The mansion at 770 Pennsylvania St. can be rented for special events or toured. For more information contact the Grant-Humphreys Mansion at (303) 894-2505; www.coloradohistory.org/ghm/.

The *Byers-Evans House,* a mansion at 1310 Bannock St. built in 1883, has been restored to its original grandeur. Admission costs $5 for anyone age seventeen through sixty-four, $4 for seniors (sixty-five and up), and $3 for young people age six through twelve. Children age five or younger are admitted free. Hours of operation are 11 a.m. to 3 p.m. Tuesday through Sunday; closed Monday. For more information contact the Byers-Evans House at (303) 620-4933 or visit www.coloradohistory.org.

Probably the best place in the city to learn about the area's history and prehistory is the adjacent *Denver History Museum* at 1300 Broadway. The museum is open 10 a.m. to 5 p.m. Monday through Saturday and noon to 5 p.m. Sunday. Admission is $7 for adults (thirteen to sixty-four), $6 for seniors sixty-five and older and for students with ID, and $5 for children six to twelve; children under six free. For more information contact the Denver History Museum at (303) 866-3682 or visit www.coloradohistory.org.

The most sumptuous of all the historic buildings in this part of Denver is the castle-like *Capitol Hill Mansion,* an impeccable, deluxe bed-and-breakfast at 1207 Pennsylvania. The mansion, a landmark building listed in the National Register of Historic Places, is not far from the Governor's Mansion and the Molly Brown House. The 1891 furniture is hand-carved oak and maple. The walls are decorated with original Colorado landscape paintings. Some rooms come with four-posters and mountain-viewing balconies. All rooms come with fresh flowers, high speed Internet, cable TV, and gourmet breakfast. For more information contact the Capitol Hill Mansion at (303) 839-5221 or (800) 839-9329; www.capitolhillmansion.com.

If there is one thing Denver does well (after more than 130 years of practice), it is the saloon. The first permanent structure in Denver was a saloon, and today there are sports bars, art bars, fern bars, outdoor cafe bars, English pubs, "Old West" saloons, rock bars, city-overlook bars, country-and-western bars, art deco bars, and even bars that don't serve alcohol. Denver, and the state in general, lead the nation in beer brewing.

In addition to a plethora of saloons, Denver has more sporting-goods stores and ski shops per capita than almost any other population center in the world and a corresponding number of recreation facilities that include free outdoor tennis courts, city golf courses, and the like. The REI flagship store at 1416 Platte St. is paradise for outdoor enthusiasts to wander and shop as they plot their next escape into nature. The climbing wall is often crawling with kids and adults testing their skills. Grab something from the Starbucks and walk outside to Confluence Park where kayakers cavort at the junction of the South Platte River and Cherry Creek.

Denver is also a serious sports spectator town. Four new facilities—***Coors Field, Invesco Field at Mile High, Pepsi Center,*** and ***Dick's Sporting Goods Park***—offer comfortable venues for watching professional baseball, football, basketball, ice hockey, and soccer. Fans flock to cheer on the Rockies, Broncos, Nuggets, Avalanche, and Rapids teams as they battle their lower-altitude competitors.

All these recreational choices may mislead visitors into thinking that Denver is all ballgames and bars. But there is much more to the Mile High City than nightlife and sports. In fact, no other city between Chicago and the West Coast can match Denver's eclectic cultural landscape. The latest addition to the arts scene is the ***Denver Art Museum's Hamilton Building.*** Designed by

"No" to Colorado Olympics

Colorado is the only U.S. state ever to turn down the Olympics. Denver was selected to host the 1976 Winter Olympics but residents voted by a 60 percent majority to prohibit public funds from being used to support the games. Concerns over cost, environmental damage, and population boom to the state were the deciding factors.

First Friday Art Walk

On the first Friday of each month, galleries and studios around town open their doors for an evening of art viewing and socializing. Art aficionados hobnob with artists, visitors chat, flirt, and network over wine and snacks, and occasionally art is sold. It's great fun, and it's free. From 6 to 9 p.m., First Fridays center around three Denver gallery areas:

Santa Fe Drive between Fifth and Tenth Avenues; www.artdistrictonsantafe.com

Tennyson St. between Thirty-eighth and Forty-fourth Avenues; www.tennysonst.com

Lower Downtown (LoDo) district (303) 628-5428; www.lodo.org

internationally known architect Daniel Libeskind, the playful, dreamlike geometry of the titanium-clad structure has changed the city's skyline. Built at a cost of more than $100 million, the new building more than doubles the museum size. Contemporary and modern, Western and Native American, Asian, and European collections, as well as temporary exhibits and a spectacular rooftop sculpture garden, offer something for everyone.

The museum is open Tuesday and Thursday 10 a.m. to 5 p.m., Wednesday and Friday 10 a.m. to 10 p.m., Saturday and Sunday noon to 5 p.m., and closed Monday. Admission for Colorado residents is $10 for adults, $8 for seniors (sixty-five and over) and students, and $3 for children six to eighteen. Children under six are free. Colorado residents can enjoy the museum for free the first Saturday of each month. Admission for non-residents is $13 for adults, $10 for seniors and students, and $5 for children.

In addition to its high-caliber art museum, Denver is home to an impressive library suited to please the most discerning bookworm. The **Denver Public Library,** with its 4.8 million total holdings, happens to be one of the best—and most versatile—in the country. It is at the library desks that you get the feeling of Denver's wide horizons. Just around the corner from the library is **Camera Obscura Gallery,** with one of the best collections of fine art photography in the West (1309 Bannock St.; 303-623-4059; www.camera obscuragallery.com.).

Denver's penchant for culture shows up in several other ways. Visitors to the state capital can take in a play at the boldly designed **Denver Center Theatre** part of the **Denver Center for the Performing Arts** (DCPA), which is the setting for a wide variety of theater productions. DCPA, at 1245 Champa St., is home to two production companies—Denver Center Theatre Company and Denver Center Productions (DCP). Among its many roles, DCP is responsible for importing touring Broadway shows and a variety of world-class entertainment.

Next door to DCPA is the nearly 2,700-seat *Boettcher Concert Hall,* where music lovers enjoy the music of the *Colorado Symphony Orchestra,* among other performers. For ticket information call (303) 623-7876 or (877) 292-7979; www.coloradosymphony.org. The season runs from September through May. Boettcher Concert Hall is located at Fourteenth and Curtis Streets in Denver. The city has come of age culturally, with its theaters, its art cinemas, its ballets, and its chamber music ensembles.

trivia

Every year since 2000 the Denver Public Library has been recognized by Hennen's American Public Library Ratings as one of the top libraries in America for population centers with more than 500,000 people.

Denver is a more interesting and diverse city thanks to the many ethnic groups living here. The long-time Hispanic population contributes a rich and proud heritage. With nearly a third of Denver's residents having Latino ancestry, the city offers a wide range of Hispanic culture in the form of restaurants, music, stores, and events such as the annual Cinco de Mayo celebration, the largest one in the country. Federal Boulevard north from Alameda has hundreds of businesses catering to the Hispanic market.

A sizeable Vietnamese population has introduced the city to the pleasures of this delightful Asian cuisine, and the 8-block stretch of South Federal Boulevard from Alameda Boulevard to Mississippi Street has dozens of restaurants, shops, cafes, and markets, including Chinese and Thai restaurants. Japanese people have long been a part of Denver's ethnic mix, and the downtown Sakura Square with its local Buddhist temple, as well as numerous area sushi restaurants, bring a taste of Japan to the city. The Korean population is sizeable, especially in the suburb of Aurora. The area around South Havana Street and South Peoria Street by Parker Road has dozens of excellent Korean restaurants, as well as stores and businesses.

Over the last few decades Denver has evolved from a meat and potatoes town into an exciting center for innovative, excellent cuisine. The city's culinary scene keeps expanding, with a wide range of tantalizing cuisine from around the globe. There's such a wide variety of eating choices that dedicated foodies could spend months exploring the many options without a single repeat.

Denver Restaurant Week in February is a weeklong celebration of culinary Denver. For seven days, 225 restaurants across the city offer a multi-course dinner for the fixed price of $52.80 (the mile high elevation of Denver is

5,280 feet) for two, or $26.40 for one (not including tax or gratuity). This fun event is a great way to enjoy excellent dining while sampling the many gastronomic destinations of the city. For more information go to www.denver .org/denverrestaurant.

trivia

The Denver Center for the Performing Arts is the second-largest complex of its kind in the United States, with ten theaters seating more than 10,000 people.

Some of these restaurants are familiar locations set in popular art and entertainment districts, while others are hidden off the beaten path in suburban strip malls and small neighborhoods. Hungry people can find American comfort food, Indian, Ethiopian, Nepalese, Middle Eastern, Korean, Vietnamese, Chinese, Thai, Moroccan, Greek, Armenian, Hungarian, German, Italian, Swiss, French, and of course, Mexican fare. Attempting to include the hundreds of good ones would require an entire dining guide. They are all worth exploring.

Of the many superb Asian restaurants, Little Ollie's in Cherry Creek consistently delivers memorable, fresh entrees. Another long-time Cherry Creek favorite is Mel's Restaurant and bar, with eclectic, innovative New American cuisine.

Denver's LoDo (Lower Downtown) district brims with outstanding dining spots. Vesta Dipping Grill offers creative American cuisine with 30 signature dipping sauces. Kevin Taylor is one of the city's best-known chefs, and his Restaurant Kevin Taylor and Kevin Taylor's at Opera House are culinary experiences you won't forget. Rioja is Mediterranean-inspired but successfully ventures into a variety of unexpected ingredients and flavors. Among the best of the city's upscale Mexican restaurants is Tamayo. Its rooftop patio has a great view of the mountains. Zengo blends Latino with Asia for a wonderful fusion experience; try some of the delicious small plates meant for sharing.

West of downtown in the Highlands neighborhood is Cafe Brazil, a neighborhood hot spot that has built a cult-like following over the years. As its name suggests, they offer all things Brazil, with bold flavors and delicious seafood. Highlands Garden Cafe works out of two restored Victorian homes combined into a single restaurant, using seasonal, locally-grown ingredients whenever possible.

Over on Federal Boulevard, among the many dozens of Vietnamese restaurants lining the street, New Saigon has been consistently good for many years. Overlook the often curt wait-staff; the food is worth the trip.

For most of the year, Denver shrugs off its reputation as a cow town, but each January the city eagerly embraces its western heritage. Of the numerous annual events that take place in Denver, the ***National Western Stock Show, Rodeo, and Horse Show*** is the biggest, longest, and most original—a yearly happening that radiates authenticity, excitement, and entertainment. More than eighty years ago, cowboys' competitions with one another were formalized into rodeos. The stock show was born in a circus tent in 1906, and these days the fast-charging riders, the antics of the rodeo clowns, and the pungent smells of the animals sometimes still remind you of a circus. For approximately two weeks every January, old Buffalo Bill and his Wild West entertainers seem to return to old Denver Town.

The National Western remains an important stock show. You can view more than 15,000 live, scrubbed, and brushed Herefords, Angus, Simmentals, Shorthorns, Longhorns, Arabian horses, Morgan horses, draft horses, miniature horses, ewes, and lambs, all in their neat pens. Watch shearing contests, breeding cattle auctions, and the judging of quarter horse stallions. Some 600,000 visitors flock to the arenas to buy, sell, learn, and socialize. Millions of dollars exchange hands here. This is a cowboy convention for real cowboys.

The rodeo competition here is among the toughest in the nation. Bull riding, bareback riding, roping, steer wrestling, team roping barrel racing, and the Mexican rodeo extravaganza are among the activities available to spectators. More than $500,000 in prizes is at stake. In addition to the stock judging and auctions, there are booths selling food and crafts, lectures, meetings, and contests for the cattlemen and -women who show up here. Money is spent on livestock supplies, raw wool, saddles, cow tags, a western art show and sale, and lassoes.

Rodeo competition takes place both afternoons and evenings. Tickets cost about the same as for a movie. And where else can you witness a llama auction, an Australian-style sheep-shearing contest, the world's largest bull show (with one animal actually selling at $300,000), and a catch-a-calf competition for teenagers, while mingling with thousands of cowboys and ranch folk? For more information write to the National Western Stock Show, 4655 Humboldt St., Denver 80216; call (303) 297-1166; or visit www.nationalwestern.com.

How would you like to dine in a historic landmark and museum? How about a steaming platter of elk steak at a table under a stuffed elk, or a plate heaped with buffalo meat, with mounted buffalos staring down? The Buckhorn Exchange is allegedly Colorado's oldest restaurant (it celebrated its centennial in 1993). It is certainly one of the most original. Moreover, it's a saloon, a magnet for celebrities and tourists, and a moneymaker.

Dinner here appeals to well-heeled meat eaters: twenty-four-ounce T-bone steaks, fourteen-ounce New York steaks, buffalo meat, baby back ribs, Rocky Mountain oysters, rabbit—all at hefty rates in a noisy, congenial atmosphere.

The saloon is upstairs, complete with a giant oak bar that was shipped here by oxcart. Nearby walls are filled with 1902 photos of hunting parties; even the men's room has historic pictures of stagecoaches.

The downstairs restaurant-museum is cluttered with more than 500 taxidermy pieces, including antelopes, deer, bears, wolverines, mountain goats, moose, weasels, zebras, and birds of all kinds, shapes, and plumage. More than a hundred rifles, pistols, and other weapons are on display

The **Buckhorn Exchange** was begun in 1893 by owner Henry H. Zietz, a cowboy and scout with Buffalo Bill; personal bodyguard of Leadville's silver millionaire H. A. W. Horace Tabor; and hunting guide of President Teddy Roosevelt, who arrived in his private train in front of the Buckhorn. The restaurant's official history relates that Henry Zietz "catered to cattlemen, miners, railroad builders, Indian chiefs, silver barons, roustabouts, gamblers, the great and the near-great." In December 1900 a masked gunman rode up to the restaurant, waved a .45, and demanded all money and valuables to be placed on the bar, "and be quick about it!" The fellow's horse had been tied to the Buckhorn's hitching post, but when the gunman rode away at a gallop, he found himself pursued by Zietz's rifle-raising customers, who "handily dispatched the miscreant to greener pastures."

After the Zietz family's death, the restaurant-museum passed into the capable hands of several historically minded Denver investors, who put large sums into restoring the building and its contents in 1978. They also raised the prices to twentieth-century levels. The Buckhorn's redbrick building is easy to find at 1000 Osage St. The location is between Colfax Avenue and Eighth Avenue, 5 blocks west of Santa Fe Boulevard.

The Buckhorn Exchange is open for lunch Monday through Friday from 11 a.m. to 2 p.m., and dinner is served seven nights a week, starting at 5:30 p.m. Monday to Thursday, 5 p.m. Friday, Saturday, and Sunday. For more information or reservations call (303) 534-9505; www.buckhornexchange.com.

The **Forney Museum of Transportation** is the perfect place to see some old vehicles, including 1915 Cadillacs, 1905 Fords, old surreys, a locomobile, an ancient electric car, carriages, bygone cycles, rail coaches, steam engines, and old airplanes. The notable exhibits include Theodore Roosevelt's Tour Car, Aly Khan's Rolls-Royce, and Amelia Earhart's Gold Bug Kissel. With more than 500 exhibits ranging from buggies and bicycles to tractors and trains, it's a collection devoted to just about anything on wheels. The Forney Museum of Transportation is located at 4303 Brighton Blvd. Call (303) 297-1113 or log on to www.forneymuseum.org. Admission is $7 for adults, $6 for seniors, $4.50 for youth (eleven to fifteen), and $3.50 for children five to ten. The museum is open Monday through Saturday from 10 a.m. to 4 p.m.

Larimer Square is a carefully renovated, eighteenth-century downtown oasis with a national reputation. Along with the Sixteenth Street pedestrian mall, it's one of the most popular destinations in Denver. In 1858, Denver's founder, General William E. Larimer, erected the city's first building here, a modest log cabin. Apparently the general had an odd sense of humor; the doors were coffin lids. As the city grew, Larimer St. became one of the most famous thoroughfares in the West. Saloons, gambling houses, and brothels catered to a steady stream of customers. It was a wild place during a boom time. The restaurants, hotels, and theaters of its heyday were renowned. Stories of what happened when the greats, near-greats, and desperados of the West met made good newspaper copy. And tales of what went on behind closed doors in the neighborhood shocked a nation. Gambling and boozing were rampant.

As the years passed, Denver gradually moved uptown, and Larimer Street became a skid row area. Thanks to the gin mills and flophouses, the handsome Victorian buildings were forgotten, although amid the grime and dirt, their architectural beauty remained. Razing was a frequent threat.

More than one hundred years later, a group of Colorado businesspeople founded the Larimer Square Association for the purpose of restoring the old buildings. The excitement that once was historic Larimer Street soon returned, and today the entire lower downtown area, known as LoDo, is the city's hip epicenter. Restaurants, cafes, bars, coffeehouses, boutiques, businesses, and hotels fill the district, with many residing in renovated buildings well over a century old. The Tattered Cover is one of the best bookstores in the country. At the northern edge of LoDo is Coors Field, home to the Rockies baseball team. Especially on Friday and Saturday nights the district buzzes with energy as hundreds of people come in search of good food, drink, and fun, but any time of the day or evening is good for strolling and discovering the charms of this historic area.

Larimer Square and nearby streets contain outstanding examples of early Denver Victorian architecture, complete with gaslights, hand-wrought leaded-glass windows, stairways, historic markers, restored cornices, and handsome outdoor benches for resting and watching. In the restaurants and shops, you find Tiffany lamps, cherry wood bars, rosewood paneling, old wallpapers, and lead or pressed-tin ceilings. Sadly, many historic buildings were destroyed during the urban renewal development of the 1960s and 1970s, but of the ones that remain, a number date back to the 1880s and 1890s. If more of these buildings had been preserved during that development period, Denver's downtown would look very different today.

Larimer Square is now a Landmark Preservation District, and it's listed in the National Register of Historic Places. For more information call (303) 534-2367; www.larimersquare.com.

The ***16th Street Mall,*** Denver's ultramodern, $76 million pedestrian thoroughfare, is the best people watching spot in the city—a place where you can be entertained by a juggler or a bagpiper or a classic violinist, shop in large bookstores or small exclusive boutiques, or just sit on one of many benches and watch Denver go by. A dozen fountains, two hundred red oak trees, and frequent flower planters make this milelong, well-lit mall an attractive shopping and entertainment street. Whenever you get tired of walking, hop on one of the free, eco-friendly hybrid shuttle buses that travel the length of the mall. Three pedestrian bridges at the west end of the mall connect to the Highlands neighborhood, which has the massive REI flagship store, excellent restaurants, hip bars, and coffee shops. For more information contact the Denver Metro Convention and Visitors Bureau at (800) 233-6837 or (303) 892-1505; www.denver.org.

From its international debut in 1892 up to the present, ***Denver's Brown Palace Hotel*** has lived up to its motto, "Where the World Registers." Indeed, this historic hotel is a classic. Nearly every U.S. president since Theodore Roosevelt has spent time here. Winston Churchill, Elvis Presley, and the Beatles all slept here—though not on the same night.

"The Brown," as Denverites have nicknamed it, is a remarkable example of Victorian architecture. The hotel lobby impresses the most. Upon entering, your eyes look up the six tiers of wrought-iron balconies to the stained-glass cathedral ceiling. The decorative stone on the pillars is Mexican onyx. Changing displays of historical memorabilia decorate the luxurious lobby. Old guest registers, menus, and photographs take you back to relive the role the Brown Palace played in the history of Denver.

The hotel is named for its builder, Henry Cordes Brown. As Brown watched nineteenth-century Denver grow, he saw the need for a fine hostelry for visiting easterners who came to do business with Colorado mining companies and railroads. The builder envisioned this hotel to rise from a triangular plot of land he owned near the center of the city. Henry Cordes Brown examined and studied the blueprints of the world's deluxe hostelries before he developed his "palace."

A prominent Denver architect, Frank E. Edbrooke, designed the building in the spirit of the Italian Renaissance. Because of the geometric pattern of Brown's land, the edifice took on an unusual shape. Edbrooke gave the building a tri-frontage and then planned it so that each room faced a street. Without any interior rooms, every guest could have a view, plus morning or afternoon sunshine. The contractors constructed this soon-to-be famous landmark from Colorado red granite and warm brown Arizona sandstone.

Completed in 1892, the 10-story building had 400 rooms. Fireplaces were standard for each room, as well as bathroom taps yielding artesian water straight from the hotel's wells (as they still do today). The finest achievements in steam heating and electricity were incorporated into the structure. The Brown was also noted as the second fireproof edifice in the country.

After four years and $1 million, Henry Brown's luxurious dream was completed. Cool water flowed from the taps; steam heat provided warmth. Ice machines kept the wine chilled and the produce fresh. Turkish baths, hairdressing parlors, billiard rooms, and a library were available for guest use. Linens, china, glassware, and silver came from the finest craftsmen. Denver society was formally introduced to the Brown Palace soon after its opening when the Tabors threw a fancy ball. In the years since, the Brown has hosted thousands of such glittering evenings.

Today the Brown Palace Hotel is listed in the National Register of Historic Places. Even in modern times it continues to provide guests with historical authenticity, Victorian charm, and good service. The original decor has been preserved, especially in the restaurants, and walking through the hotel doors feels like stepping back in time. The Brown Palace Hotel is at 321 Seventeenth St.; (303) 297-3111 or (800) 321-2599; www.brownpalace.com.

The circa-1880s *Queen Anne Bed & Breakfast Inn* is actually two Victorian homes side by side. Originally owned by the Tabor family, it opened as Denver's first urban bed-and-breakfast in 1987. Recently remodeled, each of the fourteen guest rooms is uniquely furnished by a local designer. The B&B incorporates green practices throughout, and serves organic and local breakfasts. Many of the breakfast ingredients come from the on-site vegetable and herb garden. They are located at 2147-51 Tremont Place in the Clements Historic District. For more information contact Queen Anne Bed & Breakfast Inn at (303) 296-6666, or (800) 432-4667; www.queenannebnb.com.

Since Denver's first house was built in the 1850s, the city has expanded into a variety of unique neighborhoods, each with its own flavor. These are places where locals go to relax over a meal, meet friends, and enjoy themselves. There are dozens of interesting neighborhoods to explore around the city, some sprawling for blocks, and others no more than a couple of cafes, a bar, a bookstore, and a coffee shop tucked away in a leafy back street. Here are a few places to begin.

The Uptown neighborhood just east of downtown is a mix of Victorian and Queen Anne homes with great views of the city skyline. The restaurant row along Seventeenth Avenue is lined with cafes, bars, and coffeehouses. East Colfax Avenue has some of the city's best music venues (Fillmore, Ogden, and Bluebird Theater), as well as numerous restaurants and a newly opened Tattered Cover Bookstore. Cherry Creek North, running about eight blocks long by three blocks wide, is the upscale dining and shopping district.

The Golden Triangle Museum District has eight of the city's museums, including the spectacular Denver Art Museum, and the Denver Public Library. The Riverfront neighborhood borders the South Platte River, and includes Elitch Gardens Amusement Park, the Downtown Aquarium, and the Children's Museum. The Art District on Santa Fe, just south of downtown, has more than 40 galleries, restaurants, and shops. It's the largest concentration of galleries in the city, and is one of four First Friday Art Walk sites. Five Points is one of Denver's oldest neighborhoods with blocks of Victorian homes and buildings. The main thoroughfare, Welton Street, has 75 businesses and a light rail system, and is one of the few predominately African-American owned commercial strips in the country.

For a slice of the Vietnamese community, drive along Federal Boulevard between Alameda and Mississippi Avenue. Dozens of restaurants and shops with signs in Vietnamese line the street. The Far East Center at 333 S. Federal Ave. has the highest concentration of Vietnamese stores, with an Asian market, restaurants, a bakery, and a large gift shop filled with unusual items. For more information on these and other neighborhoods visit www.denver.org/metro/neighborhoods.

Few American cities come close to matching Denver's 850 miles of biking, jogging, and walking trails. This substantial network of off-road paved and packed earth trails covers seven counties, traversing a variety of urban and rural environments. Walking or biking along these routes, you will see why Denver appears on lists of physically-fit cities. These pathways are used year-round by all ages, shapes, and sizes. Here are some of the more popular ones.

Starting north of Denver, the South Platte River Greenway Trail follows the river for almost 30 miles, connecting several riverside parks on its way from Confluence Park to Chatfield Reservoir. South of Denver, the High Line Canal Trail follows the historic High Line Canal. More than 65 miles long, the canal has a wide, mostly dirt trail for much of its length. The Cherry Creek Trail begins at Confluence Park in Downtown Denver and follows Cherry Creek south for 15 miles to Cherry Creek Reservoir. The Bear Creek Bike Trail has few bears these days, but this 20 mile route from the South Platte River to the town of Morrison offers side trails connecting to Chatfield, Red Rocks, and Bear Creek Lake Parks. Stop in Morrison for ice cream and browse the antiques shops.

If you'd prefer to laze away an afternoon on a quiet piece of green earth instead of hiking or biking, you're in the right town. Denver has more than 4,000 acres of traditional parks and parkways ranging in size from tiny to sprawling. Considered one of the largest park systems in America, Denver's green spaces provide locals and out-of-towners a relaxing reprieve from city life. Here are some of the more well-known parks.

Civic Center Park at Colfax and Broadway lies at the heart of downtown, close to the State Capitol Building, Denver Art Museum, Denver Public Library, and the 16th St. Mall. Beautifully landscaped and bustling with life, this is the location for events such as People's Fair, Cinco de Mayo, Taste of Colorado, and Martin Luther King Day. At lunchtime when office workers flock here, this is a fun people-watching spot.

At 314 acres, *City Park* is the largest in Denver. Located a few minutes drive east of downtown at Seventeenth Avenue and York Street, this milelong park has flower gardens, fountains, two lakes, a historic boathouse, and lots of grass for picnics, soccer games, Frisbee, and snoozing under a tree. Paddleboats can be rented in summer. Every Sunday at 6 p.m. from June through early August, City Park Jazz presents free jazz concerts in the park. The park is also home to some of the city's top attractions, such as the Museum of Nature and Science and the *Denver Zoo.*

The Denver Zoo has nearly 400 animals, representing 650 species. Natural habitats, winding paths, and large trees are spread over 80 acres, giving the zoo an open feeling. The zoo is open daily. Hours from March through October are 9 a.m. to 5 p.m., and from November through February, 10 a.m. to 4 p.m. Admission from March through October is $12 for adults and teenagers twelve and older, $9 for seniors sixty-five and older, and $7 for children three to eleven; children two and younger free. Admission from November through February is $9 for adults and teenagers twelve and older, $7 for seniors sixty-five and older, and $5 for children three to eleven; children two and younger free. For more information call (303) 376-4800; www.denverzoo.org.

One of the city's top museums, the *Denver Museum of Nature and Science* (DMNS) (800-925-2250; www.dmnh.org), is also located in City Park. DMNS includes both temporary and permanent exhibits, such as "Egyptian Mummies," "North American Wildlife," and "Botswana: Safari to Wild Africa." In addition, the museum is home to the Phipps IMAX Theater, a Discovery Zone with hands-on activities for children, and the Gates Planetarium.

DMNS is open daily from 9 a.m. to 5 p.m. except on Christmas. General admission is $11 for adults and $6 for children three to eighteen, students with ID, and seniors (sixty-five and older). IMAX tickets are extra. For more information call (303) 322-7009 or (800) 925-2250; www.dmns.org.

Cheesman Park, located at Franklin Street and Eighth Street, attracts joggers to its crushed granite loop trail around the park. The large grassy expanses are popular with sunbathers and small groups enjoying a quiet afternoon. Families come for the large playground. A large, white-columned memorial fountain on top of the hill is a picturesque landmark and a good place to sit and contemplate those big mountains looming to the west. This is the spot to be in the evenings for one of the best sunset-over-the-Rockies spots in the city.

Just south of downtown in a neighborhood filled with early twentieth-century homes, **Washington Park** is one of Denver's most popular year-round parks. Know as Wash Park by locals, these 165 acres contain two lakes, 54 flower beds, a two-mile loop with separate lanes for foot and wheeled traffic, boat house, fitness center, soccer and tennis courts, and plenty of big trees. You'll see lots of people working out here, but if you're not inclined to join in the activities, just find a shady spot on the grass and watch it all go past. The park can be accessed at South Downing Street and East Louisiana Avenue.

trivia

The Denver Zoo got its start when an orphaned black bear named Billy Bryan was given to the mayor as a gift in 1896.

Located at Sheridan Boulevard and West Seventeenth Ave., **Sloan Lake Park** attracts a mixed clientele: retired folks, young parents pushing strollers, joggers, picnicking Vietnamese families, soccer players, bicyclists, and sunbathers. With 177 acres to spread out, there is plenty of room for everyone. At the center of it all is enormous Sloan Lake. Quiet during the week, it comes alive on summer weekends. Each July the Dragon Boat Festival celebrates Asian American culture and traditions, and dragon boats race across the lake.

Venturing just beyond the actual city limits, Red Rocks Park, Genesee Mountain Park, Chatfield State Park, and Cherry Creek State Park are all outstanding parks. For more information about Denver's parks, contact the Denver

A Stroll along the South Platte River

Early pioneers deemed the **South Platte River** "too thick to drink, too thin to plow." As Denver grew, the local river became a dumping ground, polluted, abused, and neglected. In 1974 a major clean-up effort began, and today it's a 30-mile greenway of parks, trails, trees, and wildlife habitat. A paved riverside path is shared by walkers, bicyclists, birders, skaters, and joggers. Whitewater boat chutes provide thrills for kayakers and fun for spectators during spring snowmelt. Any stretch is pleasant, but some favorites are the urban section heading upriver from the confluence with Cherry Creek (by the downtown REI flagship store), and the lower section from the crossing at Alameda Avenue to the trail end just north of Chatfield State Park. For more information contact **Denver and Metro Convention & Visitors Bureau,** (303) 892-1505; www.denver.org/metro/features/bike-trails.

Parks and Recreation Department's Parks Division, 201 West Colfax Ave., Dept. 605, Denver 80202; (720) 913-0642; www.denvergov.org/parks.

If you want to look down onto Denver from above, take a hike in one of the mountain parks. The Denver Mountain Parks system consists of 31 named parks and 16 unnamed areas totaling around 14,000 acres of mountain and foothills owned by the city of Denver. These parks offer a wide variety of geography and activities, and a great escape not far from the city. For more information, (303) 697-4545; or go to www.denvergov.org, click the Parks and Recreation link, and navigate to Mountain Parks.

Finally, before you leave the Denver Metro area, delight your children (or your inner child) with a stop at the ***Butterfly Pavilion and Insect Center,*** located in Westminster—a short jaunt up U.S. Highway 36 off I–25 heading north from Denver. This 11-acre attraction, which opened in 1995, is one of only a dozen or so similar institutions in the United States. This "zoo" houses more than 1,200 free-flying butterflies from more than fifty species around the world. In addition, numerous other insect species, turtles, tortoises, birds, fish, and tropical plants round out the pavilion's holdings.

Open daily from 9 a.m. until 4:15 p.m., the Butterfly Pavilion offers an escape from wintry weather with its climate-controlled, 7,200-square-foot tropical conservatory. Admission is $7.95 for adults, $5.95 for senior citizens sixty-five and older and Westminster residents, and $4.95 for children four to twelve. Two children three and under free if accompanied by adults. The pavilion is located at 6252 West 104th Ave., Westminster. Take the Church Ranch Boulevard/104th Ave. exit off US 36 and head east on 104th. For more information call (303) 469-5441; www.butterflies.org.

The Eastern Plains

Many visitors are surprised to learn that not all of Colorado is filled with mountains, lakes, and alpine scenery. In fact, the flat Eastern third of the state looks more like neighboring Kansas and Nebraska than it does the rest of Colorado. Even though it's part of this quintessentially Western state, many consider this vast landscape of rolling plains more Midwest than West. Eastern Colorado is one of the most sparsely populated places in the United States. The Dust Bowl period of the 1930 was hard on the region, with 2.5 million people moving out of the Plains states. Although Eastern Colorado eventually saw a return to agriculture in the 1960s to 1980s, dropping agricultural prices combined with rising farming costs led to a decline in population throughout the region.

Unlike the Western two thirds of the state, the Eastern third lacks exciting scenery. Wide open spaces stretch to the horizon, broken by an occasional grain elevator, weighing station, or windmill. The shortgrass prairie greens briefly in the spring and is home to a number of bird species. The air is cleaner here than in the cities. Small towns with feed stores, cafes, and churches are scattered across the plains. Places like Punkin Center, Last Chance, Cope, and Otis hunker beneath the winter winds and pelting summer hail, fragments of Americana far removed from the big cities. At night main streets close down and fall silent.

Although there are few visual thrills here compared with the rest of the state, Eastern Colorado has some interesting sights. Probably the most prominent landmark on the Eastern Plains is the ***Pawnee Buttes.*** Part of the 200,000-acre Pawnee National Grassland, these twin buttes are can be seen from many miles away.

A gravel road leads up to the Buttes trailhead. From there, a 1.5 mile path takes you on foot or by mountain bike to the first butte, the western one. The eastern butte lies ¼ mile east. From a plateau the trail drops to the prairie floor, crossing open pastureland before dropping again into a deep ravine. Cream-colored chalk cliffs form the promontories. This is short-grass prairie, not much higher than tundra. The steady winds keep plant growth low to the ground. Prickly pear cactus, blue gramma grass, sagebrush, and buffalo grass grow no higher then 6 inches. This constant wind, combined with poor farming practices, combined to create the ecological Dust Bowl disaster of the 1930s, when drifts of wind-driven topsoil piled up like snow over fences, closing roads and killing crops. The Pawnee Grassland and the Comanche National Grassland in southeastern Colorado were created when the federal government withdrew the land from agricultural use and consolidated the parcels into protected grassland.

In his book *Centennial,* author James A. Michener renamed these landmarks the fictitious "Rattlesnake Buttes." The book is based on life in the area during pioneer days. About the buttes Michener wrote "They were extraordinary, these two sentinels of the plains. Visible for miles in each direction, they guarded a bleak and sad empire."

Lack of water and trees do not stop the many prairie species of birds from flourishing in this country. Lark buntings—the Colorado state bird, with its distinctive white wing patches against a black body—thrive here. So do horned larks, meadowlarks, kestrels, larkspurs, mountain plovers, common nighthawks, and long-billed curlews—some of the 200 species recorded here. A 36-mile self-guided birding tour is a great ride over the prairie in a car or on a mountain bike. Cattle share this area with pronghorn antelope, you will see occasional windmill-powered water tanks for stock. For information contact Pawnee National Grassland, 660 O St., Greeley 80631; (970) 346-5000; www.fs .fed.us/r2/arnf/about/organization/png/index.shtml.

The city of **Greeley** (named after Horace Greeley, the newspaper publisher) is 49 miles northeast of Denver, surrounded by agricultural farmlands. The town is infamous for its fragrant feedlots, and the fields beyond the town limits grow sugar beet, barley, and other crops. The twelfth most populous city in the state, it is home to the **University of Northern Colorado** (UNC). The late James Michener was one of the UNC's famous alumni and later a teacher there. He was inspired to write his bestselling novel *Centennial* through his familiarity and on-location research in Greeley and surroundings.

trivia

Horace Greeley's original concept for his namesake town was a utopian agricultural colony modeled after the Oneida, New York, experimental settlement.

Much of the local sightseeing relates to Greeley's past. At the **Centennial Village,** you can visit dozens of historic exhibits, including a sod house, a homesteader's wagon house, and a one-room rural school. In addition, Centennial Village has graceful Victorian homes. In all, some thirty structures take the visitor through the history of the High Plains, spanning the years 1860 to 1930. Open mid-April through mid-October; Tuesday through Saturday, 10 a.m. to 4 p.m. Admission is $7 for adults and teenagers twelve and older, $5 for sixty and older, and $3 for children six to eleven; children five and younger are free. Centennial Village is open free to the public on the first Saturday of each month. For more information call (970) 350-9220; www.greeleygov.com/museums/centennialvillage.aspx.

For another historic look at the area, visit the **Meeker Home Museum,** formerly the home of Nathan Meeker. Nathan Meeker was the founder of Greeley, and the agricultural editor of Horace Greeley's *New York Tribune.* This graceful, two-story adobe home built in 1870 contains many of his furnishings and the plow that turned the first sod in the Union Colony. Learn about his untimely death in the White River Massacre, and how his family

Those Western Doings in Greeley

The **Greeley Stampede** is held from the last week of June to the first week of July, with nine rodeos, parades, and fireworks, as well as events on all downtown plazas. The rodeos are at Island Grove Park, Fourteenth Avenue and "A" Street. For more information call (970) 356-2855 or (800) 982-2855; www.greeleystampede.org. The **Weld County Fair** takes place in late July at the same location, with horse shows and livestock displays, plus various contests. For more information call (970) 356-4000; www.co.weld.co.us/weldcountyfair.

Try a Yurt Vacation!

Within the *Colorado State Forest State Park,* 75 miles west of Fort Collins, the *Never Summer Nordic Yurt System* offers highly unique opportunities to cyclists.

Consider staying in a yurt here. Yurts are portable, round dwellings that were first used by nomadic Mongols in Central Asia; they sleep six comfortably and are well situated as push-off sites for some great rides.

One such bike trip is the *Grass Creek Loop.* It's a tough 16 miles round-trip. Along the way you will pass the North Michigan Reservoir and the 10,000-foot Gould Mountain.

For more information about Never Summer Nordic, Inc., log on to www.neversummer nordic.com or call (970) 723-4070. For information about Colorado State Forest State Park, log on to http://parks.state.co.us.

struggled to survive without him. It's listed in the National Register of Historic Places. Open from May through September; walk-in visitors are free. Call for hours, (970) 350-9220, or visit www.ci.greeley.co.us.

To the west, nestled against the foothills, **Fort Collins** may well be the most sophisticated community in northern Colorado. With 130,000 inhabitants, it is the fifth most populous city in the state. Colorado State University is here, and as with many larger college towns, the city has no shortage of good restaurants and cafes, bars, bookstores, and shops catering to 20-somethings. The city shows up on those annual "Best Small Towns To Live In" lists, and a stroll through the pedestrian Old Town Square and neighborhoods to the south and west will soon show you why. Large shade trees, historic preservation of homes and buildings, outdoor sculptures, fountains, shops, and art galleries give visitors and residents alike plenty of reasons to linger.

In a state famous for its wealth of microbreweries, **Fort Collins** shines. Two of the best-known, New Belgium Brewing Company and Odell Brewing Company, offer inside looks at how these finely-crafted brews are created. Each is a must for beer lovers. New Belgium is at 500 Linden St.; (970) 221-0524; www.newbelgium.com. Free tours are given on weekdays. Odell is at 800 E. Lincoln Ave.; (970) 498-9070; www.odells.com. Free tours are given Monday through Saturday. For both breweries, call ahead for tour times.

To see how beer is brewed on a large scale, take a free tour at the Anheuser-Busch Brewery at 2351 Busch Dr.; (970) 490-4691; www.budweiser tours.com.

River Adventures in Northern Colorado

A *Wanderlust Adventure* in Fort Collins will give you the opportunity to see and feel the Poudre River firsthand. Since 1982, more than 120,000 people have enjoyed trips run by this Fort Collins–based outfitter. From three-hour trips for the whole family to daylong and multiday paddling affairs guaranteed to give anyone a workout, Wanderlust will have a trip to fit everyone (minimum age of seven for easiest trip). Trips run from May through August and range in price from $46 to $99 per person. For more information contact A Wanderlust Adventure (800) 745-7238 or (970) 484-1219; www.awanderlustadventure.com.

For beer aficionados, the Colorado Brewers' Festival in Fort Collins is the place to be during the last week of June. More than 50 Colorado beers and 400 kegs will be ready for visitors. The event takes place in the historic downtown area, with food and live music from great Colorado bands. For more information call (970) 484-6500; www.downtownfortcollins.com.

The Fort Collins region is known for its nearby fly-fishing possibilities. Among others, you might head up the scenic **Poudre Canyon** and the Cache la Poudre River, which is consistently recognized as having some of the finest trout fishing in the state. For more information contact Canyon Lakes Ranger District, Arapaho & Roosevelt National Forests, 2150 Centre Ave., Building E, Fort Collins, 80526; (970) 295-6700; www.fs.fed.us/r2/arnf/.

For camping and boating, try **Horsetooth Reservoir** west of town. Horsetooth has 1,900 acres of water, which attracts summer crowds with camping, boating, biking, and climbing. To reach Horsetooth Reservoir, drive west on County Road 38E (Harmony Road) from its intersection with Taft Hill Road in Fort Collins. Park permits are available from stations throughout the park; cost is $6 per vehicle. For more information contact Larimer County Parks and Open Lands, 200 W. Oaks St., Fort Collins, 80521; (970) 498-7000; www.co .larimer.co.us/parks/horsetooth.htm.

There are many single-track and paved trail biking options in and around Fort Collins. Pick up a free map of the city's bikeway system, illustrating the 56 miles of local bike trails, lanes, and routes. Maps are available at most Fort Collins bicycle shops, or download it online at www.fcgov.com/bicycling/ bike-maps.php.

Lory State Park offers great hiking, as well as single tracks for more advanced bike riders. This former ranch is now a 2,400-acre park that tempts bikers with challenging mountain biking almost year-round; snow is frequent in winter, but abundant sunshine keeps the trails relatively clear.

Just beyond the park entrance at the Timber Recreation Area is the Timber Trail. This single-track route is not very technical, but loose gravel adds a challenge. Take U.S. Highway 287 north from Fort Collins through LaPorte. Turn left at the Bellvue exit onto County Road 23N. Turn left again (23N turns). Go 1.4 miles and take a right on County Road 25G. The park entrance is another 1.6 miles away. The park is open daily and hours vary according to the season. Cost is $5 per vehicle.

Horsetooth Mountain Park at the southwest side of Horsetooth Reservoir has a variety of jeep roads and single-track trails that are popular with local mountain bikers.

Just south of Fort Collins is **Loveland.** It's only about half the size of Fort Collins, yet it has carved a national name for itself. Loveland calls itself "Colorado's Sweetheart City." Each year hundreds of thousands of sacks of Valentines are packaged inside larger envelopes and re-mailed here. Town volunteers hand-stamp them with a Valentine's verse and send them on to the lucky recipient, postmarked Loveland. Cupid has worked here since 1947, making sure that Valentine's cards have that extra touch on the outside of the envelope. Around 200,000 Valentines are sent out annually.

Loveland is a pretty city with a small-town atmosphere. With a historic downtown, antiques shops, 27 public parks, and year-round events and entertainment, it's worth stopping in "Cupid's Hometown." For more information contact the Loveland Chamber of Commerce at (970) 667-6311; www.loveland.org.

The Eastern Plains of Colorado saw much travel activity and bloodshed in the early days of this country. Indians, trappers, traders, settlers, Mexicans, and the Spanish used what was called the Santa Fe Trail, which followed the Arkansas River for many miles. After cutting across the southeast corner of what is now Colorado, the trail reached the area around present-day La Junta, then turned south over Raton Pass into New Mexico.

Bent, St. Vrain & Company, a frontier trading and retailing business, built and owned **Bent's Old Fort** near what is now La Junta. Beginning in 1833, for the next 16 years it was the only major permanent white settlement on the Santa Fe Trail between Missouri and the Mexican settlements to the south. The fort was a trading destination for Mexicans, Indians, adventurers, and trappers. It was a place to repair wagons, get supplies, livestock, food, and water, and rest awhile after a long and dangerous journey. The famous scout Kit Carson was a hunter for the fort from 1831 to 1842.

The fort provided goods for several groups. Mexico obtained quality manufactured items from the United States. Native Americans got cookware, metal, rifles, and other goods. Trappers obtained supplies, a market for their furs, and the company of other people following lonely months of hunting.

Bent, St. Vrain & Company traded with all these folks and among themselves. Furs from the trappers and buffalo robes from the Arapahoe and Southern Cheyenne made their way back east, where they were sold at a handsome profit.

In the mid-1800s, Bent's Old Fort was caught between resentful Indians and the whites who were moving in on them. The Indian wars began and trade faded away. Charles Bent was killed in a revolt in Taos, New Mexico, while serving as governor of the state, and St. Vrain left to do business further south. Cholera spread through the Indian tribes.

The fort was destroyed under mysterious circumstances in 1949. Most historians believe that after William Bent tried unsuccessfully to sell the fort to the U.S. Army, he mined the fort with explosives and gunpowder and blew it up. What was left of the fort was abandoned and fell into ruins.

Original sketches, paintings and diaries, and archeological excavations were used to rebuild the fort in 1976. Designated by the National Park Service as a National Historic Site, Bent's Old Fort has been rebuilt as close as possible to its original design, using authentic materials and tools. Today, the adobe structure remains a monument to past and present-day craftspeople whose skill and patience built and rebuilt it again.

Just outside La Junta, Bent's Old Fort stands much as it did more than 160 years ago. To preserve the authentic atmosphere of this trade center, visitor parking is ¼ mile from the building. The long paved walk toward the fort, with its backdrop of cottonwood trees by the Arkansas River, is a stroll into history. In deference to realism, there are no concessions for food, drink, or curios.

Uniformed park employees are often on hand to answer questions. But to get into the spirit of the place, join one of the $3-per-person ($2 for children six to twelve) guided tours conducted by an individual dressed in period clothes. These "interpreters" stay in character, thanks to the authentic costumes. The tours, which run from June 1 to September 1, are fun and informative, giving visitors a feel for life around the fort in the 1880s.

Scheduled special events take place throughout the year, such as the Living History Encampment in June and the Fur Trade Encampment in October. For more information contact Bent's Old Fort, National Historic Site, 35110 Hwy. 194 East, La Junta 81050; (719) 383-5010; www.nps.gov/beol. Open every day except Thanksgiving, Christmas, and New Year's Day. Open June 1 through August 31 from 8 a.m. to 5:30 p.m.; September 1 through May 31 from 9 a.m. to 4 p.m. From U.S. Highway 50 in La Junta take Highway 109 north 1 mile to Highway 194. Go east on Highway 194 for 6 miles to the fort.

For a trip even further back into history—150 million years further back—visit **Picket Wire Canyonlands** in **Comanche National Grasslands,** about 25 miles south of La Junta. Picket Wire opened to the public in 1991. The attractions? The clear footprints of dinosaurs on a solidified limestone shelf just a few feet over the Purgatory River, as well as Native American rock art and pioneer ruins. In a quarter-mile stretch there are more than 1,300 dinosaur footprints in four different layers of rock.

Though the area is considered extremely fragile, mountain biking and hiking are allowed in Picket Wire. From a parking area near a cattle pen, an 8-mile ranch road takes bikers and hikers across a high mesa, then drops suddenly into the canyon. Alongside the trail, the relics of abandoned adobe houses, a church, a graveyard, and ranch buildings hold up against the dry climate.

On your way along the dusty trail you may catch glimpses of the current inhabitants: coyote, badgers, kestrels, orioles. Stay out of the tall grass, which is ideal snake habitat. The dinosaur tracks are marked by small signs pointing the way. Right next to the river, you come to a shelf of limestone that looks like someone mucked around in it while it was wet. On further examination you will discover that these muddlings are dinosaur tracks. Two different types of dinosaur left these track. The immense brontosaurus left big holes like you'd expect from an elephant, only much larger. The meat-eating allosaurus left distinctive three-toed, wicked-looking footprints. Many scientists consider this site to be a national treasure.

Petroglyphs are scattered around the rock canyon walls. These etchings aren't identified by signs; you have to find them on your own. This rock art is anywhere from 375 to 4,500 years old. These are precious ancient artifacts, and they should not be touched; leave them so others can enjoy them. If time is important, do this trip for the dinosaur tracks alone.

This area gets very hot in summer. Take plenty of water and a hat. To prevent rattlesnake encounters, watch where you put your hands and feet. Solo travel is generally not recommended; if you go alone, let someone know where you are going and arrange to check in when you return. The distance to the dinosaur tracks one way is 5.3 miles. Overnight camping is prohibited. Contact the Comanche National Grassland, 1420 East Third St., La Junta 81050; (719) 384-2181; www.santafetrailsscenicandhistoricbyway.org/pwdino.html.

Places to Stay in Denver and the Plains

The rating scale for hotels is based on double occupancy and is as follows:
Inexpensive:
Less than $75 per night
Moderate:
$75 to $100 per night
Expensive:
$101 to $150 per night
Deluxe:
More than $150 per night

DENVER

Brown Palace Hotel,
(excellent downtown location)
321 Seventeenth St.;
(303) 297-3111 or
(800) 321-2599
www.brownpalace.com
Deluxe

Capitol Hill Mansion Bed & Breakfast,
1207 Pennsylvania St.;
(303) 839-5221 or
(800) 839-9329
www.capitolhillmansion
.com
Deluxe

Castle Marne Bed & Breakfast,
1572 Race St.;
(303) 331-0621 or
(800) 926-2763
www.castlemarne.com
Expensive to Deluxe

Curtis Hotel,
1405 Curtis St.;
(303) 571-0300 or
(800) 525-6651
www.thecurtis.com
Deluxe

Denver Marriott City Center,
1701 California St.;
(303) 297-1300 or
(800) 228-9290
www.marriott.com
Deluxe

Hotel Monaco,
1717 Champa St. at Seventeenth;
(303) 296-1717 or
(800) 990-1303
www.monaco-denver.com
Expensive to Deluxe

Hotel Teatro,
1100 Fourteenth St.;
(303) 228-1100 or
(888) 727-1200
www.hotelteatro.com
Deluxe

Hyatt Regency Denver at Colorado Convention Center,
650 Fifteenth St.;
(303) 436-1234
www.denverregency.hyatt
.com
Deluxe

Magnolia Hotel,
818 Seventeenth St.;
(303) 607-9000 or
(888) 915-1110
www.magnoliahoteldenver
.com
Deluxe

Oxford Hotel,
1600 Seventeenth St.;
(303) 628-5400 or
(800) 228-5838
www.theoxfordhotel.com
Deluxe

Residence Inn Denver City Center,
1725 Champa St.;
(303) 296-3444 or
(800) 593-2809
www.marriott.com
Expensive to Deluxe

Queen Anne Bed & Breakfast,
2147-51 Tremont Place;
(303) 296-6666
www.queenannebnb.com
Deluxe

FORT COLLINS

Armstrong Hotel,
259 S. College Ave.;
(970) 484-3883 or
(866) 384-3883
www.thearmstronghotel
.com
Moderate to Expensive

Best Western University Inn,
914 S. College Ave.;
(970) 484-2984 or
(888) 484-2984
www.bwui.com
Inexpensive to Moderate

Colorado Cattle Company & Guest Ranch,
70008 WCR 132, New Raymer;
(970) 437-5345
www.coloradocattle
company.com
Deluxe (all-inclusive)

SELECTED DENVER AND PLAINS AREA INFORMATION RESOURCES

DENVER

Denver Metro Convention & Visitors Bureau,
1555 California St., Suite 300, 80202;
(303) 892-1505 or (800) 233-6837
www.denver.org

GREELEY

Greeley Convention & Visitors Bureau,
902 Seventh Ave., 80631;
(970) 352-3567 or (800) 449-3866
www.greeleycvb.com

FORT COLLINS

Fort Collins Area Chamber of Commerce,
25 South Meldrum, 80521;
(970) 482-3746
www.fcchamber.org

LOVELAND

Loveland Chamber of Commerce,
5400 Stone Creek Circle, Suite 200, 80538;
(970) 667-6311
www.loveland.org

Edward House Bed & Breakfast,
402 W. Mountain Ave.;
(970) 493-9191 or
(800) 281-9190
www.edwardshouse.com
Moderate to Expensive

Hilton Fort Collins,
425 West Prospect Rd.;
(970) 482-2626
www.hiltonfortcollins.com
Expensive to Deluxe

Sheldon House Bed & Breakfast,
616 West Mulberry St.;
(970) 221-1917 or
(877) 221-1918
www.bbonline.com/co/
sheldonhouse
Moderate

GREELEY

Country Inn and Suite by Carlson,
2501 West Twenty-Ninth St.;
(970) 330-3404 or
(888) 210-1746
www.countryinns.com
Expensive

Fairfield Inn Greeley,
2401 W. Twenty-Ninth St.;
(970) 339-5030
www.marriott.com
Moderate to Expensive

Sod Buster Bed-and-Breakfast Inn,
1221 Ninth Ave.;
(970) 392-1221 or
(866) 501-8667
www.thesodbusterinn.com
Expensive

LOVELAND

Best Western Crossroads Inn & Conference Center,
5542 E. US Hwy. 34;
(970) 667-7810
www.bwloveland.com
Inexpensive to Moderate

Budget Host Exit 254 Inn,
2716 SE Frontage Rd.;
(970) 667-5202
www.budgethost.com
Inexpensive

Candlewood Suites,
6046 E. Crossroad Blvd.;
(970) 667-5444
www.ichotelsgroup.com
Inexpensive to Moderate

Places to Eat in Denver and the Plains

The rating scale for restaurants is as follows:
Inexpensive:
Most entrees less than $10
Moderate:
Most entrees $10 to $15
Expensive:
Most entrees $16 to $20
Deluxe:
Most entrees more than $20

DENVER

Buckhorn Exchange,
(steak, game, wildfowl)
1000 Osage St.;
(303) 534-9505
www.buckhorn.com
Deluxe

Cafe Brazil,
4408 Lowell Blvd.;
(303) 480-1877
Moderate to Deluxe

Highland's Garden Cafe,
3927 West Thirty-Second St.;
(303) 458-5920
www.highlandsgardencafe.com
Moderate to Expensive

Il Posto,
2011 E. Seventeenth St.;
(303) 394-0100
www.ilpostodenver.com
Inexpensive to Deluxe

Little India,
330 E. Sixth Ave.;
(303) 871-9777
www.littleindiadenver.com
Inexpensive to Moderate

Little Ollie's Asian Cafe,
2364 E. Third Ave.;
(303) 316-8888 or
(720) 941-5009
www.littleolliescherrycreek.com
Inexpensive to expensive

Lucile's Creole Cafe,
275 South Logan St.;
(303) 282-6258
www.luciles.com
Inexpensive to Moderate

Mel's Bar & Grill,
5970 South Holly St.;
(303) 777-8223
www.melsbarandgrill.com
Inexpensive to Deluxe

Mezcal Restaurant,
3230 East Colfax Ave.;
(303) 322-5219
www.mezcal-restaurant.com
Moderate to Expensive

Mizuna,
225 E. Seventh Ave.;
(303) 832-4778
www.mizunadenver.com
Deluxe

My Brother's Bar,
2376 Fifteenth St.;
(303) 455-9991
Inexpensive to Expensive

New Saigon Restaurant,
630 S. Federal Blvd.;
(303) 936-4954
www.newsaigon.com
Moderate to Deluxe

Panzano Restaurant,
909 Seventeenth St.;
(303) 296-3525
www.panzano-denver.com
Moderate to Deluxe

Restaurant Kevin Taylor,
1106 Fourteenth St.;
(303) 820-2600
www.restaurantkevintaylor.com
Deluxe

Rijoa,
1433 Larimer St.;
(303) 820-2282
www.riojadenver.com
Inexpensive to Deluxe

Steuben's,
523 E. Seventeenth Ave.;
(303) 830-1001
www.steubens.com
Moderate to Expensive

Strings Restaurant,
1700 Humboldt St.;
(303) 831-7310
www.stringsrestaurant.com
Deluxe

Vesta Dipping Grill,
1822 Blake St.;
(303) 296-1970
www.vestagrill.com
Deluxe

Wynkoop Brewing Company,
1634 Eighteenth St.;
(303) 297-2700
www.wynkoop.com
Inexpensive to Moderate

Zengo,
1610 Little Raven St.;
River Front Park
(720) 904-0965
www.modernmexican.com
Moderate to Deluxe

OTHER ATTRACTIONS WORTH SEEING IN DENVER AND THE PLAINS

DENVER

Art District on Santa Fe,
828 Santa Fe Dr.;
(303) 292-3455
www.artdistrictonsantafe.com

Children's Museum of Denver,
2121 Children's Museum Dr.;
(303) 433-7444
www.mychildsmuseum.org

Colorado History Museum,
1300 Broadway;
(303) 866-3682
www.coloradohistory.org

Elitch Gardens,
2000 Elitch Circle
(303) 595-4386
www.elitchgardens.com

Kirkland Museum of Fine & Decorative Art,
1311 Pearl St.;
(303) 832-8576
www.kirklandmuseum.org

Lower Downtown (LoDo) Historic District,
1616 Seventeenth St.;
(303) 628-5428
www.lodo.org

Museum of Contemporary Arts
1485 Delgany;
(303) 298-7554
www.mcadenver.org

16th St. Pedestrian Mall,
Sixteenth and California Streets;
(303) 534-6161

United States Mint,
320 West Colfax Ave.;
(303) 405-4761
www.usmint.gov/mint_tours/

Wings Over the Rockies Air & Space Museum,
7711 East Academy Blvd.;
(303) 360-5360
www.wingsmuseum.org

FORT COLLINS

Lincoln Center,
(970) 221-6735
www.ci.fort-collins.co.us/lctix/

GREELEY

Fort Vasquez,
(970) 785-2832
www.coloradohistory.org

FORT COLLINS

BeauJo's,
(American, pizza)
100 North College Ave.;
(970) 498-8898
www.beaujos.com
Inexpensive to Moderate

Canino's Italian Restaurant,
613 South College Ave.;
(970) 493-7205
www.caninositalian
restaurant.com
Inexpensive to Expensive

Coopersmith's Pub and Brewing Company,
5 Old Town Sq.;
(970) 498-0483
www.coopersmithspub
.com
Moderate

Rio Grande Mexican Restaurant,
143 West Mountain Ave.;
(970) 224-5428
www.riograndemexican
.com
Moderate

GREELEY

Coyote's Southwestern Grill,
5250 West Ninth St.;
(970) 336-1725
Moderate

Fat Albert's Food & Drink,
1717 Twenty-Third Ave.;
(970) 356-1999
www.fat-alberts.com
Inexpensive

Rio Grande Mexican Restaurant,
825 Ninth St.;
(970) 304-9292
www.riograndemexican
.com
Moderate

LOVELAND

Black Steer,
436 N. Lincoln Ave.;
(970) 667-6679
www.blacksteerrestaurant
.com
Moderate to Deluxe

Monaco Trattoria,
218 E. Fourth St.;
(970) 461-1889
www.monacotrattoria.com
Moderate to Expensive

Peaks Restaurant,
(breakfast and lunch)
405 E. Fifth St.;
(970) 663-7288
www.thepeakscafe.com
Inexpensive

Index

About the Author

Eric Lindberg is a Denver-based travel writer and photographer specializing in adventure travel, culture, and off-beat, far-flung destinations. A member of the Society of American Travel Writers, he has won numerous awards for work published in magazines and newspapers nationwide and abroad. For more information, visit www.ericlindberg.com.